A Place Called Maine

Other books by Wesley McNair

The Faces of Americans in 1853

The Town of No

Twelve Journeys in Maine

My Brother Running

The Quotable Moose: A Contemporary Maine Reader (editor)

The Dissonant Heart

Talking in the Dark

Fire

Mapping the Heart: Reflections on Place and Poetry

The Maine Poets (editor)

A Place on Water (co-author)

The Ghosts of You and Me

Contemporary Maine Fiction (editor)

A Place Called Maine

24 authors on the Maine experience

Edited by Wesley McNair

Down East

ISBN: 978-0-89272-760-5

Printed on acid-free paper at Versa Press, East Peoria, Illinois

5   4   3   2   1

Down East
BOOKS·MAGAZINE·ONLINE
www.downeast.com

Distributed to the trade by National Book Network

Library of Congress Cataloging-in-Publication Information: A place called Maine
: 24 authors on the Maine experience / edited by Wesley McNair.
    p. cm.
  ISBN-13: 978-0-89272-760-5 (trade hardcover : alk. paper)
  1. American prose literature–Maine. 2. Authors, American–Homes and haunts–
Maine. 3. Maine–Social life and customs. 4. Maine–Description and travel. I. Mc-
Nair, Wesley.
  PS548.M2P55 2008
  818'.54082–dc22
                              2008004696

Contents

Introduction

A*Place Called Maine* showcases the contribution the state's authors have made to the personal essay. It is the third in a trilogy of anthologies recently published by Down East Books, each devoted to a genre of Maine writing and concentrating on contemporary work. The trilogy also includes *The Maine Poets* (2003) and *Contemporary Maine Fiction* (2005), which will soon be available as a paperback titled *Today's Best Maine Fiction*.

Each of these anthologies pays tribute to Maine, of course, but none more fully than the one you are holding in your hands. In fact, there has probably never been a book that contains more perspectives on the Maine experience than *A Place Called Maine*. Its personal stories, written by newcomers and natives, tell what it is like to settle or grow up or simply live day to day in this state, including adventures and misadventures with neighbors, creatures of the wild, and extremes of weather. Here, too, are accounts of lost traditions, reflections on Maine's interior meaning, and tributes to the state's unique people and natural beauty, from the coast to the northernmost border.

Though this anthology centers on today's writers, it also features well-known essayists from the past. In these pages are entries about Maine by Henry Beston, Rachel Carson, and E. B. White. Don't be surprised if you find yourself rereading the nonfiction of *A Place Called Maine* simply for the pleasure of artful description or storytelling. For the work assembled in this volume is not only among the best Maine has to offer, but also as good as writing anywhere.

Wesley McNair
Mercer, Maine
January 2008

Settling In

I'm New Here

Richard Ford

Most people come to endure the edgy status of newcomer because of what I would call traditional American reasons: A job makes us leave where we're well ensconced and go where we're strangers. Or bad luck (a divorce, a bankruptcy, a shooting) makes unexpected removal to some place where we're not known seem attractive. We settle in unfamiliar places to escape our loved ones or to find them, to be near our grandkids or to flee them, to seek happier weather, to enter the Witness Protection Program, or just to take our minds off things we don't want to think about anymore. It's normal.

I moved to Maine inspired by variants of these good reasons: I didn't feel like the places available to me were where I wanted to be. Nowhere I'd been seemed good enough. Where I was born, Mississippi—a natural destination in some minds—seemed way too specific to me. And other choices—Kansas, or its generic equivalents in undesirability, Indiana, Alabama, Florida—were okay for somebody else, but not me.

Maine I chose because I'd heard it was pretty, and also pretty cheap. And I didn't already know something bad about it, or for that matter much about it at all. It seemed sort of remote, but not too remote (maybe the rich hadn't bought it all up yet). Plus, I once had a favorite teacher from Maine, and I remembered I liked the way he talked: "The glit-tuh of the fi-yuh-flize lit the daaak haaabor pahst midnight." And I guess I'd heard the siren call of the ocean. Who knows what that Melvillean mystery's about: electrolytes; the malaise of continental socked-in-edness (I'd been living in Chicago) sponsoring a need for a more defined sense of east; a desire for a longer, colder view of life at a reckoning point just beyond the middle. I don't know. I like seafood, but I'm not crazy about boats. I'm not even that strong a swimmer. In the *Manifesto of Surrealism*, André Breton wrote, "Our brains are dulled by the incurable mania of wanting to make the unknown known." Some things, though, you just do.

But, Maine. And being a newcomer.

Because I'm a recent arrival here—four years, now—chances are anything I think about Maine is wrong. This is the dilemma newcomers face: being wrong a lot. Though if you have to be wrong a lot, Maine's not a bad place to be. People here don't seem to mind your being wrong. ("Are those red and white floating things called buoys? . . . It's pronounced *Bang*-er, right? . . . What sort of duck is that? . . . Oh. Okay. I thought a loon was something else.") Mainers tolerate. It's as if they'd intuited something crucial about the human condition just by living here—that we're all wrong a fair bit, but being wrong in behalf of figuring things out can be good. It keeps you humble, allows for interesting mystery and surprise, gives you something always to look forward to—being right. You probably wouldn't put any of this on the state license plate: "Maine: Where Being Wrong Keeps You Humble." But it's true.

It's hard, of course, to generalize about human beings (a definite signal I'm about to do it). But my instinct tells me that the happier and more satisfied people feel in their places, the better they treat outsiders; and the more resourceful people are in their lives, the less aggravated they're made by strangers. And the more manifestly wonderful a place is—like Maine—the more its natives are willing to share (within limits) their appreciation of it with like-minded people from away.

These observations may be only further proof of how wrong I am. I'm a novelist and long disposed to embroidering upon the natural human baize and to inviting my readers to agree or disagree, but ultimately to letting them weigh the evidence themselves. Truly, though, the only thing my Maine neighbors seem seriously bothered by and to treat with disdain is somebody showing up acting like he owns the place, or somebody helping himself to a big two-pounder out of some other guy's lobster trap set just off the end of a convenient dock. Everything else is more or less your business.

I've been transient or around itinerance most of my life, so that being a newcomer has by now become pretty familiar. My father was a traveling man, a drummer, who worked out of his car across seven southern states, and he often took my mother and me with him. His mother was an immigrant. My mother's father was a step-lively hotelier in Little Rock and in Oklahoma and Kansas City. Before that he worked on the Rock Island. Personal circumstances often required strategic repositionings in our life, and ordinary permanence never became much of a concept. Eventually, I beat it out of Mississippi to go to college in Michigan, then mostly stayed gone, living in Montana and New Jersey and Louisiana and lots of places in between. Probably I'll live in other places before I'm done. I seem to like that better than whatever is its opposite– being a what? A veteran in some dull burg? A native? A lifer?

Back in Mississippi in the 1950s, I was always surprised to learn which of our permanent-seeming, permanent-acting neighbors had, themselves, moved in just a year before we had. *Newcomer* isn't a highly regarded American epithet, whereas being a *permanent* and a stayer is good—which is odd when you consider that most of us here are newcomers in one sense or other. We are *this* way, I guess, but we want to lay claim to being *that* way. But it's always the newcomer who brings trouble, unsettles the still waters of fixity, sets people on edge and against other people. Few of us are comfortable being perceived as an allergen. But the friction between the quiet village life (the old European model) and the urge to go somewhere new (the fresher American model) is the germinating heat in much stirring American literature (think of *Winesburg, Ohio*; *The Great Gatsby*; all the suburban stories you ever read by John Cheever, Richard Yates, Raymond Carver, Ann Beattie). This is because being new to a place is inherently dramatic—things can swing importantly this way or that based on our ignorance or given opposition from the natives. Emotions can get frayed, character be put on gaudy display. We readers like that—from a distance of the page, anyway. We see life rendered judgeable.

My own belief about newcomer status is that in America—where I *am* a lifer—I'm fully entitled to be a newcomer wherever I please, no matter what human forces disapprove or oppose. This freedom to show up anyplace and stay is one of the small cornerstones of our citizenship, though you'll always find hard cases—dimwits—who'll dispute it, complain that you're "from away," disrespect you and tell you to leave. Mainers, I've noticed, tend not to do this, as though my liberty were somehow plainly akin to theirs. Which is a better and truer understanding of liberty than the one that proclaims you free to conform, or free to leave. Real liberty is the will to grant another the freedom to do or be what you yourself wouldn't care to do or be, and that includes the freedom to be new here.

And yet, sovereign rights aside, being new can prove tricky. Where I live, in East Boothbay, it's been easy enough to stake out a provisional place for myself and feel comfortable. I've picked up some of the local savvy: I've learned to dive out of the way of those gleaming Connecticut Volvo bumpers that target me as I cross the lot at the P.O; I've mastered the minor art of not getting trapped behind big, chuffing vacationer Winnebagos with Michigan-blue plates at the Irving pump. I'm indulgent of the two-week renters from New Jersey who take their morning walks down my road during which their dogs rile up my dogs, but who then won't speak to me when I speak to them—as if they owned the place and I was the renter. This insider lore I've accumulated regarding *other* strangers confers a clubby-cozy sensation of belonging, a currency I turn to anecdotal gold at Conley's Garden Center and the Carriage House bar and the general store—where the proprietor's from New Hampshire. ("I mean it," I say proudly. "I see those red, white, and blue Spirit of America plates in the rearview, and I just pull right off the road and head home before he rear-ends me. Yep.")

This kind of easy familiarity isn't real belonging, of course. It's pretend. When the locals sit through warm autumn mornings on the front porch at the general store, drinking coffee, reading the *Boothbay Register*, and saying precious little, I hear what they say. But I don't know what they don't say. I don't know who lost a son to drowning off Matinicus 10 years back, or who was once married to whose sister, or who went belly-up fishing for sea urchins, or who made a bundle on account of native prudence, or who went to the university at Orono on a hockey scholarship, or what building stood here before the store came. My neighbors don't say much by way of straight exposition, so I don't know how they feel about most things, or about me—except that they seem friendly. I could make it my business to find out more facts, and maybe if I'm here long enough I will. Though what would that confer? A person might live here 60 years, be born right down the road, and not feel he belonged. Really belonged. Pretend may just be good enough, since belonging—whatever that elusive ether may be—is a rarer substance than birthright. Plenty of great American literature starts from that premise, too. Think of William Faulkner.

Rightly assessing the newcomer's status, then, requires more art than analysis, I think: How do I balance my entitlement to be new here with the recognition that others were here before me and know more, have a firmer, even more significant hold on things—and yet are no more entitled to be here than I am, and are likely not even so different from me, despite their tenure. Newcomer and long-stayer are really just veneers upon the complex human interior. How can I strike this balance without isolating myself and stifling my good newcomer's curiosity, by which—if I could—I would alchemize being wrong into something that's true? Not easy. Something in the place, I suppose, and in myself has to relent, give in, accept and open up and let us breathe the other in slowly. After all, in a place you like and would consider staying, you don't want to be a newcomer forever, even if—like so many of us—you're never entirely certain what you do want.

from *The Road Washes Out in Spring*

Baron Wormser

We resolved to build our house ourselves. Though my wife had studied architecture for a time and was a capable designer, the world of practical carpentry was a mystery to us. We knew what a two-by-four was and what a hammer was, but we didn't own a Skil saw, much less a table saw. Perhaps we would do the whole thing with a handsaw and an ax. What did we know? We had read a do-it-yourself book or two that showed how houses were built. We would follow the instructions just as we did when we encountered a new recipe. As college graduates, we could learn whatever we had to learn.

It's hard for me to fathom how simple-minded yet determined we were. I look back at us at the beginning of our sojourn in the woods as somewhat holy fools—serendipity will provide. It did. Illumination, to say nothing of practical help, appeared in the form of a Maine carpenter and jack-of-most-trades named Caleb. Word must have gotten out in the neighborhood that some hippies were building a house or camp or cabin or something utterly unspeakable in the woods. Caleb was curious enough to brave the morass of our road. He got out of his battered, mid-1950s pickup and sauntered up to our site, a man in his early sixties with a limp, a potbelly, a ruddy complexion, and very steady blue eyes. We (which meant myself, Janet, and her younger brother Dave) were pondering the mysteries of concrete—not actually pouring any, but pondering it. We had the old dug well from which to draw water. We had a wheelbarrow to mix the stuff, and we had a lot of empty tubes to fill on which the house would reside. Due to heavy rains, the holes in which those tubes sat were mostly full of water. Small frogs were hopping about everywhere with what seemed like great abandon.

Caleb's Maine accent had a musical twang. His voice moved slightly up and down as he spoke his introductions, though his tone was steadily bemused. We chatted about the weather (we all agreed it had been rainy) and how it seemed as though more and more young people were moving to Maine. Then, very politely, Caleb looked the scene over and asked us in a mild, wry voice if we had ever built a house before. "Well, not really," we replied. We didn't even bother with some qualifying "but." "How," he asked after a brief, respectful pause in which he tugged at the visor of his green cap, "would you like me to build this for you? Take a couple of weeks. A jiffy." He halted. "You can help." My wife and I deliberated for a few seconds before nodding wholeheartedly. Caleb smiled a false-toothed smile. "We'll get her up before you know it. You just see." We talked over a few details about mixing concrete and what we had for lumber. Caleb shook our hands; he was missing the tips of two fingers on his right hand. Then he headed back to his truck. We never talked money.

The next day we started very early—around six. Caleb favored the cool hours of the morning. He'd get up in the dark of four or five, eat a bowl of oatmeal, then head off to work. He was still very strong; when he worked it was with a kind of reckless determination. I'd never until that day seen anyone work the way Caleb worked. He kept moving constantly while directing Dave and me (we were manning the wheelbarrows) and two of his relatives (a grandson and grandson-in-law) who knew how to carpenter. He didn't pause. He didn't look around. I don't even recall him excusing himself to take a leak behind a tree. I was surprised he didn't finish the whole job in a day. As it was, we poured all the concrete and started cutting the sills that day. If he hadn't been so good-natured, I would have thought he was possessed. Dave and I collapsed with fatigue as soon as he left.

The Maine that we wanted to be close to was personified in Caleb.

He had finished school after seventh grade ("had enough of sittin' at a desk") and had gone to work in the woods. He had worked in lumber camps and carpentered his whole life. Though various construction companies had employed him, he preferred being his own boss. He loved to build rough structures—barns, chicken houses, outbuildings. Finish carpentry held no allure for him; his favorite phrase was "close enough—spike it." An eighth of an inch didn't keep him awake at night. Though he used a spirit level, he didn't let it deter him.

Caleb lived down the road from us and, with his devout wife, had raised six daughters. He never went to church ("for women") but was a clean-living man. "I seen too much of what liquor does to people." Caleb believed in the gospel of work. Until he knocked off around three o'clock, his energy never flagged. Then he went home, took a brief nap, accepted visits from his enormous clan, ate dinner, and read a tattered Western by the likes of Zane Grey before turning in around eight. He was at it again the next morning at six.

Like a number of old-timers we were to meet, Caleb had little use for authority. That's where, despite our very different backgrounds and despite our ages, we clicked. We never talked politics for a second. There wasn't much need to. Caleb had little use for anyone in a suit and tie. "What kind of work can a man do in a suit and tie?" Caleb snorted. He had never voted. He wasn't proud of it, nor was he ashamed. To get excited about promises from people you'd never met was wishful at best, childish at worst. A speech was puffery; anyone could tell people what they wanted to hear. Anyone could wave a placard and cheer. To an independent Yankee cuss like Caleb, the very notion of cheering seemed ludicrous. He was that bracing blend we were to come across in rural Maine of the upright and the anarchistic. His moral code was utter honesty and frank contempt for anyone who didn't live up to that code. He wasn't cut out for latter-day, corporate America, and he knew it. That was fine with him. As long as he could limp along (his hip was going) and work, he was happy.

What Caleb liked to do during lunch or while we were waiting for the lumber truck to show up was tell stories. He had been all over New England as a young man. If he didn't like a situation, he left that situation. Once when he was walking down the main street of a town in northern Maine, he realized he only had a quarter to his name. Caleb promptly threw it away because he'd earn that and more. He had eaten every food known to man. "Ever eat woodchuck, Red?" he asked me one day. "Worst knot in my stomach I ever had." A great bestower of nicknames, Caleb had deemed me "Red" for my hair, and my brother-in-law "Lightning" for his sometimes dilatory work habits. Caleb had never gone west, but he was a part of that American restlessness that always had to be doing something. The only stillness he recognized was fatigue. He loved exertion, but he also loved the thinking that went before the exertion. He was ever considering what had to be done next. For all his bluff ways, he was thoughtful.

Our modest Cape-style house was done in a month, and not long afterward we moved in with our two-year-old daughter. Featuring cedar shakes from a local mill, six-over-six windows, and a back porch with hemlock posts I had cut in the forest, it was a testament to the beauty of wood. Caleb came by regularly to check on us. There was no telling what such naïfs might do. He would wink at us when he inquired how we were getting along. We had no idea what we were up against. He did, but never let on. From the out-set he understood us; our romanticism appealed to his. Despite his air of practicality, he loved the freedom of following his own nose. That was how he'd shown up in the first place. It was as if he'd been waiting.

The length of the road from our neighbors' farmhouse to our house measured almost exactly a half mile. It was, when we built the house, a discontinued road, which is to say a road that no one lived on anymore and was not maintained by the town. "Maintained" meant plowed and worked on to whatever degree was deemed sufficient by the de facto road commissioner to keep a road open for year-round driving. No one said that year-round driving on a gravel road was easy, only that it could, more or less, be done.

Our road ran first through a field with a distinct dip in it that required a culvert to channel the water. Because they often were not buried in the ground deeply enough, the metal culverts had a way of heaving with the frosts. In spring, the run-off flowing madly in the ditches and out of the woods would go under the culvert, the culvert would sink, the soil on both sides of the culvert would wash out, and a modest chasm would open up. This happened any number of times. Many an afternoon on the way back from work, I would pause before the culvert and ascertain whether or not I could get across. More than once we put two hardwood planks across a good-sized gap and drove our car across, Janet beckoning as to where to put the wheels, with me driving very, very slowly.

The field was actually the best part of the road. Most of it was flat, exposed to the sun, and dried out reasonably quickly in the spring. From the field, the road headed uphill and was bordered by trees. On the upper part of the road, steep banks stood on both sides. Anyone who has ever examined a road has noted that the road wants to be above rather than below its banks. Alas, our road was never going to reach such heights. In addition, the last two hundred or so yards of the road went up a modest hill. The hill was shaded by large pines and some years did not thaw out until late April or early May. When it did, holes would open up that made driving a distinct challenge. More than once we buried a wheel in mud over the top of the tire. Stanton, our old neighbor who prophesied that we, as know-nothing hippies, would never last more than a year or two "up there in the woods," would come along with his pre–World War II tractor, attach a chain to our front bumper, and pull us out. He would make an understated remark about the road ("This road ever see daylight?") and smile a resigned smile. He lived on the level portion of the road that didn't wash out, fall in, or buckle.

I never knew how alive the earth was until we had to deal with the road up to our house. In winter the road was plowed, and because the ground froze, we didn't have to worry about getting stuck in mud. It did, however, ice over and lead to sudden lurches on the drive downhill. I became adept at veering and then correcting that veer while keeping up a conversation with my wife. On the uphill drive, it led to the great question, "Can we get up the hill?" If the answer was "no"—and it was sometimes—then it meant backing down the road, a head-twisting, literal pain-in-the neck process. Frequently, getting up the hill meant gunning the Subaru while in first gear and frantically wiggling to the right and the left as the car staggered and whined. Since the driveway into our house represented a slight incline, the driver had to regain enough control and momentum after cresting the hill to make it around the corner of the driveway and up into the driveway itself. When my steering attempts failed, I wound up parking the car in a cleared area on the other side of the road. Because that area was the turnaround for the plow truck, I couldn't stay there but would have to get into the driveway before the next snowstorm. When the plow came along it blocked the mouth of the driveway with packed snow, but that was nothing to take personally. It was The Way of the Plow.

Winter was a cakewalk compared to spring. Washouts from rain left deep runnels. The road collapsed in some places, creating formidable sinkholes. I realized that the word "abyss" was not simply a metaphor. Sucking, swampy mud covered areas where the ditch and the road were indistinguishable. We often left the car at the beginning of our portion of the road and walked the half mile. I remember Janet and I carrying a futon (a clumsy thing that is hard to get a purchase on) up the road in a rainstorm. Every step felt like ten. Being educated and young, we compared ourselves to characters in a play by Brecht—Mother and Father Courage. We carried laundry, groceries, children, lumber—you name it.

On clear days in the spring we could be seen throwing stones into holes in an attempt to give the road some foundation. It was peaceful, satisfying work chucking those stones in. I could imagine how the farmers had chosen each stone to make the walls that ran everywhere and that had once designated boundaries and enclosed the fields that were now woods. They had taken what was at hand; though New England didn't have much topsoil, it had plenty of stones. A stone wasn't going anywhere. The *splat* or *kerchunk* it made when we dropped it was pleasing.

Our endeavor no doubt would have seemed crazy to most people who had better things to do. Yet the road, in all its ingloriousness, was our necessity. We came to understand how roads were named for the families that had lived on them. They existed for human purposes and were, in their changes from season to season, not-too-distant members of the family. They were of the earth, and they had their moods. As we shored our road up, cleaned the ditches, and dug around the culverts, we were crafting it.

You didn't, by and large, craft a road, however. It wasn't macramé. You brought in heavy machines and bulldozed to make a ditch or spread some gravel or put in a new culvert. The town did what it could. We weren't a high priority; there was no reason we should have been. The so-called main roads in town often were so badly rutted during mud season as to be barely passable. Nine miles an hour would have been a sane maximum speed. As you sedately bounced along, you could feel your vehicle's shock absorbers giving up the hydraulic ghost. We had, after all, chosen to live on what had been a discontinued road. That was our affair.

And it was. Driving the last mile on a summer's night with the windows down and the rich, warm, earthy air pouring in was sublime. The lights would be out in our nearest neighbors' farmhouse. Stanton and Ella were asleep by nine o'clock. As we headed up toward our place, the saplings on the side of the road almost grazed the car. A fox might dart across or, more often, a skunk or porcupine would be briskly waddling off to one side. "Where are we going?" we used to say to ourselves and to our children as we drove past the last electric pole into the darkness where no one seemed to live. Playfulness and wonder were in our voices. "Where are we going?"

Our landing in rural Maine was part of a historic moment that was known more or less as the Back-to-the-Land Movement. The capital letters seem somewhat ridiculous since there was no organized movement, only a demographically tiny number of people who felt the same vibration emanating from the 1960s, namely, to abandon the metallic hubbub of urban life and try to live with the earth. Although we were only in our twenties, we had already had our fill of the galvanism that was trumpeted by the tireless word "new." It seemed no accident that America had been heralded in Europe as the "New World." If the scene in the movie *The Graduate*, where Dustin Hoffman is given one word of sage advice—"plastics"—spoke for that New World's contribution to what was once called "civilization," we wanted no part of it. The economy we wanted to practice, however effaced it seemed, was a long-standing, handmade one. *The Whole Earth Catalog*, that oversized compendium of practical, esoteric, and funky lore, was its printed portal.

We reaped a serious amount of scorn for our actions. Our parents informed us that we were throwing away our educations, if not our lives, by going off to live on a dirt road. They had labored to get ahead in this country. They had put together savings accounts over decades and learned to play the stock market and invest in properties so that they could take vacations, buy big cars, and send their children to college. They had believed that each generation materially improved on the previous one. As we indulged a useless fantasy and rejected what they had striven to create, we were going backward. In their calculating yet optimistic eyes, we were spoiled, callow youths who had read too many books, seen too many movies, and had far too many romantic notions.

Their viewpoint made good sense. We attempted to put a positive face on our actions, stressing that rural life would improve our characters and make us stronger people. It didn't fly with our parents. They had not been born yesterday; they knew that we were pursuing an unofficial and not ballyhooed (though basic) American freedom— the freedom to go off and, from the point of view of happiness as the pursuit of what money can buy, screw up. We were hopelessly existential when, according to our parents, we should have been pointedly economic. Money brought comfort, security, and leisure, all of which helped to avoid pain, an avoidance that constituted, according to that sage of happiness Thomas Jefferson, "the art of life." Individual desire meshed neatly with public opinion—"I want this, too!" The national genius was perennial novelty. As in Las Vegas (the nation's alternative capital), anyone with the cash could buy in.

Living in a house in the woods that lacked the bare amenities was another story, one that had more to do with the pursuit of old realities than with glossy happiness. We figured that, since everyone was busy getting ahead, there was room for us to stay behind to savor the breeze and go blackberry picking. One less car on the freeway wouldn't be noticed. Amid the whirlwind of modern, abstract energy, there was room for some people to work hard at simple endeavors.

Our way of life meant, among other things, that until our daughter reached the threshold of adolescence and balked at the indignity of it, we didn't have a telephone. When I filled out a vital information form at work and left the space blank where it asked for your phone number, the secretaries were polite but baffled. "That means you don't have a phone, Baron?" "That's right. I don't have a phone." Pause. "Okay," in a very uncertain tone of voice. Everyone had a phone. Why would a person not want a phone? I dressed conservatively, drove to work in a car (rather than coming by horseback), did my job conscientiously, but no phone? Was I on a most-wanted list?

Now and then we called our parents, siblings, and friends from a pay phone outside the general store in the next town. We wrote letters. We savored the stillness. The sounds in the house were modest ones— a window closing, a match being struck, a fire whooshing in the stove, a pump sucking up water. We had nothing against anyone. We loved some people dearly. We didn't want, however, the jangling intrusion. In turn, we were told we were selfish; we were thinking only of ourselves. Probably we were. What communications came to us were communications we wanted to come to us. We had decamped in order to live deliberately. Why choose distraction when living on the earth was the sweetest experience?

We hadn't rejected everything the United States offered—far from it. Europeanized America was the place you ran off to. Once there, you were free to start running off again in pursuit of whatever gimcrack scheme or notion inspired you. Like many thousands who lit out for the territory, we were seekers who were fleeing. That we didn't know what awaited us was part of the charm. We had heard rumors and read stories—elsewhere existed. Our parents shook their heads ruefully. They had wanted their children to be thoroughly American. Alas, we were.

Cold Spring Nights in Maine, Smelts, and the Language of Love

Alice Bloom

"Gettin' any?"

"Nope."

"Checked out the other end yet?"

"Nope."

"Aren't goin' through Flying Pond are they?"

"How about Four Corners?"

"Nope. Nothin'. Might not be tonight."

"Christ Almighty, my feet are freezing already," says Hilde, our friend.

Hilde is tall for a woman, but she also weighs more than she would like to. She is thinking of going on the Zen macrobiotic rice and vegetables diet because eating Weight Watchers is too expensive, but right now she's sucking a Tootsie Roll Pop, to which she is lately addicted. It's a night in late April. The snow is still deep in places, but spring is here. We have parked on a back road, which at this point skirts a large black pond, to talk to some other fishermen; but now she and my husband and I are headed down a path into the woods alongside the pond. It's ten o'clock at night; we are carrying a Coleman lantern, a net on a long stick, and a bucket. We are following, between snow banks and down a muddy path, an invisible, rushing, splashing stream to the point where it feeds into the larger waters. We are after smelts.

We—my husband and I—have never caught or eaten a smelt and when, weeks later, we finally do, there isn't much to them. They're too small to gut or bone. Cut off the heads, dip them in egg then corn meal, fry them fast, and the little bones crunch right up like potato chips. We've been smelting every night for a week, under a full navy sky, a foam of stars, a small white hard moon, cold hard winds, and all around us every night the freeway roar of invisible, just released water. It's that invisible roar that we hunt.

We've been ice-locked since November, not a sound in our world but wind and cold birds, not a movement visible but wind and birds, bare trees, cars, and chimney smoke. But now it's spring and melting, all heaved up, and we're out in it, the nightly chase of the elusive smelts, which don't swim, but "run." But when? If we're at the right place the right night, we'll get enough fish for breakfast the next day.

We have never eaten fried fish for breakfast, but are willing to go along with most anything these days, any new rules or news, because we're "from away," fresh from fifteen years lived in Midwestern faculty ghettoes where, by and large, people tended not to go fishing with buckets and nets at ten o'clock at night. Anything now seems possible. Every night all the possible places must be checked.

These smelts run through at small water mouths, where one lake feeds into another or a stream narrows into a pond. A bridge makes a good spot. The mouth funnels all the smelts together so that if you're there when they come through that spot, all of a sudden the cold water is replaced by what looks like one shivering silver animal, oily with life, thousands of smelts, each no longer than a small hand, all running through at once, headed out, no slackers.

You can't smelt in the daytime because you can't see them. Lantern, in this case, is a stronger beam than sun. Like so much other lore about living in the country, this turns out to be true. The sap won't run when the wind blows, either, and the sap stops running at night. Birch logs burn good. My first batch of maple sap turns into sludge on the stove. The second batch turns to lumps that would crush healthy molars. I want so much to be here. I bottle up jars of each, take them to town for advice. The first person I ask, Carl, looks at the jars, shakes them, holds them up to the light, shakes his head, hands them back to me, says, "Well, I think you must of tapped a hog." The thing about lore is that there's so much of it, and you don't know any of it because you never needed it before, and then you hear a piece of it and it happens. Or, you do it.

As we stumble through the woods, my husband going ahead with the lantern, me in the middle, Hilde behind, the person of Bart Stone figures in the general air of spawning, breaking up. Hilde, watching in the lantern's erratic swing for deep mud, and sucking the lollipop, confesses, and cheerfully so, to "going almost all the way" with Bart Stone, "several times."

"When?" I scream back. "How? Where?"

"In a dark corner," shouts Hilde, pulling the sucker from her mouth with a pop. "At the party after town meeting!"

"*That's* why you didn't want to leave!"

"At your party last week, too!"

"Where?"

"By the front-room door!"

"Does that unnerve you?" I yell. (Her husband Everett is out of town, taking his parents someplace. Otherwise, Everett would be with us tonight.)

"Nope!" Hilde yells. "Should it?"

Voices, clank of lantern handles and buckets, slog and suck of mud, lights ahead through the trees. Roar of wind and water, moonlight, the fish. Where are they plotting up? What rush of blood or signal do they obey, and how do they know it? One night, a week ago, all of a sudden, the frogs are back—spring peepers. It doesn't begin with one or two peeps a night, then several more the next, building to a chorus, but all at once, all peepers where there was nothing but silence, wind, snow. When we walk outside the kitchen door that night to smell the new wind, there the peeps are, coming from the swamp down the dirt road. "Listen to that," someone says, "the frogs thawed out." Is that lore? Have they? I would have thought they had just been born.

"What I'd do if I was doin' it, is, I'd glue her in the joints first. But do it in the back. If you don't she's not gonna take the stain even and wherever she's got that glue on her is gonna show up like a sore thumb when you stain 'er."

"How'm I gonna keep 'er stain from gettin' on the wall then, get somebody else to do it?"

The old gent looks around the hardware store to see if we'll all laugh at this witticism. We all do.

"Stain her first," says the hardware clerk, "stain 'er first, then nail 'er together. She goes right up. Looks real good."

I can't resist. "I wonder," I say softly, "how come men talk about boats and cars and engines and stuff, projects, I guess, as 'she,' 'her,' do you think?"

"Never noticed," says the old gent, "just do I guess."

"Women don't, at least I don't think so," I say.

"Maybe," he winks at the clerk, "may be 'cause women don't have no projects!"

I haven't learned how to boil sap but I've learned a little something about keeping my mouth shut. Women, I think, refer to projects as "the," or "it," or "my," as in "I take my material and lay it this way on the bias," or as "your" as in "first you take your flour then work your lard into it until your dough is real fine crumbed." I have not yet heard a woman refer to an engine or to a pie as having any particular sex at all. "Gimme a quarter-inch drill bit, please," I say, wanting to add, "she broke yesterday while I was tapping a hog," but I don't.

If I'm willing to believe I'll behead fish to fry them for breakfast, I'm willing to sit at the feet of nearly any lore. "Yes-ma'ms, he had some trouble drivin' over the yes-ma'ms," says a man about his son who's just home from the hospital, his back, industrial accident, been operated on. Out the first day coming home a hundred miles in the car, he had trouble when his wife, driving, hit the "Yes-ma'ms."

"What did you say?"

"The . . . ups and downs, the, what do you call it, the potholes, the little dips and such, you know. Always called them the yes-ma'ms' but don't have *any* idea why."

Lore makes cosmic sense, I'm sure of it. And it makes visions, and the vision of this nightly smelting event is one of overlapping nets: the fish spread, submerged, invisible, dog-paddling probably, waiting, unfocused, ungathered, just thawed out, maybe. About to gather, about to pour and tumble together through chutes of stream and creek mouths, about to become a net. But now they're lying patternless, in a net of lakes and ponds. We wait. The water, thawed out, now everywhere, makes a net; threading and pouring from one lake into another, from new mud to trickle to creek to pond to river to the mighty ocean, all the water connected and spreading out under the net of blowing black naked trees, under the net of the sky, the stars at steady random, a million sparkling fish above us.

Between these nets we creep, us fisherfolk, following lore and the once-a-year craving for this spring tonic, this rank, oily bony titbit of a fish; crossing paths, moving up back roads, across bridges, stopping out on broken docks, on mushy ice floes, driving to the next spot, getting out of the car, walking, lantern-lit, lantern bobbing, checking, peering, waiting, not talking much, moving off again, back into the car, all with our dots of light like fireflies in late June. A patient, eager dance of lights, tying the knots of nightly movement across and around the net of lakes, in and out of the sound of breaking creeks. From very far above, it would be a net of nets, in pursuit, and spring causing them all.

"You think I'm stupid, don't ya?" yells Hilde.

"Oh no," I yell back. "I just wanted to know how you feel about feeling this way."

She slides in the mud, but catches herself against a wet tree. My husband's gotten too far ahead with the lantern for us to see the path.

"God-damnit. God-damn mud. I thought you were trying to tell me I was crazy."

"Oh no, I don't think you are!"

Our world has not had any smell but chimney smoke since October and the first hard frost then, which deadened the air. Actually what the first hard frost did was freeze up the last things of the year that smelled—mashed apples on the ground, rotting leaves, rotting marigolds, deer droppings, rain-soaked cabbages left in the garden. Hard frost has no smell, neither does snow. Though it's true that you can smell snow coming.

"I don't love him," Hilde continues, "but I sure like him. I couldn't feel this way about somebody I didn't like. And Everett knows how I feel. I think."

"Well, it's hard to avoid those feelings in this town," I say, a little grimly, feeling a little grim, trying to imply that one is taxed by these eternally rambunctious circumstances.

"That's for sure," she says.

She's gotten far behind me. "What?" I scream.

"I say, *that's* for sure."

And this seems to tie up the subject. It hasn't happened, but it almost did. Maybe it will still happen. There's another dance next week for someone's birthday. We'll all go. We slosh on, after the bobbing light. Where is the creek mouth?

I think, sidestepping a bog, of the intricacy of language that rightly ought to form the details of this investigation into the facts and feelings of wanting Bart Stone. Bart Stone, currently unmarried again, is about thirty, has hundreds of white teeth, white as a wolf's, rubs musk oil in his hair for parties in emptied sheds, or garages, and after the first dance has stripped down to his thermal underwear shirt that, in cut and charm and cling, is curiously like Calvin Klein's cashmere sweatshirt-style sweaters. Bart Stone gets sweaty at dances because he dances with all four limbs and dances every dance. In between records, he goes outside and stands in his sweat in the snow, drinks whatever's at hand, someone else's hand, and yells several times at the sky. How far ought Hilde and I to go with this language? "I went almost all the way," intended to be a confessional delicacy despite the wind and water noise, really sounds brutal if you think about it. Like a car wreck; totaled, "all the way." I want to start netting the subject with some details.

They can't have met in private because there's no place to go in private up here. Is necking in a dark, late, but public corner—the town meeting dance in the wooden Grange Hall—called an "affair"?

We have only naked space here in the country, against which no one's car or truck is anonymous. And otherwise, only these sweaty public events. "Affairs" are urban. They take place in good clothes in small, tasteful, dim, empty bars on late afternoons after your last seminar, in a part of the city not your own; and affairs are largely composed of talk. Whatever it is that takes place with your head against a splintery upright, in a large damp crowd smelling of wet wool and felt-packs (a crowd that sometimes includes your own children, as children also come to the town dances and dance), while wearing a thermal undershirt, while holding a can of warm beer stiffly, politely off to one side during the kiss, while overhearing bits of argument still hot about the further outrage perpetrated at today's town meeting over using revenue-sharing funds for filling spring road potholes or the unwarranted and totally unnecessary and undeserved raise in the dogcatcher's salary, whatever it is that happens during all this seems to need a word other than "affair." But then I'm not sure that Hilde would care that much right now about figuring this out, and exploration in this case seems finished, anyway. It's too noisy to talk. Nature makes too much noise for talk. At least we've understood each other.

"And I just want you to know, I don't care if you think I am crazy. I think I would've gone all the way if he'd've wanted to."

To this, I attempt no reply. "Wait!" I yell at the lantern, my husband, who's dancing ahead down the muddy path. He dances back.

"Wow, we live here! This is not a vacation! I went to work today!"

"That's just what Everett and me were saying last night," says Hilde. "Ten minutes from your back door, and all this beauty."

The next afternoon, the children are home from school. It's the week off called "mud vacation," and truly, the school buses can't get down the country roads. Together, Hilde and I have seven children. They're all here at my house. She and I are sitting at the kitchen table drinking tea. We have propped the kitchen door open to let the sunshine in, sun shines on the melting snow and mud, little insects—snow fleas—play in the bar of light. Things outside hiss and trickle. Maple sap burbles on the woodstove, two canning kettles and one turkey roaster full. Everything is sticky and muddy. We've stopped cleaning anything for the duration: the tops of things, the floor, the kids.

The thawing mud is so deep that nobody can drive anywhere near to the house, so we can't hear cars. That's a loss, because hearing cars is always an event out here where we live, and sends the dog to one kitchen window and the children to another. There's no place for cars to be going but to this house. In winter the snow plow stops at the edge of our yard and turns back. So in winter even the oil man coming is fun.

But now, with the mud, we can't hear the cars, they have to park so far up the road, and so suddenly there's a great spawn of men on foot: Bart Stone, Marshall, P.D., Spider, Timmy Coffin, Freddie Ferber, and an unknown friend in a red hunting hat—filing largely into the afternoon through the spillway of the sunny door. They are muddy and tolerably drunk, in good spirits, each one carefully wrapped around a 16-oz. beer. They fill up the kitchen with an energy beyond their number and literal size. The dog leaps up and down. Hilde and I move our chairs together, offer tea. They don't want tea. "Tea! tea! Oh, yes Jeesus, tea!"

They have been out visiting all day, here and there, house to house. They are full of plans, and have come to engage whoever they found at home. It's Patriots' Day, but no one knows what that signifies except that none of them is at work. "I thought Patriots' Day was in November, man!" "No man, that's *War* Day in November."

First they talk about Freddie Ferber's troubles with Mrs. Marmelot, an elderly foreign lady from whom he's rented space for a lunch counter, the only one in the village, up front in the building in which she also lives, out back. She has lately retired from running the lunch counter and has given Freddie the lease. He is cook, manager, and the sole waiter and dishwasher. He's been running it for three weeks. It's housed in an old airy studio built and then abandoned by a taxidermist sometime in the 1930s.

"He rents her place, pays rent, he pays, man, to be her fuckin' manager. Do you know what he *makes* a week? Take-home? About one fuckin' quarter!"

"I can't put up with it much longer," says Freddie, shaking his head, with an early Beatles haircut, and looking down into his empty beer can.

"You know why she's so fuckin' crazy and tough? She was in the war, man, that's why, she was a fuckin' Chesso-sov-lakian gorilla, man, that's why!" Much play on "go-rilla." Bart Stone imitates a gorilla, scratching his ribs, showing his teeth, and falls off a stool laughing.

Freddie looks up, happily, inspired, forgets about his empty can. "That's what I'll tell the customers I got out back! A go-rilla! But ah, man, she's gonna ruin the breakfast crowd, comin' in in her night-gown at 7:30 in the morning. 'Don't mind me, boys, I'm just getting myself some coffee!'" Freddie mincingly imitates Mrs. Marmelot's Hungarian voice, her lordly girth, her ladylike demeanor. "You know what she says to me yesterday? She says 'I guess I'm going to have to give you your marching papers!'"

"Oh man, *why* do you *take* it?"

A fight, Freddie now explains, has taken place with Mrs. Marmelot over the proper way to make a beef stew. Freddie is frying each piece "separate, with onions." But Mrs. Marmelot objects, wants him to add "lima beans and vinegar and all kinds of shit."

"Man, how can you let her do that, it's supposed to be your fuckin' place, she's got no fuckin' business bein' out there at all, telling you what to do!"

"That's right! that's right!" says Freddie, now properly outraged. "When she ran it, would anybody with any brains even eat in there? You don't see me fixin' coffee in a frying pan, warming up that old crap from the morning, using two-day-old bread and five-day-old hamburg."

They've forgotten that Hilde and I are there. Much loud advice, head nodding, commiseration: "I'd kick her fat Russian ass right to Russia, Freddie, right back to Russia." "Let's hog-tie 'er and have a party in there tonight and then you can fuckin' quit, Freddie." Netted with all this, talk of the coming Saturday night's birthday party, the beer supply for today, the adventures of today. "Let's liberate the bridge in Chesterville for Patriots' Day!" "Let's liberate Camp Bearspaw and have a party in that fuckin' big lodge of theirs." "Yeah man, let's do that, but what about them people up the head of their road in the chicken farm there, though?" "Fuck it, man, we'll park way down and walk in." "Who can fuckin' walk, man?"

The stub of an already used joint passes back and forth, burning fingers and lips. The kids swarm through the room, out into the mud, and back in again. Some of the men are standing, some on stools and chairs, one in the open doorjamb, two on the edge of the lit woodstove. All of them talk at once. And sex, it runs like the major thread. "How about Faith Coffin, she's about what do you think, eighty-five? Eighty-six now?" "That don't make no difference, I can go for a hot old lady anytime." "How old's *she* now?" They point their beers at and tease Hilde about Patty, her nimble, blonde ten-year-old, whose face, blank and friendly as a school slate, pops into instant grin at this incomprehensible but adult attention. "*She's* old enough. When did you start, Hilde? Thirteen? Fourteen? Fifteen?" "I was married when I was seventeen," says Hilde, primly. "Ah, man, twelve, then!" They wave their empty cans, pound the furniture, fall backwards with laughter. The kids have no idea what's going on—does anyone?—except that it's exciting, better than the oil man.

"When you gonna teach me t'dance?" asks Marshall, turning my way.

"You have to come to a party first, don't ya?"

"He's been on the wagon since New Year's Eve," says Hilde in a loud *sotto voce*. But I knew that. Marshall "goes overboard," everyone says. He's married to his high school sweetheart. He's avoiding the temptation of parties. His wife has already gone home several times to her mother, home being almost next door, and Marshall is not drinking, won't dance, and watches TV every night. Now he's so drunk his eyes roll, his eyelids are transparent lavender. He keeps rubbing his thick beard, forgetting that he has a lit cigarette in his hand.

One of them, Bart Stone, being a bachelor these days, has been invited out to supper. He asks to borrow the phone and calls the woman who invited him to tell her to expect fourteen. Then they all get up to leave. Marshall gives one rub to the top of my head while going through the door and groans with ritually acknowledged frustration. They're leaving because they've run out of beer and we don't have any. Of course, no one says this. It wouldn't be polite. Hilde and I stand in the sunny doorway and watch them go, and we talk a little of what we'll now fix for our respective suppers. And we know, though we do not say so to each other in the quiet, that they'll get back in the one crowded car and talk about us sexually. Not intricately, nor much, but with sighs and brief agreements. They won't use our Christian names: "she," "her," "the big one," "that little blonde kid."

They'll talk about us, and some of our children, as "lays." The raucous, elaborate flirtations of the kitchen like mere spray on the larger creek of their deeper feelings, and those, they share only with each other, not with women. At least, not with women that they don't know. And not much with each other, and never in mixed company. Their deepest feelings may not be known.

They will squeeze and settle into the car, and in the lull of opening new beers, looking out the rear window and slowly backing out the quarter-mile of still-passable road to the tarred road, they'll talk. "A little to the left, a little to the left! Watch it!" Not hard to imagine their heavy, gloomy insinuations, the language of their serious formulas: "Yeah, I could sure go for that." "Oh yeah, man, couldn't you though." The afternoon is over. It's time for everyone's supper at home. Hilde begins to gather up her children. "I'll have to hose you bunch down," she says.

Next day, seen singly in the village store, buying gas, bread, screws, stain, baby cereal, each man is subdued, circumspect, stiff, polite, perfunctory, eyes kept down, parsimonious, shy, Yankee. This is store decorum, and lore that I don't know yet controls it. It is as much ritualized, however, this decorum, and as much agreed-upon as are the protected ceremonies of abandon, to which we all move in and out the days as to an invisible music, a minuet, that calls the spring dance.

Settling Twice

Deborah Joy Corey

I n Penobscot, Maine, I often travel a stretch of road similar to the one that ran past my childhood home in New Brunswick, Canada. It wanders the same easy way through scattered country houses, a Baptist church, abandoned barns, and a general store. On the southward stretch, I pass the tiny rectangular field like the one where my older brother Dana was shot on Halloween night, when he was twelve.

In Bangor, Maine, there is a replica of the five-story brick mental hospital where my maternal grandmother died. It has stacked, barred windows identical to those one of *her* daughters would stand in years after her mother's death, crying and clinging to the bars, her head tucked beneath one reaching arm like that of an ibis. Some of her family who had just visited were driving away. I was in that departing car. I was five and remember feeling afraid for my aunt. Something about the still and paralyzed look on her face, and the swirl of the greenish yellow paint on the visiting room's walls had made me feel as if life in that place was racing out of control.

The clammy July heat made my legs stick to the vinyl car seat, so I had turned my head only slightly to look back at my aunt. The sun was shining on the window where she stood, and it made her appear ghostly behind the bars. Earlier in the visiting room, a thin male patient had put his face close to mine and stuck his tongue out. His tongue looked like the pointed tongue of a sparrow and his breath smelled both metallic and sour. His brown hair was wild and looked as if it had been singed by fire.

My father drove that day. My mother sat close to him and cried. "We need to get her out of there. She'll die in there just like my mother." Dad took one hand off the steering wheel and pulled Mom close to him, which made her cry louder. Her shoulders were round and white in a sleeveless dress and they heaved up and down as if her heart was trying to escape. I thought Dad might sing one of the many songs he often sang to Mom while he was driving, but he was quiet. Still, I imagined him singing:

> *Daisy, Daisy, give me your answer do*
> *I'm half crazy all for the love of you*
> *It won't be a stylish marriage*
> *I can't afford a carriage*
> *But you'll look sweet upon the seat*
> *Of a bicycle built for two!*

My younger brother Aubrey sat next to me, staring down at his open palm, which held a black, skeletal key. It looked exactly like the one the nurse had used to open my aunt's locked door. I reached over to touch it, but Aubrey closed his hand quickly and stared at me as if to say, *You never saw that.*

I wondered if he had stolen the key to my aunt's room or if he had just taken some random key left on a table or a wooden bench in that hideous-colored waiting room. Or did one single key work for all the rooms? Could a boy steal a key, and then unlock every door, freeing the patients like birds from a cage?

"What did you think of that man?" I whispered. "The one who stuck his tongue out at me?"

"What a spook," Aubrey said, and then looked away. "They're all a bunch of spooks."

Before we turned onto the main road, I looked back at the hospital. All I could see was a bright sunspot in the window where Aunt Anna had stood. It was as if she'd been zapped away and nothing was left of her but a bright gleaming stain. When we moved beyond the black iron gates, I saw the name of the hospital written on a plaque, *Fairview*.

As the road ahead twisted and curved towards home, I listened to my mother, whose crying had turned to sighing, while quietly reciting all the provinces of Canada with their capitals, one of the many things besides reading and arithmetic my now barred aunt had been teaching me. *The capital of Nova Scotia is Halifax, the capital of Prince Edward Island is Charlottetown, the capital of Newfoundland is St John's, the Capital of New Brunswick is Fredericton . . . .*

When I finished all ten provinces plus the Yukon and the Northwest Territories, I began again, for in the exercise of remembering and repeating, I could see my Aunt Anna's broad-cheeked face before me instead of the lonely road ahead. I could see her lips, which were always plump and moist, but had on that day resembled two dried worms.

Driving through Bucksport, Maine, to reach Castine, I pass a paper mill reminding me of the one that promised progress to my small stretch of Canadian road in the late sixties. First, heavy machinery called harvesters clear-cut a large swath of forest near the Saint John River. The machinery did not cut the trees, as was the usual custom, but yanked out every tree in its path by the roots until a whole section of forest lay decimated, the roots twisting up like old arthritic hands. The decimation disturbed my father. He was a landowner and made his living from the forest, too. A respected cruiser, he knew the woods intimately and many companies called on him for his estimates and advice. Dad could pace out a tract of the forest and judge to the cord what could be cut and how much the stumpage would bring. He believed in selective cutting and replanting. He also believed in only taking what was needed, and he knew the roots of the great trees on the banks of the Saint John River held everything in place. Without them, the spring melts would bring flooding and erosion.

After the huge trees had been hauled away, a barren, dusty patch of land remained. Black crows flew and pecked about. Looking at it, I thought of Golgotha, that place I'd heard about in church.

In the months that followed, a high, steel building was slowly erected and then fenced in like a prison with barbed wire. One crisp fall day the progress began, signified by white, sulfur-smelling smoke that billowed into the blue sky. If I were to give the smell a color, it would not have been that white, but the greenish yellow of the visiting room walls at *Fairview*.

One Sunday, beneath the smoke, a line of local men with lunch pails walked behind the fence to begin their shift. Driving the family to church, my father slowed down to watch them enter the mill, a towering grey wall of a building without windows. Aubrey leaned over the front seat and asked Dad what they did in the mill. *What they made?*

"They're making clouds," Dad said, and then lit a cigarette. In the shadow of the great cloud-maker, the smoke my father expelled seemed wispy and insignificant.

Outside of Bucksport, Maine, is a long stretch of road with a railroad track crossing, much like the one where my father's car was hit by a speeding train. He had just dropped Aubrey off at hockey practice in the new arena paid for by the paper mill and was returning home. The cold, moonlit night was white with crusty snow, the sky clear and starry. When the train hit my father's car, it carried him half a mile along the tracks and into the woods before coming to a complete stop. The train tracks were also new, courtesy of the paper mill, and while speeding home, my father completely forgot about them. Since the wigwags and warning lights had yet to be installed, there was nothing to remind him.

After, Father's new Ford LTD resembled crumpled paper. Volunteer firemen worked almost an hour before they were able to pry him out from under the dash. Fortunately, he had known enough to duck. Rescued, he punched his fedora hat back into shape before placing it on his head, and then walked away unscathed in his dark green car coat, as the train sat still and steaming on the tracks.

When my father reached the road, he could hear someone calling, *Dad, Dad, Dad.* Aubrey had run the three miles from the arena after someone reported to him that his father's car had been hit by a speeding train. Years later, Aubrey would tell me he took a short-cut across the frozen river to get to the railroad tracks. Although snowmobiles and even cars sometimes ventured on the frozen river, we were warned to stay away. Our father said that one could never predict when a body of frozen water might decide to open. I thought how my younger brother could have disappeared into the great river that night, trapped beneath a layer of ice. I thought how on his way to find what he expected to be his dead father; *he* could have been lost forever.

At the church suppers in Castine, Maine, where I live, three and a half hours from my home of origin, I often see my many aunts who are now deceased, stalwart women whose affection and goodwill lifted me up as a child. I have found a twin for every one of them. Aunt Anna, Aunt Verta, Aunt Marguerite, Aunt Ginny, Aunt Ethel, Aunt Nina, Aunt Elma. They still wear the starched, bibbed aprons of years ago, of sisterhood, of baking white cakes that rise up like castles and sweet rolls that are made for butter, of exchanging recipes, some for food and some for life. They are the women of good causes and of lives surely not quite what they dreamed they would be, even though their carefree smiles always suggest otherwise.

Many of these women are descendants of the Loyalists, just as I am. When some of my ancestors came north from Boston in the late 1700s on their way to British territory, they landed on the shores of Castine. One story is that they thought they were on the St. Croix River in New Brunswick, and did not know they had landed on the Penobscot River a day's sail south of their planned destination. They built houses and planted crops, only to learn years later that they were not under the protection of the British Navy. Immediately, many of them dismantled their houses, loading them and their families and possessions on ships so they might sail north to the banks of the St. Croix River, then called the Quoddy.

One of the history books I read as a child said the Loyalist men were gallant gentlemen who wore powdered wigs and plum-colored coats and three-cornered hats, and that on their ships, along with their slaves and livestock, they carried priceless mahogany, silver, damask linen, and family portraits in heavy trunks. When the Indians saw the white-sailed ships of the Loyalists on the horizon, they thought they were great birds coming across the water, for no ships had ever ventured that far along that river. *So did the white man come to the waters of the Quoddy.* There, they settled and named the town St. Andrews, Shiretown of Charlotte.

Often, my family and I visited St. Andrews. The Loyalist houses that had been dismantled in Castine and rebuilt in St. Andrews were marked with plaques, and my parents loved to walk by them and think of the Loyalists' journey from the Penobscot to the St Croix.

"Imagine," Mother often said, "moving your whole life on a ship. What a job. Those poor women—having to settle twice."

After my mother died, I found in the bottom of her hope chest two large linen pieces with red stitching. Redwork, it is called, and the pieces are signed by my grandmother, Nora Taylor, the one who died at Fairview, the one who was a descendant of those grand yet once-displaced Loyalists. Her Loyalist ancestors who remained in America were ancestors of the 12th President of the United States, Zachary Taylor. Recently, *U.S. News and World Report* voted him one of the worst presidents ever to have served. Although he was a brave soldier, the article said, he could be "unaware to the point of innocence."

One of those pieces of redwork from my mother's hope chest shows a young girl sleeping, accompanied by the stitched words, *I slept, and I dremed that life was beauty.* I love that the word "dreamed" is spelled wrong. The second linen is of a young woman sweeping, with the words, *I woke, and I found that life was duty.*

One corner of the *duty* linen is frayed as if worn, but was probably discovered by a mouse who no doubt wanted to line her *new* nest with red linen thread, working vigorously to retrieve it. I suppose most women end up working harder in their lives than they ever *dremed.* I know many of my Loyalist ancestors did, as surely as my mother and my teacher-aunt, and those women of good causes and church suppers.

At my first church supper in Castine, a woman whom I likened to my Aunt Verta because of her rotund, solid shape and smiling, tilted round face, welcomed me and later asked if I knew the story of the Little Drummer Boy.

"The one who didn't have a present for Jesus?" I asked.

"Oh no," she said, "the one who was abandoned here in 1779. He was American, and when the Loyalists fled, they left him locked up in the barracks of Fort George." I pictured Fort George high on the hill. I had already been there a few times to explore, so was familiar with the barred room dug into the side of the hill on the southwest corner.

"They say he played his drum until he died. When they excavated a number of years ago, they found a small skeleton drooped over a dusty drum."

"Really?"

The image took my breath away, not the image of a young boy dying, but the image of my ancestors, my blood, having abandoned him.

In the emergency room at the hospital in Blue Hill, Maine, where I have waited with each of my daughters on different occasions as they spiked a temperature or cradled a broken arm, there is an extra-wide interior door that says ICU. Seeing it always reminds me of my brother Dana who once lay behind such a door in a New Brunswick hospital. He was packed on a bed of ice and bleeding from every orifice of his body, dying at the age of twenty-two from alcohol and prescription drugs. The demons of being shot on that Halloween night when he was twelve, and then dragged into the shooter's house and held hostage, had never stopped haunting him.

We, his family, had been instructed to say good-bye as he hemorrhaged, but our mother refused to say good-bye to one of her children, keeping a prayer vigil over him for twenty-four hours until his bleeding stopped and the doctor pronounced his obvious recovery a miracle. My father had stood behind Mother the whole time she prayed, his hand resting on her shoulder like a flightless wing, but as far as I know, his legs never once buckled the way they had when the doctor first announced my brother's pending death.

Dana wasn't the only member of my family who lay afflicted behind that door marked ICU. Ten years later, my father would lie behind the same door, his body refusing to heal after surgery for intestinal cancer. It would take days for the hospital staff to discover that a pair of surgical scissors had been left inside him, post op. Recently, I read the chances of this happening are one in fifteen thousand. A doctor who is a MacArthur recipient was studying such things, the article said, in the hope of improving the odds against medical mistakes. I couldn't help wondering what the odds were of having your car struck by a train, and what were the odds of surviving such a wreck? What were the odds of getting intestinal cancer at the age of fifty and then surviving the embedded surgical scissors for weeks? Such was our father's intestinal fortitude, we often teased, for he was so courageous and resolute that we never dreamed he'd really die. But thirty years after the surgical scissors were removed, my father would lie behind that same ICU door, his cancer having recurred so aggressively that it had eaten the bottom of his spine away. His fortitude remained, even though morphine kept him restless and sometimes confused. "I can't remember your name," he confessed to me in tears the morning before he died.

My mother and my six siblings had been gathered for fifty-four days and nights, taking turns keeping a vigil over Dad. We did not want him to die alone. The doctor had noticed a slight improvement, a rallying, and my family suggested that I take a break. "You need to go home and sleep in your own bed," my sisters said. "You're exhausted." Before leaving, I asked the doctor how long he thought my father would live. "He's very sick," the doctor said, "but he's also very strong. His heart is like an athlete's." It was no wonder. One of his favorite things was to head out into the untrailed forest with a compass around his neck. Several miles was but a stroll for him.

Yet on the night that I arrived back home in Maine to rest, my sister called at 3:20 in the morning to say Dad was gone.

Dad, Dad, Dad.

"Jesus," I cried, "dear Jesus."

"He's all around you," my sister said. "Just feel him." I did not know if she meant Jesus or my father.

I did not ask.

To this day, I am often haunted by my father's suffering and sorrows, and how I contributed to some of them. One always occurs to me when I pass the curving on-ramp along I-95 at Orono, Maine. It resembles the entrance ramp where two good friends of mine were killed on the night we graduated from high school. At the time of the accident, I was back at the party house, having refused to leave when they coaxed me to go eat an early breakfast at an all-night diner out on the Trans-Canada highway. I don't know why I refused to go. True, the driver of the car and my date for the night had been drinking, but I was young and had already taken many other chances. Had I accepted their offer, I too would have been hit by the oncoming tractor-trailer. As it turned out, my girlfriend Carol sat between the two boys and was killed instantly along with her date, Greg.

The car crash was so loud that it woke many residents along the river and a phone chain began, finally reaching my father who rushed to the site. The emergency crews had already removed the passengers and the howl of the distancing ambulances could still be heard. A friend at the site said when my father saw the crumpled car, he dropped down on the eroded treeless river bank and wept. Of course, he recognized my date's car and of course, he had no way of knowing I wasn't in that car.

When I was eighteen, I wanted nothing more than to escape my stretch of road with wrecked cars, barred windows, and ICU doors, first landing in Toronto, where I studied acting, and then much later, after I was married, Boston, and finally north like my Loyalist ancestors to Castine, Maine.

At eighteen, I wanted to leave the field of gunshots. I wanted to forget that my maternal grandmother, Nora Taylor, had died in that mental hospital after she visited a Pentecostal church for the first time. During the service, a young zealous preacher insisted that she stand on a chair and try to speak in tongues. Perhaps like one of her infamous American ancestors, she too was unaware to the point of innocence, climbing on that unsteady chair. The result was she fell, hitting the front of her head so hard on the altar that she began to convulse. The preacher thought she was *having a fit* and drove her to Fairview two hours away, where she died a week later of a cerebral hemorrhage. She was forty-nine years old, the same age I am now.

The story goes that my grandfather brought my dead grandmother home and laid her naked on their bed, studying every inch of the body that had given him nine children, the body that had been with him since she was a young girl sleeping and *dreaming* of a life as beauty. It was the descendant of another woman's body that had once also unknowingly landed on the wrong shore.

My grandfather was afraid that my grandmother had been beaten to death, as was often the custom then in lock-down facilities. A police officer, he was aware of these things. He was also Scottish Catholic and did not believe people should attempt to speak in tongues. He died one month and one day later, while cutting firewood for the kitchen stove. According to my mother, he died of a broken heart, which was only a saying then, but recently has been proven to be a very real physical response to sudden loss. Maybe the doctor who proved that should get a MacArthur grant as well. For in this world of sorrow, proof of one's broken heart might be a worthy diagnosis, a condition to take precautions against.

At the time of my grandfather's death, his children ranged from two to twenty years of age. They were eventually divided up like candy among their relatives. My mother, who was the two-year-old baby, went to live with her aunt who was going blind. My mother's oldest brother became a painter like his mother, and later did many paintings of that family before they were split apart. My favorite is of all the siblings, bundled up for the winter cold and chopping wood outside.

The boys hand-saw the wood while the little girls stack and secure it under their tiny chins as their colorful scarves blow sideways in the wind. In the frosty window of the small cape behind them, a toddler's face peers out, *my mother*, and above her in another frosty pane is an older face which resembles that of a mother's, but is the face of her sister, Anna. She is frowning. Watching the children, she must have felt their desire to stay together, their little hands and arms working to keep the fire going, still *dreaming of a life of beauty*, yet already training for their lives of duty. Of course, Aunt Anna knew staying together would be impossible. She couldn't take care of them all. My mother said the unjustified feeling of abandoning her siblings never left Aunt Anna. And eventually she died of a broken heart, too, although some called it a heart attack instead.

Among the sorrows I wanted to forget at eighteen was that when Aubrey finally reached my father on the night of the train crash, he had vomited so badly that my father had to take him into the woods and strip his putrid outer clothes away. Afterward, Dad removed his own coat and wrapped it around his son.

Apparently, the volunteer firemen offered to drive them home, but Dad said no. He said they'd like to walk. *It's only a few miles.* And that is what I see when I remember that cold moonlit night, the back of a tall man in a fedora hat, his wing-shaped hand resting on the shoulder of a skinny-legged boy in an oversized car coat. If I were a painter like my grandmother and uncle, I'm sure I would have already painted several variations of this scene. It is as real to me as if I'd been there, so real that sometimes I could reach out and touch it, not the scene so much, but the feeling I have imagining it.

Recently, I saw the Edvard Munch exhibit at the MOMA in NYC. I have always been drawn to his well-known painting, *The Scream*. Seeing it in a photograph for the first time many years ago, I got the same terrifying feeling as on that day when we sat in the visiting room with Aunt Anna at Fairview. In the background, Munch has used the same swirling greenish yellow of the waiting room, creating a speeding swirl of fear. The figures in *The Scream* are still, but the world around them is rippling out like a vast stone thrown into a still pond, visually echoing the scream.

Yet after spending the afternoon with Munch's work, I came to the conclusion that perhaps *The Scream* was one of his lesser works. Like the waiting room at the mental hospital, the painting had the feeling of horror without the balm of compassion. It was ghoulish in both its central image and the sound I saw and imagined rippling around it.

After visiting the exhibit, Munch's paintings *Death in the Sick Room* and *The Sick Child* were supreme in my estimation. In these paintings, love embraces the suffering. "I do not paint what I see, but what I saw," Munch said. "My sufferings are part of myself." And although the horror is present in these less famous paintings, it is lessened by an echoing compassion, far more powerful than a sickening yellow swirl.

These paintings are neither spooky nor ghoulish.

As Munch's sister Sophie was dying, she asked to be taken out of a bed and put in a chair. Munch's 1893 *Death In The Sick Room* captures the emotion of that scene. "It's not the chair that should be painted," Munch wrote, "but what a person has felt at the sight of it."

In the painting, just the slight crook of Sophie's arm is visible. It is mainly the back of the black high-styled chair she has been placed in that the viewer sees. To me, as in *The Scream*, it is a painting of echoes, but gentler, like a familiar hymn being hummed over and over. In a chair behind the dying girl sits another girl, red-headed as Sophie was, with her head bowed. Both of these figures are attended by somber yet obviously loving parental shapes. One shape is praying. There is the exquisite feeling of wholeness in this painting. Why, I wondered, standing before *The Sick Child*, if one was going to admire a Munch painting, would one not admire this one? Why choose a scream rather than a hymn?

At eighteen, en route to Toronto, I wanted to forget that the simpleton who shot my brother on Halloween night was our school bus driver. As a Halloween prank, they had wanted to let the air out of the school bus tires. What boys of twelve wouldn't want to do that? I'm sure in their giddy enthusiasm, it never crossed their minds that a gunman might lie in wait near the bus, nor that after shooting my brother, this man would drag him into his house, threatening to finish him off. "If you don't stop screaming, I'll take you to the river and drown you." Dana shook and screamed, *Dad, Dad, Dad*, until my father, retrieved by my brother's friend, broke into the tiny house and lifted his son off the floor.

After spending one night in jail, the shooter continued to drive my siblings and me each day to school. How I hated his pin-point eyes, his round wire glasses, his beaky nose and black hole for a mouth. How I avoided the sight of him when the bus door snapped open. How I wanted to run. No wonder Dana eventually quit school, remaining home with my mother, who home-schooled him with such love and care that we his siblings have often voted him the smartest of us all. She taught him to record his dreams and think in metaphor; she taught him to bake biscuits, to discuss religions, and to recite poetry; and she taught him to love the sound of quiet and to read critically and to rest. And by listening to his anguish, she taught him to listen to the anguish of others, one of his traits that I now value most.

In acting classes in Toronto, I studied the Stanislavsky method, training myself to visit my family memories over and over, then turning them into the scenes I was asked to play. As Maria in *West Side Story*, I reacted to a brother's death while recalling my own brother's bleeding body one Halloween night. I became Amanda Wingfield in *A Glass Menagerie*, thinking of my Aunt Anna and the feeling of abandonment she must have felt that day we drove away without her. Each time I used some deeply buried and difficult memory to replicate an emotion, I also grew closer to the character my acting coach wanted me to create. For a time, he nicknamed me "Deborah the distraught." I grew closer to my family's pain and as frayed inside as the edges of that embroidered linen in my mother's hope chest bearing the words, *I woke, and I found that life was duty.*

One day, my acting coach asked for joy rather than despair, and I found that emotion impossible to give. "For God's sake, Deborah," he said, "it's your middle name. Can't you give the character some joy?"

I felt paralyzed—held in a scream.

I thought of the word joy, saw its jumbled letters in front of me, then scurried inside myself, looking for the precious thing tucked at the bottom. I remembered how my mother had given me the middle name Joy, because she had labored all night long to give birth to me. When telling me of the night I was born, she always quoted the chosen psalm, "Weeping may endure for the night, but joy cometh in the morning."

Beneath my acting lay much joy, but my heart and mind refused to access it. What if I wore my joy memories out, or rubbed them bare as I had been doing with my difficult memories? I had allowed the echoes of my families' screams to repeat openly on stage, but my joy belonged to me.

That very day, I quit acting and took up modeling. On runways and photo shoots, I painted my face with such care that nothing of my past shone through. I learned to keep my eyes cold and concentrated, I learned to let clothing become the chameleon's skin, which allowed me to strut down a runway. Walking with loose hips, I felt all that truly mattered to me was still hidden deep inside. My joyful memories were like gardenias in a sealed room, unbelievably beautiful, and yet so pungent they could make me weep whenever I opened the door.

Much later, and a week before my father died, I spent the night at the hospital with him. He'd been moved from the ICU to Palliative Care. Disease had played hide-and-seek in my father's body for many years, yet the odds had always worked in his favor; so his medically predicted, pending death was impossible to accept. Hadn't he always survived? Hadn't we all?

As I sat by his side, the night light made his hospital room seem grey, yet somehow iridescent. It felt as if we were in the gloaming, as if time had been magically rolled back and the two of us were old friends sitting together on the branch of a big tree. We were suspended. Held in love is the only way to describe it, as silly as that sounds. I had long left modeling behind and was married with a daughter of my own, living on the coast of Maine and writing fiction.

In that hospital room, I leaned forward in the blue vinyl chair beside Dad's bed and rested my hands on the white sheets. He patted and rubbed my fingers as we talked, and I looked down at his worn gold wedding band. It was as thin as golden wire. He and my mother had been married fifty-nine years. After a while, Dad moved over in his narrow hospital bed and made room for me. I knew it hurt him to move, but he didn't wince. I climbed in under the sheet and laid my head on his chest. His heart was thumping like a distant drum, which I would come to remember as the slow steady beat of death, as ominous as the sound of a boy drumming in his deathly barrack.

Dad's emaciated hip bone curved into my stomach. He smelled of a pine forest. "Your mother's eyes," Dad said, "I'm worried about her eyes."

Mom had macular degeneration and was no longer able to drive her car nor read her adored books. She often missed a step and fell.

"It just seems so unfair."

"Daddy, we will take care of Mom."

He wrapped his arms around me tighter and held me to his side as close as he could, and I felt all of his lovely green forest coming from his wasted body into mine. I felt joy. I felt wholeness. "And who will take care of you?" He asked.

"My husband," I said

"Yes," Dad said, "Yes, Bill will." He kissed my forehead and I said, "Daddy, will you please sing *A Bicycle Built for Two*?"

Not only had it been a song he often sang to my mother, but for my sixteenth birthday he had bought me a bicycle built for two and we had ridden it late into the night, singing and laughing, as the summer cicadas' wings hummed in the air, a hymn that lit a string of golden light between my heart and his.

Dad pulled me closer and started to sing, but then his voice cracked and he stopped, so I sang for him while his fingers drummed out the tune on my shoulder:

> It won't be a stylish marriage
> I can't afford a carriage
> But you'll look sweet upon the seat
> Of a bicycle built for two.

On the night that Aubrey and Dad walked home from the train crash, they entered the kitchen and stood for a moment like strangers. A rush of cold air came with them. I was drawing a pile of decimated trees on white paper. The roots of the trees reached up to the heavens as if they were delivering a prayer. Mother was next to the kitchen window starching and ironing pillowcases. She had been wondering about Dad's whereabouts for some time, glancing out the dark window as she ironed.

Looking at Dad and Aubrey, her lips slowly shaped in an O, she suddenly rushed across the kitchen and wrapped her arms around them. Her white apron strings tied at her back were like ribbon. Aubrey began to cry, so I rushed into the circle and cried, too, and among us there was a feeling of great gratitude even though things were yet to be explained. The overriding fresh smell of my mother's starched apron was like a clean bed. And there was the feeling of joy. There was wholeness.

On the night that Dana was shot, rather than wait for help to arrive, my father rescued him and loaded him into the car, rushing to the hospital. Mother remained home with Aubrey and me. The police had been called but had not arrived. Although no one said it, I think my parents felt that night the world had turned on their family and was a dangerous place, swirling about.

Aubrey and I lay with mother in her bed, one on each side, crying and shaking while she brushed our foreheads and hummed a familiar hymn. I thought of the words as I listened: *It is well with my soul. It is well with my soul, it is well, it is well, it is well with my soul . . . .*

The phone on the nightstand rang.

Aubrey and I turned rigid beside her as we listened to the bus driver's voice blare through the receiver, threatening to come and kill us all.

"Mr. Bates," my mother said, sitting up straight in the bed, "if you have a little time on your hands just now, I suggest rather than shoot any more children, you get down on your knees and pray for mercy."

Mother slammed the receiver down, then cuddled back down and pulled us to her chest. She smelled of baking bread and her heart was racing, almost buzzing like the wings of summer cicadas. Soon, she began to hum again.

After a while I began to hum and then Aubrey did too, and for a time we were tucked beneath the wings of a loving, humming mother, suspended. The night rolled back to its gloaming, to the happy time before the world had turned.

Many years later, I would read about a troop of Boy Scouts on a camping trip in the Northwest Territories. I remember them as being seventy miles from the capital of Yellowknife, although I'm not sure that is accurate. In the night, a grizzly bear entered their tent and began mauling one of the boys. The others in their terror began to hum. I suppose their humming was no different than my mother's. Faced with the death of one child, she managed to keep the fear of her other children at bay with humming, no different than a little drummer boy beating his drum or a dying father tapping out a favorite tune on a daughter's shoulder.

In so many ways, Maine is New Brunswick's twin sister. They line up together, shoring each other like siblings. Like the settlers who landed in Castine in 1773 believing they were in Canada, I often think I am in Canada as well. The similar places I go by allow me to remember my past. In these settings, the jagged cracks of my family's lives are still visible, but more importantly, so is their joy. I see the iridescent gloaming in each familiar scene. I know now it was not that my father was almost killed by a speeding train, but that afterward, he walked with his hand on the shoulder of a shocked son. It is not that my father lay dying a painful death in a hospital bed, but that he found the strength to move over and make room to hold me so I could breathe in the fleeting green of him. It is not that my brother was shot, but that after, my mother was courageous enough to hum my frightened brother and me to sleep. It is not that my grandmother died an unnecessary death in an insane asylum, but that my grandfather retrieved and cared for her body. And it is not that my brother lay dying, but that Mom prayed until there was hope, while Dad's reassuring hand rested on her shoulder. When my family and I look back, we do not see the dying brother, we hear the prayers like cicada wings in the air, and we feel the golden light of such devotion lit between our hearts.

Sometimes when we remember, we weep. Not because we are sad, but because we know joy. Our parents wove it in us like red linen thread in a nest. And *what, dear Jesus, what were those wonderful odds*?

As Munch said, it is not the death chair that should be painted, but what a person has felt at the sight of it. How sturdy those feelings make us. Like the roots of the great trees that held everything in place on the banks of the Saint John River, our parents' love supported our family hardships, and it continues. For that kind of love never leaves, *it is all around*. We simply need to *feel it*.

In Maine, some may see me as a settler on the wrong shore, but all that is familiar makes it feel just right. There is no need for a ship to take me and my precious possessions farther on. This is where I'll stay with my family. Joyfully passing the places that remind me of home.

"Why Don't You Write a Book?"
from *We Took to the Woods*

Louise Dickinson Rich

During most of my adolescence—specifically, between the time when I gave up wanting to be a brakeman on a freight train and the time when I definitely decided to become an English teacher—I said, when asked what I was going to do with my life, that I was going to live alone in a cabin in the Maine woods and write. It seemed to me that this was a romantic notion, and I was insufferably smug over my own originality. Of course, I found out later that everybody is at one time or another going to do something of the sort. It's part of being young. The only difference in my case is that, grown to womanhood, I seem to be living in a cabin in the Maine woods, and I seem to be writing.

There is nothing that I so greatly admire as purposefulness. I have an enormous respect for people who know exactly what they are doing and where they are going. Such people are compact and integrated. They have clear edges. They give an impression of invulnerability and balance, and I wish that I were one of them.

I wish that I could say that, from the moment I first thought about this kind of a life to the moment almost two decades later when I finally began living it, I had been working single-mindedly toward it. But it wouldn't be true. Actually I'd forgotten all about it long before. I did a lot of things—graduated from college, taught school, worked in an institution for the feeble-minded, went to Europe—but none of it was in preparation for an end. At the time it seemed end enough in itself.

I was shocked, therefore, to receive not long ago and within the same week, letters from two old friends saying virtually the same thing, although the writers are strangers to each other. What they said, in effect, was this: "Isn't it wonderful that you're at last doing what you always said you wanted to do! It proves that anything is possible, if one wants it enough to work for it."

My two friends, I thank you for your high opinion of my character, and I hate to have to disabuse you of it. It is wonderful—far more wonderful than you know—that I am doing what I once, without really believing it, said I was going to do. But if it proves anything, it is only that some people are fools for luck. Let me admit that not only is my living in the woods and writing an accident on both counts, but that until I received your letters I had been so busy coping with the situation that I hadn't even realized that I was living my old dream. It's a very queer feeling to wake up and find that the dream has sneaked up on you and become the reality.

There are differences, of course. My idea was a little log cabin in a sort of spacious park. There is nothing park-like about this northwestern-most corner of Maine. Here, between two ranges of mountains, the Boundary Mountains and the Blue Mountains, lies a high, wild valley, the basin that holds the Rangeley Lakes. The country is crisscrossed with ridges, dotted with swamps and logans, and covered with dense forest. There are very few people living here, and no roads down into what we call The Outside. There are a few narrow trails, but travel through the woods is so difficult, with the swamps and blowdowns and underbrush, that the lakes have remained what they were to the Indians, the main thoroughfare.

I like to think of the lakes coming down from the north of us like a gigantic staircase to the sea. Kennebago to Rangeley to Cupsuptic, down they drop, level to level, through short, snarling rivers; Mooselukmeguntic to the Richardsons to Pond-in-the-River, and through Rapid River to Umbagog, whence they empty into the Androscoggin and begin the long southeasterly curve back to the ocean.

I like to say their names, and I wish I could make you see them—long, lovely, lonely stretches of water, shut in by dark hills. The trees come down to the shore, the black growth of fir and pine and spruce streaked with the lighter green of maple and birch. There is nothing at all on the hills but forest, and nobody lives there but deer and bear and wildcats. The people keep close to the lakes, building their dwellings in narrow clearings they have made by pushing the trees a little way back from the water.

Our own clearing is on the Rapid River, just below Pond-in-the-River Dam; and because Rapid River is not navigable, being the swiftest river east of the Rockies—it drops a hundred and eighty-five feet in three miles, with no falls, which is some kind of a record—we amazingly live on a road. It doesn't go anywhere. It's really a carry between two lakes, so it is sensibly called the Carry Road. It starts at Middle Dam, on the Lower Richardson, and roughly follows the course of the river five miles to Sunday Cove, on Umbagog.

Middle Dam is quite a community. There is the dam itself, a part of the system for water control on the Androscoggin, with the dam-keeper and his family, Renny and Alice Miller and their three children, in year-round residence. Then in summer the hotel is open. We only call it a hotel; it's really a fishing camp. In winter it is closed, but there is a caretaker, Larry Parsons, who stays in with his wife, Al, and a hired man or two. So the permanent population of Middle Dam hovers at around nine, and that is comparative congestion. We get our mail and supplies through Middle, and it is the point of departure for The Outside, so its importance is all out of proportion to its population.

Sunday Cove, the other end of the carry, is something else again. The rutted, grass-grown road dips down a last steep hill and ends in the lake. There is an abandoned lumber camp rotting down on the shore, and a pair of loons living in the Cove, and that's all there is to it.

And halfway along, between road and river, is Forest Lodge, the sole address on the Carry Road, and our home.

When I said we lived in a cabin in the woods, I was speaking loosely. Forest Lodge is in the woods all right; there is nothing north or south of us but trees for so many miles that sometimes it scares me to think about it. But actually it consists of one cabin, one shack, one large house in the worst cracker-box style, and an assortment of lean-to's, woodsheds, workshops, and what are euphemistically known as outhouses. These latter are necessary because we have no plumbing, and therefore no bathroom.

We get our water from the river and from a spring up back in the woods. We do our bathing in washtubs in front of the kitchen stove, and for other uses of the bathroom, we resort to the outhouses. This is no great hardship in summer, but in winter, with the snow knee deep, the wind howling like a maniac up the river, and the thermometer crawling down to ten below zero, it is a supreme test of fortitude to leave the warmth of the fire and go plunging out into the cold, no matter how great the necessity. We like to think, however, that it builds character.

The cabin, hereafter to be referred to as the Winter House, was the original Forest Lodge, built for a fishing camp. It is a low building with a porch and an ell, set on a knoll with a view up the river to the Pond-in-the-River. From the outside, it's not a bad little house, but everything that could possibly be wrong with it inside is wrong. The ceilings are too high and the windows are too small, although Ralph, my husband, ripped out the old ones and doubled the window space the first year we were here. The living-room, where we spend much of the time in winter, is on the north side, toward the woods, while the bedrooms, which we use only at night, are on the sunny, open side toward the river. The reason for this irritates me. In the country, the living quarters are always on the road side of a house, so that the inhabitants can keep tabs on the passersby. In winter there are normally about three passersby in seven months, here, but still the old rule holds. Apparently it's preferable to sit forever in sunless gloom than to lose one opportunity to speculate about someone's identity, starting point, destination, family connections, and probably discreditable purpose. We can't do anything about the arrangement, because the chimney is in the living-room, and that's where we have to have the stove.

That chimney is another wrong thing. It rises out of a fireplace—

which is too shallow to draw properly—and instead of being in the wall, it is set out into the room about four feet. This splits the room into two parts, making the attractive and comfortable arrangement of furniture impossible. In winter the fireplace itself is of no use whatsoever, as anyone who has lived in the country in winter knows. A fireplace is pretty, and on chilly fall evenings, will keep you warm enough; but what you need in winter is a stove. So we have a stove. We boarded up our pretty fireplace, punched a hole in the side of the chimney, and set up an air-circulating wood heater. It isn't very attractive, and it takes up a lot of room, and set cheek by jowl with the fireplace, it looks silly. But it keeps us warm.

The only advantage of that half-witted chimney arrangement that has appeared to date is that the otherwise wasted space behind it can be used as a woodbox. Ralph, known in these parts as "an ingenious cuss," cut a hole in the house, fitted it with a beveled door like an ice-chest door, and now we can put the wood in from outdoors. This doesn't sound like much of a triumph, but it is, nevertheless. Nothing will cool a house off quicker than opening and closing the front door forty times, while armloads of wood are brought in; and nothing will enrage and discourage the housewife more surely than the pecks of dirt and snow inevitably tracked onto her clean-swept floor. This little woodbox door, therefore, contributes largely to the peace and comfort of the Rich ménage.

Why don't we just burn the Winter House down and forget about it? Because it's the only house that can be heated in really cold weather. Ralph has insulated it properly and finished the inside with really beautiful hand-rubbed pine paneling, and in spite of all I have said against it, it's not half bad, actually. It hasn't any kitchen, either, which is a point in its favor, odd as that may sound. We use the kitchen ell of the Big House all the year round, so the cooking odors that always collect in small country houses in the winter, no matter how often they are aired, never get into the Winter House.

About the last of May, or as soon as it is warm enough, we move down into the Big House, and the Winter House becomes the guest house for the summer. The Big House was built at a later date for a summer camp, and that is all it is good for in its present state. It is big and airy and the walls are too thin for warmth and it sprawls all over the place. I like it because it is on a high bluff over the river, with a view and sunlight and space to spread out in; because it has a huge stone fireplace that will take four-foot logs and really heat the living-room in the wettest, coldest September rain storm; because there is a wide porch over the river; because if I decide to eat some crackers and cheese before going to bed, I don't have to climb into a mackinaw and gumboots as I do in winter, and cross a clearing in the cold to get them. And most of all I like it because I like to go upstairs to bed, instead of into the next room. For these reasons, we always put off moving out of it in the fall until the last possible moment, and we are re-building it so we can live in it all the year. Since Ralph is doing the work himself, for economic reasons, this is a slow process. At the moment the whole structure is balanced precariously on poles over the cellar he has dug beneath it. It looks both dangerous and sloppy, but he says it's perfectly safe, and when you're in a house, its external appearance needn't bother you. In fact, I should think a good way to buy a house would be by the looks of the house across the street, which is the one you see most of.

The house across the street here is the Guide's House, or what would be the servants' quarters, if we had servants. It's called the Guide's House because most people living in a place like this would be summer people, and they would employ a registered guide, who would live in the house across the road. It's a nice little shack, with a living-room and two bedrooms, and Gerrish lives there.

Gerrish works for us, but he is in no sense a servant. He has a guide's license, but that isn't important, because so have Ralph and I. It's a handy thing to own, around here. What Gerrish is, I suppose, is the hired help. We pay him to do certain things, which is the hired part. But since he is practically a member of the family, he does a great many other things for which we don't, and couldn't, pay him. That's the help part. We couldn't ever pay him, for example, for being so good and patient with our four-year-old Rufus, who, not to mince words, is often a pest, un-motherly an observation as that may be.

Gerrish has to take his pay for that out of Rufus's adoration of him. We couldn't pay him, either, for being so dependable, and for always giving us a dollar and a quarter's worth of work for every dollar of his wages. We are very lucky to have found him. This is not a place that many people would care to work in. It is remote, not only from movies and stores, but from other people. There is nowhere to go except hunting and fishing, and nothing to see except woods and water. But luckily Gerrish likes it, and I think that he considers the Guide's House, his own undisputed realm, as home. Perhaps that is pay of a kind.

The one building here that looks as though it belonged in the deep woods is Ralph's shop, an old log cabin from long before our day. I can't say much about it, as it comes under the heading of sacred ground. It is full of tools and pieces of board that look like any other boards, but which have something special about them, so that they must never be touched, or even looked at. Hanging from the rafters are old car parts, lengths of rope, chains and boat seats, all of which are going to be used some day for some important project. In the middle is a pile of invaluable junk, and around the edges are kegs of nails and bolts. In my bridal innocence I used, when I needed a nail, to go and take one out of a keg. But it always turned out that I had taken (a) the wrong kind of nail for the job on hand, and (b) a nail that was being conserved for a specific purpose and was practically irreplaceable. So now when I need a nail I find Ralph and ask him to get me one.

He's usually easy to find. I have only to listen for the sound of a motor running. He is completely infatuated with gasoline motors, and collects them from the most improbable places. Once he brought home an old motor that someone had hauled into South Arm for a mooring anchor and then abandoned. It had been underwater all summer and frozen into the ice all winter, but he dragged it the seven miles home on a hand sled, brooded over it, took it to pieces and put it together again, and now it runs the saw that saws our firewood.

We have only five miles of road to run a car on, but we are a four-car family. They aren't new models—the newest is a 1930 Model A and the oldest a 1924 Marmon—but they run, and they pay for themselves. All summer long Ralph hauls canoes and duffle across the carry for camping parties, and in the spring and fall the lumber company finds it convenient to hire him to tote their wangans up from Sunday Cove.

This lumber company is our privacy insurance, our guarantee that we won't wake up some morning and find new neighbors building a pink stucco bungalow down the river from us. With the exception of our two acres and a strip owned by a water power company, they own every foot of land for miles around. And they won't sell an inch to anybody. I won't go into reasons and company policy. All that matters is that, come hell or high water, they will not sell.

So here we sit in what amounts to a forest preserve of some hundreds of square miles; and in that "we" the reality differs again from the dream. I was going to live alone, remember. I don't, and that's quite all right with me.

Besides Ralph, Rufus, and Gerrish, there is Sally, Ralph's sixteen-year-old daughter by a previous marriage, and further proof that I am a fool for luck. A stepdaughter could be a thorn in the flesh, which Sally certainly isn't. And there are Kyak and Tom, the dog and the cat.

We ourselves wouldn't have named Tom that, but we got him from a lumber camp that was moving out and didn't know what to do with him, so we had to take him as equipped. We compromise by saying that his full name is Thomas Bailey Aldrich, which isn't very suitable. He is the sort of cat that should be called Tom, regardless of banality. He is big and tough and mean, and he'd as soon as not fight the whole family at once. His idea of an average day is to get up at noon, trounce the dog for looking at him, go out and chase a deer away from the clearing, and set out the two miles for Middle Dam, there to visit with his girl, the Millers' cat, after half murdering her other three suitors. Then he comes home, looking so smug you could shoot him on sight, and sleeps until noon the next day.

Kyak, though we love him dearly, we have to admit is strictly an Art Dog. His grandmother was with Admiral Byrd at the South Pole, and his great-grandfather helped carry the serum to Nome. If they could see him, they'd turn in their graves. He is a very good example of the Siberian husky, with a white wolf mask, a rangy big body, and a curling plume of a tail; but he is completely nonfunctional. Try to put a harness on him, and he will lie down with all four feet in the air. Try to teach him to retrieve game, and he will look sorrowful and broken. The only thing he is good for, besides looking beautiful, is a watch dog, and he doesn't even do that well. He barks horribly at nothing, or at members of the family, and then amiably lets strange woodsmen walk right into the house. Then after they are in, and for all he knows, we are lying in a welter of blood, sometimes he remembers his responsibilities and stands outside barking hysterically. There's no use trying to do anything with him, except love him.

Around the blank space on the map where we live are some towns and some things that look like towns, but aren't. South Arm is one of these. We simply call it the Arm, and it's important, because it's at the beginning of the road to The Outside. Once you get off the boat from Middle Dam at the Arm, you have begun to leave the woods behind. There is still a long drive to Andover, the first village, but you can't help knowing that if you follow the road far enough you will land, not at a lonely cove tenanted only by loons, but in Boston or New York, or Butte, Montana. It makes a difference. The Arm itself is not imposing, consisting of a huddle of ramshackle wharfs and a string of tired sheds where people in here keep their Outside cars. But its implications are enormous.

Andover really is a town, with a school, two or three little stores, and a post office, whence comes our mail. Upton is a town, too, and our civic center, where we send Sally to school and where we go to vote. Most of the land around here is wild land, or unorganized territory—just squares on the map labeled C Township, or North C Surplus, or Section 37—but the back line of Upton runs north of us, so technically at least we live in organized territory. Upton has one hundred and eighty-two inhabitants and the loveliest view in Maine.

The only other town that concerns us is Magalloway, which is too small to be on the road map or to have a post office. But it does have the Brown Farm, where our telephone line ends. Let me say at once that the Brown Farm isn't a farm, and our telephone line isn't a telephone line, in the modern sense of the word. It is a fifteen-mile-long piece of wire, frail and uninsulated, strung haphazardly through the woods from tree to tree, and the private property of the lumber company, for communication with their various operations. We are hitched onto it only because once they cut down some of our trees by mistake, and extended this courtesy as reparation and apology. If it hasn't snowed lately, or the wind hasn't blown any trees down across the line, or if the wire hasn't sagged wearily into one of the many brooks it crosses, we can, by cranking three times on the battery-powered telephone which hangs on the kitchen wall, talk to the Millers. Or we can ring four times and talk to Cliff, an old hermit who lives down on Umbagog. Or we can ring twice and get the disembodied voice that is all I know of Joe, at the Brown Farm.

Although not a farm, the Brown Farm is a number of other things, including a hospital and delousing station for lumberjacks, a bunkhouse and mess-hall, a rest-cure for work-worn horses, and a storehouse for the tremendous amounts of food and equipment necessary in the lumber camps. There used to be a clerk in that storehouse who had a splendid graft. At that time the lumber company was using a brand of canned goods that gave premiums for the labels off the cans—a pickle dish for ten labels, a baby carriage for five hundred, and, I suppose, a Rolls Royce for a million. The clerk isn't there anymore, though. His label-removing activities—they buy canned goods by the car lot—left him no time for his duties; and besides, the cooks in the camps got bored with having to open twenty anonymous cans before they happened on the sliced beets they were looking for. He was about to retire, anyhow. He'd sold the things he didn't fancy himself, and had money in the bank.

Once, seven years ago, I saw the Brown Farm, but I didn't know then what it was going to mean in my life, so I didn't pay much attention. I don't remember what it looks like. I was the schoolteacher-on-vacation, and my sister and I and some friends came up through this country on a canoe trip. We went through the Parmachenee section, and then we debated whether we should come back through the Rangeleys and along Rapid River or not. The guide insisted that this was the way to come—that although it involved a lot of work, the country was wild and beautiful and unspoiled enough to be worth a few paddle blisters, pack sores, and lame muscles. So we finally gave in, not too enthusiastically, being travel-frayed already.

And that offhand decision, in which I didn't even have a major part, was the accident by which I now live in a cabin in the woods. As we walked along the Carry Road, we saw a man splitting wood in the yard of the only house we had seen in days, and we stopped to talk to him. He had just arrived there that morning, and he was about to build his first fire and cook his first meal. He invited us to stay and eat with him, because he felt like celebrating. He'd bought the place for a summer camp during the boom years, but he hadn't been able to come East from Chicago, where he lived, since 1929. Now, however, he'd sold some patent rights and not only was he going to spend the summer there, but if things turned out right, the rest of his life. We were all touched and amused, I remember, by his enthusiasm.

Now that I know Ralph better, I know that there was nothing strange about his inviting us all to spend the rest of the week with him. Since that day, eight years ago, I've known him to invite a week-end guest, whom he liked, to extend his visit from week to week until it lasted more than two years. But at the time I thought, and I guess all the others thought, that he was crazy. We stayed, though.

We stayed, and we had a lovely time. We fished and sunbathed and swam, and in between times I found out why a man so obviously dry behind the ears should want to bury himself in the woods for the rest of his life. Ever since he was twelve years old, he had been spending his summers at Coburn's, and his winters wishing it were summer so he could go back to Coburn's. Middle Dam was the place in all the world where he was happiest, and he'd always told himself that some day he'd live there permanently. It took a long time and a lot of doing, but finally he'd managed. You see, Ralph, unlike me, has a single-track mind.

My mind, however, did fall into a single track before that week was over. I became obsessed with the idea that if I didn't see more— a lot more—of this Ralph Rich, I'd quietly go into a decline and die. It's a common phenomenon, I believe, both in fact and in fiction. It doesn't need any explanation, if indeed it can be explained. It's seldom fatal, I understand, so probably I'd have recovered if I'd had to. I didn't have to. Almost immediately upon my return to Massachusetts, while I was trying to think up a reasonably plausible excuse for happening back to the Rangeley region at the time of year when people just don't go there, I began getting letters, telegrams, and finally telephone calls, almost daily from Ralph. Then he began spending his time and money on the long and painful trek from Maine to Boston. It was, in short, a Courtship, and ended in the usual manner, with our deciding that this was a lot of expensive nonsense, so why didn't we get married?

I know that everybody who was ever in love has speculated along the following lines, but please bear with me while I do it once again. If, on that trip out of Parmachenee, one of us had stopped on the Carry Road two minutes to tie a shoestring, or if Ralph had split wood just a little bit faster, we would never have laid eyes upon him. He'd have been in the house, and we'd have walked right by. But the timing was perfect, and that's how I happen to live in the woods.

How I happened to be a writer was just as sloppy and haphazard. I wrote a little number about Maine guides, at my sister's suggestion, for *Scribner's* Life in the United States Contest. I finished it in May, and the contest didn't close until September, so I thought I'd try it out on a couple of dogs first. I'd get it back in plenty of time to qualify.

Now this is not mock modesty. I was absolutely stupefied when *The Saturday Evening Post* bought it. Ralph was, too. But we rallied sufficiently to write another entry for the *Scribner's* contest, since our first had been scratched, as it were, and it won a prize. This double success so went to our heads that we decided that from then on we would be writers.

We weren't, of course, because being a writer involves a lot more than just thinking it would be nice to be one. We sold our first attempt at fiction—which was probably bad for us as it gave us false confidence—and then we settled down to discover that writing is not all beer and skittles. But I think that now, at last, we are nearly writers. We don't wait for inspiration anymore, having found that inspiration is mostly the application of the seat of the pants to the seat of a chair.

We stall around, trying to put off writing, which I understand is the occupational disease of writers. We earn most of our living by the written word. And we are utterly impatient with people who say, "I've often thought I could write myself."

It's taken me a great many words, I see, to answer the first questions people always ask us when they come out of the woods and find us here, unaccountably installed in a little clearing that is always full of the smell of pine and the sound of the river. That's a question that always crops up early in the conversation—"Doesn't the river get on your nerves?"—because until you get used to it, the dull roar, like heavy surf, seems to shake the air. It is all-pervading and inescapable, and you find yourself raising your voice higher and higher above it. But after a while, unless the tone changes with the rise and fall of the water, you don't even hear it. You learn to pitch your voice, not louder to carry over it, but lower and deeper, so that it's not shattered by the vibration. And finally all the places in the world that are away from the sound of furious white water come to seem empty and dead.

I don't pretend to know all of the answers. I don't know what to answer when people say, "But isn't the way you live Escapism?" I don't even know, really, what escapism is. We haven't tried to escape from anything. We have only exchanged one set of problems for another—the problem of keeping out from under car wheels for the problem of not getting lost in the woods, for example; or the problem of being bored to death by one's neighbor for the problem of being bored to death by oneself. I don't know what to answer when someone says, "I should think you'd go insane!" It's too cheap and easy and obvious to retort, "And I should think you would."

But some of the answers, the answers to the easy, matter-of-fact questions, like "Why don't you write a book about it?," I do know. The answer to that is, "Well, I guess maybe I will."

And so I am writing a book about it.

Sightings

Edging Up on It
from *The Edge of Maine*

Geoffrey Wolff

We may reason to our heart's content, the fog won't lift.
—Samuel Beckett

I'd first come to the edge of Maine at fourteen from the sky, riding a DC-3 into Bangor a few minutes after a midsummer sunset and then by Pontiac station wagon to Castine. I was visiting a girl I scarcely knew; we'd met during a glee club concert at my school. She was fifteen, an only child, and her dad, driving along the Penobscot River, was asking questions—where did I expect to go to college and did I sail?—and his wife was trying to draw my attention to points of historical and topographical interest out there in the night. In the back seat the girl and I were already holding hands and I wasn't looking out any car windows. After Bucksport the parents clammed up the final half hour as their headlights bounced off streaks of fog swirling at the shoulders of country roads. The station wagon poked hesitantly down a finger of land bounded by the Penobscot and Bagaduce rivers, to its tip on Perkins Point. The drive must have tired them, because after feeding us hot chocolate in their big country kitchen, they sent us off to bed. My room was upstairs at one end of a long hall with creaky pine floors; their daughter's was at the other end; mommy and daddy slept between, with their door open. The next morning, anxious that I might be called on to show what I'd meant when I'd answered that I "liked" to sail—without mentioning that I had been in a sailboat once in my life, and hadn't been happy to be there—I woke soon after dawn, and before me I saw for the first time one of coastal Maine's representative prospects. The house was set on a bluff above Wadsworth Cove and my bedroom windows were aimed to look across a few miles of Penobscot Bay to Islesboro. The curtains hung still and heavy at my open windows, and for a moment I believed it was drizzling rain from my ceiling. Outside was milky, thick. Whatever sailors did, I reckoned, was not going to be done this morning. I gathered my damp sheets around my damp flannel pajamas and fell back asleep. The fog was as lazy as I; it stayed put the whole week. I had much opportunity to study this fog. Its physical properties—droplets responding sluggishly to gravity and stirred gently by an occasional breeze—were dynamic, but the affective atmosphere of the matter—gloom, dampness, a shutoff of the world—was static and unrelenting. A couple of days before I was scheduled to leave, my hosts didn't even try to disguise their anxiety: DC-3s weren't flying into or taking off from Bangor. I manfully volunteered to hang around till the murk burned off, but these considerate folks wouldn't hear of monopolizing more of my summer and sent me home by bus. My soi-disant girlfriend seemed stoic about my leave-taking. Rumbling along Route 1 during that long, long journey to New York—past many a roadside enterprise selling garden gnomes or lobster traps, and crossing the occasional bridge with the rumor of water below—I realized that I'd have to wait to "see" that part of Down East beyond the low-tide line. Maine was in no hurry to show its stuff to me. Meantime I began Dickens's *Bleak House*, which my hosts had given me as a souvenir:

> *Fog everywhere. Fog up the river, where it flows among green aits and meadows; fog down the river, where it rolls defiled among the tiers of shipping . . . fog in the stem and bowl of the afternoon pipe of the wrathful skipper, down in his close cabin; fog cruelly pinching toes and fingers of his shivering little 'prentice boy on deck.*

Thirty years later, asked "Do you sail?," I'd respond with a straight face: "Do I sail? Are you kidding?" In 1982, aboard our thirty-foot cutter *Blackwing*, clearing Race Point northwest of Cape Cod's tip at Provincetown, on an offshore course bearing northeast 112 nautical miles for Monhegan Island, my wife asked, "Are you sure you can do this?" I gave the only possible answer.

Priscilla and I had sailed a good deal by then, in the Caribbean and Europe and along both American coasts. We'd bought *Blackwing*, our second cruising boat, three summers before. Now she was nicely broken in, sturdy and reliable, rigged with a self-tending jib and driven when necessary by a diesel auxiliary. She was beamy and heavy, built to go offshore and stay awhile. This was to be her first overnight passage offshore. Typically we sailed her within a fifty-mile radius of Jamestown, Rhode Island, where we lived then: to Cuttyhunk, Block Island, Nantucket, Stonington. These were frequently open-ocean passages, subject to what seemed like an impressive inventory of perils: storms, heavy seas, rain, patches of fog from time to time. But we'd depart in the morning, allow generous time to alter our course or destination to adjust to the weather, sail until late afternoon, provide a comfortable margin of daylight to find a mooring or drop anchor, watch the kids fish, have the Mount Gay poured before dusk, congratulate ourselves on our prudence and competence.

So we had decided soberly to let *Blackwing* convey us in measured stages from Jamestown to Penobscot Bay. First night at Cuttyhunk, second night at Wings Neck, riding the dawn tide east through the Cape Cod Canal followed by a nice downwind sail to Race Point. The final leg would be the new experience: sailing twenty-plus hours out of sight of land with virtually no seamarks, aiming for Monhegan, a big bold island with a lighthouse.

Assuming a clear night to let the full moon shine down its nighttime consolation, our enterprise nevertheless presented for us challenges of stamina and navigational sagacity. Priscilla—bearing full-time duties as cook, lookout, and general counsel—would give limited service at the helm. My sons could each keep a steady course, but they were kids: Nicholas was just shy of fourteen, Justin was eleven.

Holding a precise course across the Gulf of Maine was no petty imperative. The currents swirl erratically, and given poor visibility an on-the-button landfall would be a matter of blind hazard. This dilemma kept circumspect sailors far from Maine. Its chief topographical attraction—rock-strewn coasts and myriad islands—makes close-to-shore sailing a grim option. Sailing Down East once upon a time separated lambs from wolves. The advent of affordable electronic navigational instruments teased the lambs forth, and here we were, bubbling "downhill" as sailors in those waters say of our course before the wind.

The state of electronic navigation in 1982 was transitional. Global positioning system (GPS) receivers, today almost as ubiquitous as the compass, were still a glimmer in the Pentagon's eye. Radar was big, clumsy, ruinously expensive, and unsuited to small sailboats. Prudent mariners who had experience sailing offshore in Maine were equipping themselves with loran. This device, using land-based signals to triangulate positions, was tricky to tune and use, and it cost a pretty penny back then, maybe two thousand dollars. We must have spent half that sum on the cases of wine now being shaken to ruin stowed in our bilge. Still, I felt good vibes, the kind I'd once felt kicking the bald rear tire of a used street-racing Norton motorcycle and telling the salesman that I had a hunch the bike (dripping oil and festooned with lightning-bolt decals) had been fastidiously cared for, so didn't he agree I was wise to buy it? Besides, I was going to use a radio direction finder (RDF), a device that was basically a little radio turned this way and that to locate the null—or dead spot—on a radio transmitter signaling at known intervals from a known position. In our case this position was a tower atop Monhegan Island. Theoretically, one could sail along the path of this radio beam to its source. Aircraft had used RDF for many years. I had practiced in daylight with an evolved version of the instrument—a silent radio shaped like a pistol and with a compass for a sight—and I was satisfied with the approximate accuracy of the outcome. Nothing was perfect, and, as experienced sailors never tired of repeating, electronics were meant to be used as backups. A far-sighted offshore mariner navigated by visual reference and DR, dead reckoning, defined by one dictionary as "predictive calculation based on inference," defined by seafaring folk wisdom as "dead wrong."

After sunset I went below to catch a couple of hours of sleep, leaving Nicholas at the helm. I could feel the steady waves lift our transom and slew us a bit windward and feel him correct in the deliberate manner—nothing panicked or forced—of someone who knows what he is doing. Justin was in the cockpit with him, looking around for traffic. Their voices were low and steady, intimate. Priscilla was below, reading by the light of a kerosene lamp, as I listened to the weather radio. The Maine coastal forecast was summer-generic: wind southwest ten to twelve knots, with a chance of fog. This hard chance was forecast in a bored, matter-of-fact voice. In the twenty-first century marine forecasts are delivered by computer-generated voices,* but in 1982, the dispassionate voice we heard was enough to chill me in my bunk. I poked my head through the companionway hatch to remind the boys that if the fog came, to wake me right away. The moon was dimmed by a screen of thin clouds, but I could see it. Went below; lay down; closed my eyes. Was gone.

Nicholas was talking. "It's here."

He sounded grim. It sure was there. My sleeping bag was heavy with it. My glasses were wet. I had no right to be surprised. Just before I went below I'd wiped moisture from the compass dome and cowl, and when I'd spoken to my boys in the cockpit I'd seen my breath. That had been more than two hours ago. Now Priscilla was sleeping.

"Did you see other boats?"

Justin said it had just happened. Not there and then there, moon blinking off like a burned-out bulb.

"But before it happened, did you see anything?" I willed my voice to hold steady. It was 3:35, and we were approaching the Portland shipping lanes. With any luck we would spot the big light on Monhegan in a few hours. Now I couldn't see the top of our mast, the bowsprit, anything out there that wasn't within touching distance.

---

* The illusory "Paul," cobbled together from ones and zeroes, sounded like a Swede. Swedes objected, scoffed that he sounded like a Norwegian. Norwegians said he sounded like a guy from Minnesota. He was replaced by "Donna" and "Craig." Donna sounds way cooler than Craig, who seems to hail from Allentown, Pennsylvania.

Like the Beaufort Scale used to grade winds systematically, meteorologists convey specific qualities by what sound to be loosely descriptive words: "fog" occurs when horizontal visibility is reduced to less than two-thirds of a mile and "heavy fog" when it declines to a quarter-mile. This was past heavy. "Dense," you might call it, "thick o' fog." To describe the experience of this degree of fog at night, Roger Duncan—coauthor of *The Cruising Guide to the New England Coast*, an East Boothbay citizen, and author of the authoritative *Sailing in the Fog*—abandons the language of exact measure and declares "you might as well have your head in a bag." *Sailing in the Fog* wasn't published until 1986, so how could we have known four years earlier Duncan's advice: "No one who goes to sea for pleasure would sail a boat among the ledges and islands of a broken coast at night in the fog. Anchor. Stay where you are."

I asked my sons again to tell me the last sights they had seen. They agreed that they'd noticed a set of fast-moving lights to seaward, heading across our bow. Pretty far ahead.

"How far?"

They couldn't say, they said. It was tricky to judge light at night, whether it was far off and bright or dim and near.

"Any other shipping?"

"Something on our course, coming up astern. A sailboat, maybe. I don't think it's moving faster than we are."

But we weren't moving. We might as well have been anchored. We were becalmed, rolling gently in the oily seas. The sails dripped dew; the boys dropped and furled them. We were "off-soundings," in water too deep to measure. That was good, I guessed. I fired up the faithful Yanmar diesel, never a missed beat these three years. Breathing felt difficult, as though a barber were holding a damp towel to my nose and mouth while I waited for a tanker to crawl into our cockpit. I posted Nick at the bowsprit, resumed forty-five degrees, smelled coffee cooking. Priscilla was looking through the hatch at the sky, ahead, astern at me.

"Priscilla . . ." I began.

"Just keep your head," she said.

Fog is: A metaphor. A bank. A blanket that makes one shiver. Wet blanket. A wall. It's a bitch, a son of a bitch, everywhere in the universe (till it scoots away as slippery as it came, "scaling it up," as sailors say). It's a scare, a horror, can blind you to the ledge that will grind your keel and tear your rudder out, stonehearted, a stone killer. It's cunning and reckless, a damned freak, a dirty trick. It's ugly or beautiful, depending on whether you're a navigator or an aesthetician. Jack the Ripper used high humidity to cloak his bloodthirsty prowlings; J. M. W. Turner found filtered loveliness in vapor, steam, and what came to be called smog, the coal-fired, greenish-yellowish-orangish-brownish infernal fog Dickens saw as "soft black drizzle." Edward Bullough, a Cambridge don, chose fog at sea to illustrate his influential theory of "psychical distance," adumbrated in 1912 in the *British Journal of Psychology*:

> *A short illustration will explain what is meant by "Psychical Distance." Imagine a fog at sea: for most people it is an experience of acute unpleasantness. Apart from the physical annoyance and remoter forms of discomfort such as delays, it is apt to produce feelings of peculiar anxiety, fears of invisible dangers, strains of watching and listening for distant and unrealized signals. The listless movements of the ship and her warning calls soon tell upon the nerves of the passengers; and that special, expectant, tacit anxiety and nervousness, always associated with this experience, make a fog the dreaded terror of the sea (all the more terrifying because of its very silence and gentleness) for the expert seafarer no less than for the ignorant landsman.*
>
> *Nevertheless, a fog at sea can be a source of intense relish and enjoyment. Abstract from the experience of the sea fog, for the moment, its danger and practical unpleasantness. . . . Direct the attention to the features "objectively" constituting the phenomenon—the veil surrounding you with an opaqueness as of transparent milk, blurring the outline of things and distorting their shapes into weird grotesqueness; observe the carrying-power of the air, producing the impression as if you could touch some*

far-off siren by merely putting out your hand and letting it lose itself behind that white wall; note the curious creamy smoothness of the water, hypocritically denying as it were any suggestion of danger; and, above all, the strange solitude and remoteness from the world, as it can be found only on the highest mountain tops; and the experience may acquire, in its uncanny mingling of re-pose and terror, a flavor of such concentrated poignancy and delight as to contrast sharply with the blind and distempered anxiety of its other aspects. This contrast, often emerging with startling suddenness, is like a momentary switching on of some new current, or the passing ray of a brighter light, illuminating the outlook upon perhaps the most ordinary and familiar physi-cal objects—an impression which we experience sometimes in in-stants of direct extremity, when our practical interest snaps like a wire from sheer over-tension, and we watch the consummation of some impending catastrophe with the marveling unconcern of a mere spectator.

Now, writing this, I'm moved by the recollection of "curious creamy smoothness." Then, afloat in it, I was utterly the creature of "peculiar anxiety," exhausted and demoralized by "fears of invisible dangers."

Fog, we learn in the ninth-grade English class introducing us to metaphor, "comes on little cat feet." But we also learn in science class that fog is not a mystery. Just a low cloud is all, a cloud that couches land, sticks to water. The wind that had been shoving us along came from the southwest, no surprise, indeed the prevailing summer wind in those parts. The south part made the air warm; passing over the Gulf Stream made it warmer still, and humid. High humidity brought a high dew point, the temperature at which the air could not hold moisture latent. As the sun dropped and the moist, warm air col-lided with the cold water of the Gulf of Maine, churned by tidal ac-tion, that dew point was reached: Bingo. Just a humdrum atmos-pheric phenomenon in the neighborhood of the fog factories of the Bay of Fundy and the Labrador Current, more common than sunshine. We felt as though we'd been kidnapped. Oh, how I had counted on the Monhegan Island Light! But the light could have been fixed to my damned bowsprit and I wouldn't have seen it. The decks were greased with wet and the gray swells were dirty. The air was like sour milk, dreadful yellow. The rigging, dripping morosely, brooded like gallows. I blew a foghorn with requisite regularity, and the dense, wet dark swallowed the doleful noise.

The night it ended I composed a log:

With Justin in the bow blowing a pitiful warning, with Nicholas below trying to recover from the night, with Priscilla deep in Duncan and Ware's Cruising Guide to the New England Coast, *day breaks. Day breaks my heart. Black obscurity gives way to pearly obscurity. Portland marine weather promises a great day ashore, sunny and hot, good beach day, maybe a little hazy. Oh, by the way, offshore? Fog.*

Priscilla doesn't say, "How did you get us into this?" But how can I fail to know what she's thinking as she reads Roger F. Duncan and John P. Ware, whose celebration of the water we now blindly bob upon bristles with warning labels of treacherous tides, rocky shoals, evil weather, fog?

Priscilla reads aloud from the humid pages something she thinks I might need to know: "The onshore tide set from Portsmouth onward is a major navigation hazard. In spite of the fact that we make a major compensation for this effect we almost always fall inside of the anticipated landfall. . . .

"Does that bear on us?" Priscilla asks.

I nod, shake my head. Confess, "I don't know."

Because the tide sets in an irregular circular motion along the course we have sailed, I haven't the least notion where I am, not the foggiest, which is why this log is all description and no exposition. No facts to transcribe, just "beats me" and "dunno" and "huh?" As I will learn, at the helm I have indulged a known fog-bound sucker's bias, always slightly favoring east over west, the sea over the coast, overcorrecting the helm when Blackwing swings to port, under correcting when she veers to starboard. The good news: I (probably) won't run us up on a rocky beach in Muscongus Bay; the bad news: Between us and Portugal are few bells, horns, whistles.

At ten o'clock, our ETA for Monhegan, the diesel coughs, sputters. Nick's at the helm; I shout at him, assume he's adjusted the throttle; he hasn't. My irritated cry provokes alarm in the people I've brought here to make happy. I feel sorry for myself; I'm ashamed; I'm scared.

I'd been in fog before, fog as thick as this. I'd run buoy to buoy from Pulpit Harbor on North Haven into Camden. That was five years before, and when I'd missed a mark, I'd known enough to motor the boundaries of a square, shutting off the engine to listen, and I'd found my way. It had been a strain, of course, cramping the neck muscles, all that tensing to hear, that fierce concentration on the compass, but I had known where I was when the world went blind and the whistling buoy I sought was four miles distant, halfway to Camden. Distance multiplies the effect of error, but earlier this year we'd been swallowed by fog running from Block Island to Newport, and I hadn't panicked, just held on course fourteen miles for the Texas Tower, and there it was, its monster spider legs rising from the sea, on the button: *There!* That wasn't so hard, was it?

This was different. I tried to find Monhegan with the laughable RDF. The null suggested it was abeam, either port or starboard. Gee, thanks. The weather radio suggested a likely possibility of thunderstorms, and we prayed for them, to blow the fog away, part the veil for even an instant. A teasing zephyr astern drifted diesel exhaust at us.

We didn't speak. We listened. I dared not shut off the engine. I now believed so powerfully in entropy—in general disintegration and systematic failure, in bad luck—that I dared not alter anything: course, throttle, helmsman. We motored forward, forty-five degrees. Time had hung up. None of us had any sense of its duration. When the engine coughed (was even that reliable thumper preparing to stab me in the back?), I dumped into the tank our last jerrican of diesel, and I worried silently that we might soon run out of fuel. How could that be? Hadn't I prepared? Done the math? I tried to do the math now in my head and it never came out the same twice. We were all seeing coronas, occasional flashes of light around us. Samuel Eliot Morison has written about the persistence of mist-shawled mystery along this coast, its sailors seeing "fantastic figures in a lifting fog, [imagining] the towers and battlements of a shimmering dream-city; and someone who knows the story will sing out, 'Norumbega!' " The strobing phenomenon that day was sometimes a comfort—was the sun about to break through?—and more often a terror: What was *that?* These items we did not see: black cans or red nuns, birds, lobster pots, seals, boats, any way out of our fix. Now and then we imagined we heard a booming sound. We were listening for anything: a foghorn, a gull crying, a ship's bell, a ship's engine, surf breaking on rocks, something.

I can recall my fear in its shaming detail all these decades later. Truth is, of course, that the terror was mostly unfounded. We had a VHF marine radio aboard, and trailed behind us a seaworthy rubber dinghy powered by an outboard. It was improbable, with my family scrutinizing what there was of a horizon, that we'd hit anything. That was the problem: There appeared to be nothing around to hit. And even if there were, our speed was four knots. We weren't mountain climbers trying to get off the summit in a whiteout, but I was near frozen with anxiety and dread, and decades later, I came upon a piece of writing that suggested the elevator-falling quality of this panic, aggravated by the added dimension of altitude.

In James Salter's memoir *Burning the Days*, he tells of training as a pilot at the end of World War II. One May evening he was sent with others in his squadron on a navigation flight to Pennsylvania, from West Point to Scranton to Reading and home. They left while it was still light and soon were separated from one another. The information they had received about the direction and velocity of winds aloft had been inaccurate, and as the sun dropped and Salter flew west at an airspeed of 160 miles per hour, with "no one to see or talk to, the wind, unsuspected, was shifting us slowly, like sand." In common with seventeen-year-old drivers and with sailors like myself, pilots at

Salter's level don't think about what they don't know, because they don't know they don't know it. Call it cockiness or call it blissful ignorance, it is dangerous. "Flying," Salter writes, "like most things of consequence, is method. Though I did not know it then, I was behaving improperly." He had failed to pay close enough attention to certain anomalies he might have noticed about the ground unspooling below, and he was unused to flying at night, "a different world" in the dark. "The instruments become harder to read, details disappear from the map." Then, as night cooled the Earth, a scrim of mist obscured the lights below. Salter, attempting to navigate by the same RDF system that I was using thirty-five years later in Maine, tuned and adjusted the volume to find a clear signal from Reading, Pennsylvania. No matter what course he flew, the signal grew weaker. Now he was watching the clock, and his fuel gauges. "Something was wrong, something serious: the signal didn't change. I was lost, not only literally but in relation to reality." Now panic attacked:

> I turned northeast, the general direction of home. I had been scribbling illegibly on the page of memory, which way I had gone and for how long. I now had no idea where I was. . . . There was a terrible temptation to abandon everything, to give up, as with a hopeless puzzle. . . . I had the greatest difficulty not praying and finally I did, flying in the noisy darkness, desperate for the sight of a city or anything that would give me my position.

Salter found in his map case a booklet, "What to Do if Lost," which he tried to read by flashlight. A half dozen steps were listed, to be performed in sequence. Some he had already tried, he thought, and in the dark, running out of fuel, he lost faith in the procedure. This was not bobbing on a gray ocean. This *would* end sooner than later. And it did, with Salter crash-landing in a field and onto the front porch of a house in Great, Massachusetts.*

---

* "Fog Kills Songbirds in Bay of Fundy," the Canadian Broadcasting Corporation recently reported. Fishermen tell of sea birds falling onto their decks from the sky; the birds—lost in fog—become wet and heavy, too cold and miserable to fly.

Priscilla heard something first. Then I imagined I heard something and throttled back. We all cupped our ears, turning this way and that. Listening, Priscilla held her finger to her lips. Then we all heard it, a low moan, like the complaint of someone left alone with a bellyache. The resigned lament would come and go. For an hour we sought it, steering box courses as I tried for a change to follow some conventional navigational routine. This required discipline, or ignorance: Often the course I was running three minutes to each leg would seem to take us away from the breathy warning signal, or perhaps this was the effect of a slight wind shift, or of the buoy (if that's what it was) ceasing to rock in those flat seas, or of an object—an oil tanker, let's imagine—coming between the buoy and us, or . . . who knew? Then it appeared and once we saw it, we couldn't imagine not having seen it. Reason told me that the whistle marked "SL" had not been placed to tell us where we were, but to mark a hazard. Nick urged me to creep up on it and I did, because I was stalking the whistle, feared I'd spook it. But it stayed put, fifty feet off, anchored. I envied it. Now it groaned frankly, excessively.

Justin took the helm and circled the mark while I went below to hail the Coast Guard on Channel 16. My voice did not reassure me. I had once had a bad stutter, and it had come back. Was there an "SL," black and white, n-n-n-n-ear Mon-hee-hee-hah-heh-huh-hegan?

That was a negative, skipper. We were circling a buoy on the Seal Ledges, a little east of Large Green Island, fourteen nautical miles east-northeast of Monhegan, which we had missed by a mile, exactly. We were in *bad* water, with a foot between our keel and a kelpy rock slab, and the Coast Guard suggested we get ourselves out of there, "with all due haste," to Matinicus Island, three miles southeast. Looking back, I guess we should have felt rescued. But our least desired course that afternoon was a course to seaward that would leave behind us the one thing we knew, yonder whining whistle. The weather radio was undecided between thunderstorms and dense fog, growing denser. We went for Matinicus and its little sister a bit seaward—Ragged—trying to pick up a red nun buoy on the Foster Ledges, R10, 155 degrees, a mile and eight-tenths, twenty minutes or so distant. No bells or whistles enhanced R10, and we missed it; it could have been thirty feet from us and we'd have missed it. We should have been near Matinicus. Priscilla was reading: "The region should be approached with caution. There are no really snug harbors . . . unmarked dangers are frequent, and tides are swift. In fog or storm the careless or inexperienced can get into real trouble."

Justin was on the bowsprit, shouting, "Look at those thunderclouds!"

I looked up, saw black, smelled Christmas. Pines on a cliff, trailing beards of gray mist. And then we were among rocks, and a rocky beach materialized yards ahead. I swung the wheel over while Nick yelled directions, and we *didn't* grind out on a ledge or tear open the hull, or even stub our toe. It was high tide.

We anchored. I got on the radio: "Anybody on Ragged Island or Matinicus. Anybody. Please come back, please. This is *Blackwing*. I am looking at a rocky beach on the west side of one of your islands. We are tired. And lost. I repeat, we are frightened. Please come back."

And there came a lobsterman, clear-voiced. Said he was pulling pots, he had us on his radar, would drop by in a jiffy, lead us into Criehaven, the harbor on Ragged. He had an extra mooring, he said, we could use it. Drink a cup of coffee, he suggested. Take it easy. Welcome to Maine, he said.

I could have wept. Asked again—"Do you sail?"—I would have responded, "Sort of, maybe, not really." Did mister manly man resent how his woman and sons already felt about the savior with radar, and sense enough to find his way to a safe haven? I did not. My he-manliness, poor pathetic thing, was back there in the Portland shipping lanes, or where I'd lost my wits somewhere near Monhegan, where I'd gone plumb numb.

When the lobsterman came alongside and saw my hands shaking, he suggested, seeing how thick o' fog it was, that he *tow* us in. That seemed to me the brightest idea anyone ever had. He towed, disappeared into the murk as the line went taut; I pretended to steer, and the boys and Priscilla went below to talk about something. Criehaven's a snug harbor, and when we entered I knew from the chart that we passed a breakwater not twenty-five feet to starboard. We never saw it. And till the fog lifted we never saw land from *Blackwing*.

We hung on a mooring in Criehaven two days, two nights. That first night it cleared, and we saw the northern lights. Snug below, I listened to Nick on the forward deck explain with the timeworn patience of an older brother that the flashes were in fact World War III.

Justin, evidently undeceived, said, "I'm glad we're here."

"Amen," Priscilla said from the cockpit.

Next morning: fog. We stayed put. If the fog hadn't lifted, we'd still be there, believe me. Back then, it was a common idiom of cruising guides to warn that a Maine fog could keep you so long anchored in one place that you'd ground on your own beer cans before you'd dare move. But the fog did lift, as it does. And way short of disaster it could have been worse. Roger Duncan has described sailing in a Penobscot Bay fog so thick that the Vinalhaven ferry coming in from Rockland with radar couldn't find her slip. As for him:

> We underestimated the tide, mistook one headland we had never seen for another equally unfamiliar, got into a nest of half-tide rocks, bounced off one, stuck on another, but fortunately sailed her clear. We anchored, guessed, speculated, blundered about from island to island for three hours, went ashore and asked a party of clam diggers where we were, and at length made a safe harbor in the falling dark. Better we had not tried it.

So now? I feel less and less like a fool, which is striking evidence of foolishness. More and more it has seemed to be a good idea to venture offshore, so we do. But never with Monhegan as a destination. Let's call it a bad vibe coming from Monhegan, a really weak signal.

A Traveling Companion
and Adams Hill
from *A Year in the Maine Woods*

Bernd Heinrich

A Traveling Companion

The route from Burlington, Vermont, to my cabin is about 200 miles long. Most of the way you travel on Route 2, through the cities of Montpelier and St. Johnsbury, Vermont; through Lancaster and Gorham, New Hampshire, at the foot of the northern Presidentials; and then to Rumford, Maine, past the great Boise Cascade paper mill. When I smell the Rumford mill, I feel I'm almost home. It's only a few more miles to the foot of Mount Blue, where big Webb Lake fills the valley below Tumbledown Mountain, Blueberry Mountain, and Little Jackson Mountain, but it's been a long ride for a baby raven.

My friend Chuck Reiss and I got him on May 13, after setting up a ladder that just barely reached to the nest in a recess on a granite cliff. The blackflies attacked us mercilessly, but the birds' parents left when we came. Chuck, who builds houses, climbed easily to the top and I watched his progress, for once quite satisfied to experience the thrill vicariously. I had already done the hard part—getting the permits.

The young bird Chuck brought down was feathered out and already close to adult weight. His wing and tail feathers had a beautiful bluish-purple sheen, but he still had a few wispy tufts of white down on the top of his head. He was clumsy, not yet a flyer, but already a good hopper. He did not appear to be afraid of us as he calmly looked us over with steely light-blue eyes. He readily seized the meat that we held in front of him. He either swallowed it right away, or spit it out and flung it violently aside as if he did not approve of its taste.

We grabbed him after he tried to hop away, and he made loud, angry, rasping calls like a chain dragged over jagged metal. But he soon settled comfortably into a nest in a cage in my living room, and there he tolerated having his head scratched. Gentle petting made him sit down and close his eyes. The rest of the time he preened a lot and stretched often. Using his thick bill, he played with the leaves, sticks, and grass stems at the edge of his nest. I had already watched him for many hours from a nest-level blind I had built in the top of a red maple tree, and he behaved now much as he had then. He had been the largest of the brood, always alert and playing. I decided to call him Jack.

On the road back from Vermont, I am feeling anxious now about having Jack up front with me in the pickup truck. My first concern is his hyperactivity. I recall the "roadkill" barred owl that once very much revived itself on my backseat before proceeding to use my steering wheel as its perch. A raven is much larger, much more active, and eats more. It's not that I lack sufficient entrees for Jack—chopped squirrel, flattened cedar waxwing—but the speed of his digestion disturbs me. Blueberries pass through in 15 or 20 minutes.

Before leaving, I put a couple of cardboard boxes filled with books and such in the bed of the truck, but the cab was reserved for us. To make the ride as comfortable as possible for Jack, I taped a tree limb as a perch between the two front seats. That way he could sit next to my right ear while still keeping an eye on the road, too, possibly looking for roadkills. As I conveniently feed his front end, his droppings should cascade onto the newspapers covering the floor. As a precaution, I taped plastic sheeting over both seats, in case he got restless on his perch.

It was evening when we began our five-hour ride. Jack settled next to my right ear after giving the cab a brief whirl or two. However, as much as I wanted him to snooze, he didn't drop off once the whole way. I often caught the glint in his eye as he kept ever alert, staring at my face. To reward him for this good behavior, I ripped apart the cedar waxwing and handed it to him in little pieces.

His throaty little murmurs told of his contentment and enjoyment of the ride. We talked for the whole while through Vermont and New Hampshire, but it was up to me to keep the conversation going. Without my prompting, Jack often lapsed into silence. I'd tell him that he was a nice bird, that I noticed him, listened to him, and liked him. He'd counter with a soft, low "mm." These "mm's" varied slightly in length and mellowness, reflecting his approval and excitement. Very low, soft, and long, almost whispering "mm's" meant that he was very laid-back. Higher, shorter, and louder "mm's" meant heightened awareness and agitation. On occasion, as Jack's anxiety increased, there was also an upward inflection of the sound. When he was mellow, there was a slight downward inflection instead.

Once in a while he'd stop to stretch—with both wings held upward while he crouched down, or with one wing and one leg (toes tightly clenched) extended first to one side and then to the other. I think Jane Fonda would have approved of these exercises, which were accompanied at times by a more assertive or emphatic "krrr" or "kn," meaning "I'm feeling *great!*" Then he might give a little cough before idling away the rest of the time preening his feathers or checking out the passing scenery.

I understood perfectly well what Jack was saying. Mostly, it was to the effect of "I hear you, you're OK; I'm listening, I'm here and A-OK." One can speak volumes with a few little sounds, given the proper context and intonation. With Jack, context is everything. A raven reacts only in the moment, so you always know what he's about.

An hour and a half into the ride, I had made my usual stop in St. Johnsbury at Anthony's Diner, a small place with barstools, featuring the "Woodsman's Burger." I only wanted coffee, but if I took Jack with me he'd walk all over the customers' plates, steal french fries, check out the coins in the cash register, and generally cause mayhem, so I had to leave him behind. As I closed the cab door, he immediately hopped off his perch and pressed against the window, acting desperate, but I didn't look back, determined to drink a leisurely cup. Besides, absence makes the heart grow fonder.

When I returned 20 minutes later, I found that absence also makes the gut run faster. There were foul streaks all over the seats, and they weren't mere white and scentless droppings. The cedar waxwing had taken the fast route, and wasn't as adequately processed as roadkill should be. He had missed me—the body doesn't lie.

Oh well. When you have a baby, such surprises are part of the bargain.

Once we were off again, Jack quickly resettled on his perch next to my ear.

"You OK, Jack? You glad to see me?"

"Mm*mm*."

"This is *fun*, huh?"

"Mm*mm*."

He was *very* glad to see me, and we journeyed on.

When we got to Maine our conversation started to lag, and he had to endure Joan Armatrading and Bruce Springsteen on tape as we drove along the Androscoggin River and finally entered the hills by Dixfield.

Adams Hill

Our destination is Adams Hill in western Maine. Once the site of a farm, it is now, except for my small clearing, all forest. When I was a boy, I used to come here with my friends, Phil Potter and Floyd Adams (a descendant of one of the Adamses for whom this hill was named), and we'd see brushy fields and woods overtaking the old apple trees.

People had lived here a long time ago, as they had on hills all around New England. Stone walls that once marked the edges of fields and pastures still braid through these forests like remnants of a lost civilization. You come upon rectangular cellar holes defined by neatly fitted fieldstones and split granite blocks. These barn sills enclose thick white birch, ash, and maple trees. On occasion you still see a bit of rusted barbed wire sticking out of a massive 200-year-old sugar maple that must have once formed a pasture boundary.

My cabin is about a half mile up a steep hill through the brush from a steep winding road, at a place once called Hildreth's Mill that now only exists in the memories of old-timers. Even after a long dry spell has drained the hill so that the path no longer doubles as a small brook, you can't drive there except with a four-wheel-drive vehicle. This path isolates me well from casual visitors, but true friends are not deterred. I like it that way and accordingly have not made great efforts at road improvement.

The cabin walls are of spruce and fir logs that I chopped down with my ax and peeled with a bark spud when they were still full of sap and when the bark still separated easily, like a skin. My former wife, Margaret, and I hired oxen to drag the shiny white logs out into the clearing. Using ropes, levers, and inclines, we hoisted up the logs, which I flattened on two sides by chopping off long, smooth flakes, and then notched at the ends with deep, smooth cuts. Gradually we assembled the structure, over the course of a summer.

It is long after dark when Jack and I arrive, but by now I can walk up the path with my eyes closed. I carry Jack in a cardboard box and he seems relaxed as we have a quiet conversation in the dark. During our first night at the cabin, he gets to stay beside my bed in the box so I can talk to him and reassure him.

Early the next morning, I awake to a wild melee of bird song. Far sweeter than any symphony I could possibly imagine, it comes from all around. The clearing surrounding the cabin grows spirea bushes, and there is a ground cover of ever-green club mosses, close relatives of the giants that produced our coal in the carboniferous ages. There are also maple, spruce, pine and balsam-fir saplings, and patches of wild raspberries and blueberries. This profusion of plants that I have been neglectful of pruning in the last several years is now a haven for white-throated sparrows, juncos, chestnut-sided and Nashville warblers, and deep-blue indigo buntings. These birds all sing at intervals, as does the phoebe that has built its nest over my window. I hear the blue jays, rose-breasted grosbeaks, and red-eyed vireos calling from the forest, and I vault out of bed, feeling like a new man.

Looking out the window on this first day in early June, I see a sea of shining green. I had not realized how varied and vibrant green, the color of life, could be. The hue is darkest where you look through several layers of the recently unfurled maple leaves, and it shines with a yellowish tinge where the sun filters through. In the clearing around the cabin, the sea of green is more uniform than it is farther in the forest, perhaps because of the vigorous stands of sugar maple around the cabin. The red maples, at the edge of the clearing, have a reddish tinge. They, like the ash, have not yet fully leafed out, but they already have flowered and are laden with red seeds that color the whole tree. The spruce tree across the clearing is a dark, almost black green, as are most conifers, although this year's new conifer shoots are bright lime colored, some with a bluish tinge.

As I step out the door, inhaling the cool air, I smell lightness and relief. The birds' calls are intense now, and I see the blue eggshell of a robin on the path—young have hatched. A blue jay flies over the cabin, carrying a twig. Walking on the path, I find tiny violets growing along it: white ones, blue ones, even a few yellow ones. These almost mono-colored miniatures of cultivated pansies are as nature made them, not as someone's whim dictated. Therefore I find them incomparably more beautiful than the domesticated varieties.

Underneath the tree canopy of luminescent green there are flowers everywhere. They are all perennials, and most are snow white: starflower, Canada mayflower, foamflower, goldthread, bunchberry, anemone, strawberry, and Solomon's seal. There is also the white painted trillium with delicate red lines in the center. I had hardly remembered the most obvious and striking spectacle of the myriad snow-white flowers now staring me in the face. It seems always easier to note the one *purple* trillium than all the many white ones.

Jack is soon clamoring for food in ear-shattering, rasping, insistent cries. I feed him, then leave him silent and contented on the branch of a pine by the cabin.

My lookout tree is a red spruce. For the last nine years, I have climbed it to watch for ravens both at dawn and an hour or so before dusk. Its solid branches are stairlike almost down to the ground, because this tree has grown so close to bare ledges that the sunlight has been able to penetrate nearly the full length of its trunk, unlike most of the spruces farther down the slope. However, all of the small scratchy side branches have long been knocked off during my, by now, hundreds of trips up and down.

No brittle-limbed pine tree, this, where strength must be gained through massive thickness. On these spruce branches, barely an inch thick, you can jump up and down and they only bend and bounce back like steel. They've already held tons of snow for perhaps 60 winters.

Red spruce is what forms the "black" tops of these hills and mountains, poking up above the deciduous forests of beechnut, birch, red and sugar maple, and red oak. Mixed in below are also a few basswood and bigtooth aspen, and there are balsam fir, red maple, and white cedar in the swamps. Pin and black cherry, quaking aspen, red maple, and fir trees spring up quickly wherever blow-downs or clearcuts have created temporary openings. All openings in these forests are quite temporary—whenever one occurs, the woods inexorably rush in, like air filling a vacuum.

The snow comes a little earlier and stays a little later up on the spruce ridges than it does below. It's cooler up here, and the thick canopy of needles shades the ground so that the sun cannot melt the snow. This is the breezy year-round home of the tiny golden-crowned kinglet, the black-capped and boreal chickadee, and the red-breasted nuthatch.

The small russet cones of red spruce are borne only near the tip of the crown. Here, under the cover of an umbrella of short, thick green branches laden with cones, I make my perch. I have cleared the live branches to provide a panoramic view in all directions. Here, on top of a hill near Tumbledown Mountain, you see an unbroken forest blanketing all the other hills and valleys. Traveling around this wilderness, you see the fresh tracks of moose and deer, as well as bear-claw scratches on the smooth gray trunks of the beechnut trees. You wouldn't guess that the pine forest below my perch was a clear hay-field 40 years ago, surrounded by orchards and sheep pastures.

The old homestead where I built my cabin is visible over there to the north. In springtime, you see a purple lilac that the first settlers planted there; in June, part of the clearing is overgrown with their pink roses as well. The clearing would have been long gone by now, but I keep it roughly trimmed. I like the lilacs and the roses, which remind me of the settlers, not to mention the view, and the space in which to grow a few blueberries.

Rhubarb planted over a hundred years ago still comes up near the square granite blocks that used to be a barn foundation. There, among the spirea bushes where I dug down to plant the blueberries, I found the remnants of plows, hay rakes, horse harnesses, and also a square blue bottle with "Hall's" written on one side and "Hair Re-newer" on the other.

What happened to the people who lived here? They left their names on the gravestones in tiny cemeteries that are hidden in wood-land all around. The weather is already erasing their names from the markers. Of all they built, only the stone walls, crumbling wells, and barn and house foundations still remain as visible reminders.

The gravestones I can still read give only names and dates. The names reflect the names of the local topography—Holman's Ridge, Gleason Mountain, Houghton Brook. The dates reflect a sad truth. Of 100 gravestones that I have read nearby, 57 are for children who died before the age of 20. Mortality between the ages of 20 and 30 remained high (13 gravestones), but then leveled off to four to seven deaths per year until people reached their 90s. Mostly the young and the very young died. The old, once old, endured their lives and missed their children. One headstone for a seven-year-old reads, "Our angel boy." There is no hint on the gravestones of what anyone died from, except one inscription: "Albert M Son of Rodney and Melissa Stearns, a Member of Co G. 17th Regt. Maine Vols., Shot Near Petersburg Va. June 20, 1864." However, I suspect that before antibiotics the same bacteria that wiped out the Native Americans also claimed some of the new settlers.

Just below the lookout to the west is a steep granite drop-off with caves. Porcupines live there now, the ones who gnaw scars onto the maple trees.

A few hundred feet down is a tarred road. You can't see it from up here, but you can hear pulpwood trucks rumble by. Each is filled with two tiers of four-foot logs, with a hydraulic lift resting on top of the load like a big claw.

The trucks go on down the hill toward the paper-mill towns of Jay and Livermore Falls. Others go through Mexico and on to Rumford, not far from here. We're also close to Madrid, Norway, Peru, Sweden, Denmark, Naples, Poland, Paris, and Berlin. The rivers that course through this country are the Androscoggin and Kennebec; the lakes include the Umbagog, Aziscohos, Mooselookmeguntic, and Parmachenee.

The big lake yonder at the foot of the rounded mountains is Webb Lake. The Webb family still has its farm over on the far north end where the lake becomes shallow and gives way to marshy meadows. Moose often come out of the woods there in June to catch the breeze and escape the blackflies.

Just to the other side of Webb Lake you see a cone-shaped mountain, Mount Blue, less than five miles away. At 3,187 feet, it's the tallest mountain around here, except on clear days when you can see all the way to New Hampshire and Mount Washington and the Presidentials, all part of the same White Mountain chain.

A lot of what exists in these woods cannot be seen from my red spruce. Most of the lives around us go on unnoticed. They leave no records. We see only bits and pieces, and then only if we look very, very close, or for very, very long. We have to decipher these other natives of the forest if we want to understand the landscape. A million scents that we never smell waft on the breezes: each of them has special meaning to some insect. If I chop this tree down in the summer, there will be hundreds of beetles of half a dozen species to smell it. They will come flying up against the wind and lay their eggs, which will soon turn into white grubs. Different kinds of wasps will then come to lay their eggs on the grubs, and woodpeckers will later feast on both. There are thousands of beetles of exquisite designs, and not a living person knows even so much as their names.

The birds we know better—at least their names. I've seen 20 species of wood warblers alone around this hill over the years. Each species has its own song, sometimes several. To walk in the woods and not recognize the songs is to not hear them. To not think of the birds' uniquely beautiful and artfully concealed nests is to have the woods seem empty. Most of us are like sleepwalkers here, because we notice so little.

Down there in the valley is a pond. Loons raise their fluffy dark chicks there in the summer, and catch trout. Some springs, they fly in from the winter spent on the open Atlantic even before the ice is out here. If so, they search for other open water and wait to return later. A pair of ravens, too, are familiar with the pond, their home. The pair has nested in the pines along the shores for perhaps 20 years, and it may nest there for perhaps twice as many more.

The indigo bunting that nests in the clearing over there by my cabin spends its winters in Central America, flying the thousands of miles at night, navigating by the star patterns. It learns these patterns as a nestling, huddled down in a little grass cup in the spirea bushes, even as I look at the same sky, so that it can return to its home that I share with it here.

Neighborhood Deer

Susan Hand Shetterly

In 1535, Jacques Cartier and his crew, stuck for the winter in the New World, took the advice of a man who was most likely a Micmac, and made themselves a tea steeped in the sprays and bark of the northern white cedar, a pungent, resinous brew that saved them from death by scurvy. They called the tree "arbor vitae," tree of life.

In my town, the arbor vitae is the whitetail deer tree. It grows best in acidic bottomlands, where its thickets can persist for centuries, holding back the bite of winter snow and wind. Our neighborhood deer own such a place in the woods across the road from my house. In the cold afternoons of late winter, they walk through the snow at the back of my yard to their yard, a tamped-down refugium where they settle in for the night.

The tree of life is also their winter food tree. If I want to know how the deer will fare in the hunger season—the long weeks of late winter and early spring—I look for browse lines on the cedars. Around my house, the tansy-scented leaves are hemmed back as far as a deer on a snow bank can reach. They have stolen next winter's food from themselves.

The does and their big fawns gathered under those cedars at the end of last winter to eat the tough green sprays, their skinny legs up to their hocks in the snow, their necks stretched into the branches, their heads hidden. Sometimes one or the other in the small herd lifted onto its back legs to reach into the higher branches. They did not care who watched them from the house, and as the winter wore down, they did not care who came out the door.

Food was what they cared about. They ate in silence. The only sounds came from the tugs they made at the branches and the sharp and sudden cracks as their hooves broke into the crusted snow.

A game trail leads across the paved road to the cedar copse where the deer have their shelter. The trail follows an old dirt road along a narrow esker, then drops to cross a stream that ushers water out of the heath two miles to the north and pours it into the salt marsh a half-mile to the south.

When a forester cut these woods ten years ago, he felled the grand softwoods, limbed, twitched, yarded them, and hauled them away. Now the land grows back in raspberries, in red maple shoots and young fir and pine, cedar and spruce and birch, which is just fine for the deer. The game trail is much older than the cutting. The deer are true to it all year long.

In the evenings, when neighbors and I walk the paved road, we sometimes see them step out from the trail. Lifting one sharp hoof after another, they walk into full view, and stand looking at us before they cross to meet the trail on the other side. We count them: three, four, five, six. One or the other of us sometimes can't help lifting a hand to wave, a small gesture of acknowledgement. Of shared community. When the deer see the waving hand, their ears twitch—one, two—as if they are waving back.

We meet the deer like this with the sun shining low on the road, which runs west, making a soft brush stroke of gold that backlights them as they travel through it and disappear.

One morning in August, on the side of the road I heard what I thought was rapid, shallow breathing. I stepped in the high grass of the shoulder and almost stumbled into the ditch where the carcass of a deer lay on its side.

It trembled all over. It looked as if it were getting its life back in fits and starts. But the life it was tending belonged to thousands of glistening cream-colored maggots engulfing the body. They writhed, climbing under and over each other a couple of layers thick, gorging on the warm deer flesh. Their bodies chafed, making the wet panting noise. No place on the corpse was free of these turgid maggots. Even the socket that once held the sleek globe of the left eye was full to overflowing like a cup, and the parts of the deer I could not see, the liver, the lungs, the ruminant stomachs and the heart were thrumming.

The deer gave itself to the task of becoming something else, which did not look easy or painful. Some days later, it flew away as blowflies and flesh flies and carrion beetles. It left a scatter of bones and pieces of stiff skin.

A neighbor of mine walked onto the deck of his house one early morning just before hunting season with a mug of coffee in his hand, took a sip and glanced down the cobbles of Patten Bay to the gunmetal water. He looked again. There, up to its belly in the tide, stood a doe. Two coyotes patrolled the beach in front of it. Back and forth they paced over the stones, stopping every now and then to fix her with their eyes. She stood with her head up, frozen in one posture, the water sloshing at her sides. Alert to every move they made, she did not look directly at them. They looked at her straight on.

My neighbor froze, too. If he made any sound, the smallest gesture, she might bolt shoreward. He was suddenly witness to something that, in the moment, gave him a rush of what he said felt like fear. He stood still until, for no reason he could tell, both coyotes stopped at once. Together they turned to look at him. It may have been a puff of wind carrying his scent because after the first hard frosts the morning wind tends from the land to the water. Whatever it was, the coyotes pinned him with their gaze. Then they raced into the brush. The doe never moved.

My neighbor took a sip of coffee, which was no longer hot. The doe didn't seem to notice him. But maybe she discounted his presence. He took another sip. He watched her shift a little in the water that had risen up her belly. Then, slowly, heavily, she waded ashore. Stood on the beach. Looked both ways.

"What the hell?" my neighbor said to no one as the doe ran in the same direction the coyotes took.

"What the hell?"

The apple tree in my yard is a twenty-year-old Northern Spy. When it begins to drop its big, scabbed, sweet-sour fruit after the first hard frost, a few at a time thud into the stiff grass.

Today a doe and her yearling buck took the windfalls into their mouths and crushed them. They stood beneath the tree, seriously chewing, their jaws moving from side to side, the juice splashing their nostrils and pouring down their chins. Their long pink tongues came out and slurped it up. I stood at the window, the imagined tartness of apple watering my own mouth.

They wore the buff-colored coats of winter. Their bellies were purest white. They had gleaming black eyes, gleaming black noses. Velvet antler buds sprouted between the ears of the yearling above a face that kept some of the round softness of childhood. The doe's head was lean and spare.

When they were done with apples, they sauntered off, swishing their tails from side to side.

A raven lifted off the bright splash of a gut pile on the snow in a clearing where a hunter had disemboweled a deer. The bird yelled as it flew, circling once over the trees.

I was walking the clearing to the east of the road, and came to the green mass of shredded rumen and blood and the loops of intestine yanked by the bird. But there was something else, something I noticed up by the trees. Something tossed aside. I walked over and picked it up.

It filled my hands. It was deeply furred, immaculately white. Parting the luxuriant hollow guard hairs, I found two bare testicles as round as reptile eggs, coal black. From them ran a sheath, just the tip of the penis showing beyond it, pink and sharply pointed.

It had been cut from the buck, and, what seemed a shabby gesture, flung. What should I do with it? Unsure, I held it in my bare hands. In the end, I dug into the loose snow under the trees. When my fingers reached dirt, I made a few scrapes, and carefully laid this purse of unspent coin inside, covered it up and tamped it in with the soles of my boots as the raven coasted over the trees once more, in silence, dipping a wing toward the gut pile.

Of Moose and a Moose Hunter

Franklin Burroughs

When I first moved to Maine, I think I must have assumed that moose were pretty well extinct here, like the wolf or the caribou or the Abenaki Indian. But we had scarcely been in our house a week when a neighbor called us over to see one. She had a milk cow, and a yearling moose had developed a sort of fixation on it. The moose would come to the feedlot every afternoon at dusk and lean against the fence, moving along it when the cow did, staying as close to her as possible. Spectators made it skittish, and it would roll its eyes at us nervously and edge away from the lot, but never very far. It was gangly and ungainly; it held its head high, and had a loose, disjointed, herky-jerky trot that made it look like a puppet on a string.

The young moose hung around for a couple of weeks, and it became a small ritual to walk over in the summer evenings and watch it. My neighbor, Virginia Foster, had reported it to the warden, and the warden told her not to worry: the yearling had probably been driven off by its mother when the time had come for her to calve again, and it was just looking for a surrogate. It would soon give up and wander away, he said, and he was right. But until that happened, I felt that Susan and I, at the beginning of our own quasi-rural existence, were seeing something from the absolute beginnings of all rural existence—a wild creature, baffled and intrigued by the dazzling peculiarities of humankind, was tentatively coming forward as a candidate for domestication. Mrs. Foster said that if the moose planned to hang around and mooch hay all winter, he'd damn well better expect to find himself in the traces and pulling a plough come spring.

First encounters mean a lot, and in the years that followed, moose never became for me what they are for many people in Maine: the incarnation and outward projection of that sense of wilderness and wildness that is inside you, like an emotion. As soon as I began going up into the northern part of the state whenever I could, for canoeing and trout fishing, the sight of them came to be familiar and ordinary, hardly worth mentioning. You would see one browsing along the shoulder of a busy highway or standing unconcerned in a roadside bog, while cars stopped and people got out and pointed and shutters clicked. Driving out on a rough logging road at dusk, after a day of trout fishing, you would get behind one, and it would lunge down the road ahead of you. Not wanting to panic it or cause it to hurt itself—a running moose looks out of kilter and all akimbo, like a small boy trying to ride a large bicycle—you'd stop, to allow the moose to get around the next curve, compose itself, and step out of the road. Then you'd go forward, around the curve, and there would be the moose, standing and waiting for the car to catch up to it and scare it out of its wits again. Sometimes you could follow one for half a mile like that, the moose never losing its capacity for undiluted primal horror and amazement each time the car came into sight. Finally it would turn out of the road, stand at the fringe of the woods, and, looking stricken and crestfallen as a lost dog, watch you go past.

Of course you also see them in postcard situations: belly deep in a placid pond, against a backdrop of mountains and sunset, or wading across the upper Kennebec, effortlessly keeping their feet in tumbling water that would knock a man down. Once two of them, a bull and a cow, materialized in a duck marsh as dawn came, and I watched them change from dim, looming silhouettes that looked prehistoric, like something drawn by the flickering illuminations of firelight on the walls of a cave, into things of bulk and substance, the bull wonderfully dark coated and, with his wide sweep of antlers and powerfully humped shoulders, momentarily regal.

But even when enhanced by the vast and powerful landscape they inhabit, moose remained for me animals whose ultimate context was somehow pastoral. An eighteenth- or nineteenth-century English or American landscape painting, showing cattle drinking at dusk from a gleaming river, or standing patiently in the shade of an oak, conveys a serenity that is profound and profoundly fragile. The cattle look sacred, and we know that they are not. To the extent that they epitomize mildness, peace, and contentment, they, and the paintings in which they occur, tacitly remind us that our allegiance to such virtues is qualified and unenduring, existing in the context of our historical violence, our love of excitement, motion, risk, and change. When I would be hunting or fishing, and a moose would present itself, it would not seem to come out of the world of predator and prey, where grim Darwinian rules determine every action. That world and those rules allow the opposite ends of our experience to meet, connecting our conception of the city to our conception of the wilderness. The moose would seem to come from some place altogether different, and that place most resembled the elegiac world of the pastoral painting, an Arcadian daydream of man and nature harmoniously oblivious to the facts of man and nature.

I suppose it would be more accurate to say that the moose came from wherever it came from, but that it seemed to enter the Arcadian region of the imagination. I found it a difficult animal to respond to. It was obviously wild, but it utterly lacked the poised alertness and magical evanescence that wild animals have. If by good fortune you manage to see a deer or fox or coyote before it sees you, and can watch it as it goes about its business unawares, you hold your breath and count the seconds. There is the sensation of penetrating a deep privacy, and there is something of Actaeon and Artemis in it—an illicit and dangerous joy in this spying. The animal's momentary vulnerability, despite all its watchfulness and wariness, brings your own life very close to the surface. But when you see a moose, it is always unawares. It merely looks peculiar, like something from very far away, a mild, displaced creature that you might more reasonably expect to encounter in a zoo.

In 1980, for the first time in forty-five years, Maine declared an open season on moose. Given the nature of the animal, this was bound to be a controversial decision. People organized, circulated petitions, collected signatures, and forced a special referendum. There were televised debates, bumper stickers, advertising campaigns, and letters to editors. The major newspapers took sides; judicious politicians commissioned polls. One side proclaimed the moose to be the state's sacred and official animal. The other side proclaimed moose hunting to be an ancient and endangered heritage, threatened by officious interlopers who had no understanding of the state's traditional way of life. Each side accused the other of being lavishly subsidized by alien organizations with sinister agendas: the Sierra Club, the National Rifle Association. The argument assumed ideological overtones: doves vs. hawks; newcomers vs. natives; urban Maine vs. rural Maine; liberals vs. conservatives.

At first this seemed to be just the usual rhetoric and rigmarole of public controversy. But as the debate continued, the moose seemed to become a test case for something never wholly articulated. It was as though we had to choose between simplified definitions of ourselves as a species. Moose hunters spoke in terms of our biology and our deep past. They maintained that we are predators, carnivores, of the earth earthly; that the killing and the eating of the moose expressed us as we always had been. The other side saw us as creatures compelled by civilization to evolve: to choose enlightenment over atavism, progress over regression, the hope of a gentler world to come over the legacy of instinctual violence. Both sides claimed the sanction of nature—the moose hunters by embodying it, their opponents by protecting it. Each side dismissed the other's claim as sentimental nonsense.

I knew all along that when it came to moose hunting I was a prohibitionist, an abolitionist, a protectionist, but not a terribly zealous one. When the votes were counted and the attempt to repeal the moose season had been defeated, I doubted that much had been lost, in any practical way. The hunt was to last only a week, and only a thousand hunters, their names selected by lottery, would receive permits each year. It had been alleged that once moose were hunted, they would become as wild and wary as deer, but they have proved to be entirely ineducable. Hunter success ran close to 90 percent in that first year, and has been just as high in the years that followed; and the moose I continue to see each summer are no smarter or shyer than the one that had mooned around Mrs. Foster's feedlot, yearning to be adopted by her cow.

Late one afternoon, toward the end of September, the telephone rang, and there was a small voice, recognizably Terri Delisle's: "Liz there?" So I went and got Liz. She's old enough to have overcome all but the very last, genetically encoded traces of telephobia—just a momentary look of worry when she hears that it's for her, and a tentativeness in her "Hullo?" as though she were speaking not into the receiver but into a dark and possibly empty room.

Terri is her friend, her crony. The two of them get together—both polite, reticent, and normally quiet little girls—and spontaneously constitute between themselves a manic, exuberant subculture. It possesses them. They are no longer Terri and Liz, but something collective: a swarm, a gang, a pack, or a carnival, having its own unruly gusts of volition. They glitter with mischief, laugh at everything, giggle, romp, and frolic; and I believe that, with each other's help, they actually lose for a moment all consciousness of the adult world that watches from within, waiting for children to draw toward it. They aren't destructive or insubordinate—that, after all, would be a backhanded acknowledgment of civilization, maturity, and responsibility. They are simply beyond the reach of reproof, like colts or puppies.

But on the telephone, with distance between them, self-conscious circumspection took over. I heard Liz's guarded and rigorously monosyllabic responses: "Yep." "He did?" "Sure—I'll have to ask Dad." "OK. Bye." And so she told me that Terri's father Henry had killed a moose. Would we like to go over and see it? "Sure," I say, all adult irony, "I'll have to ask Mom."

* * *

I knew Henry Delisle in a small and pleasant way. There were a lot of Delisles in town, and Henry, like his brother and most of his male cousins, worked over in Bath, at the shipyard—a welder, I think. But like many other natives of Bowdoinham, he had farming in the blood. The old Delisle farm, up on the Carding Machine Road, had long since been subdivided and sold, and Henry's neat, suburban-looking house sat on a wooded lot of only two or three acres. Even so, he had built himself a barn and a stock pen, and he kept a few pigs, a milk cow, and an old draft horse named Homer. There couldn't have been much economic sense to it, just a feeling that a house wasn't a home without livestock squealing or lowing or whickering out back. He plainly liked the whole life that livestock impose upon their owners—harnessing Homer up for a day of cutting and hauling firewood; making arrangements with local restaurants and grocery stores to get their spoiled and leftover food for pig fodder; getting the cow serviced every so often, and fattening the calf for the freezer. He had an antiquated Allis-Chalmers tractor, with a sickle bar and a tedder and a bailer. There are a lot of untended fields in Bowdoinham, and plenty of people were glad to let Henry have the hay if he would keep them mown.

That was how I had met him for the first time. He had come rattling up to the house in his big dilapidated flatbed truck to ask me if anybody planned to cut my fields that summer. In fact somebody did, and I told him so, but Henry had too much small-town civility, which coexists comfortably with small-town curiosity, simply to turn around and drive off. I appreciated that, and so we chatted for a while—Henry sitting up in his truck, talking with an abrupt and fidgety energy, and I standing down beside it.

He remembered my house from his boyhood: "Used to be a reg'lar old wreck of a place. They didn't have no electricity down here or nothing. Winters, they'd cut ice from the pond. Had a icehouse dug into the bank there; kept ice all through summer. Hard living." He told me a story I'd heard even before we bought the house, how one winter the eldest son had gone out to the barn to milk, as he did every morning, and had found his younger brother there, hanging from a ceiling joist. "Never a word or a note. That was a terrible thing to happen. Unfriendly people, but they didn't deserve that."

He laughed. "But they was *some* unfriendly, I want to tell you. I slipped down to the pond and set muskrat traps one fall. But they musta seen me. They pulled 'em every one out and kept 'em. I was afraid to ask—just a kid, you know. Probably still lying around in your barn somewhere." He looked at me and sized me up: "But I ain't afraid to ask now, and don't you be afraid to turn me down—would you mind me setting a few traps in that pond this fall? It used to be about lousy with muskrats." I hesitated at this—the pond was still full of muskrats, and I enjoyed seeing them sculling across it, pushing little bundles of cut grass ahead of them, or sitting out on a log, grooming themselves with a quick, professional adroitness. But I liked him for the way he had asked it, and there was something else. His country-bred practicality and local knowledge gave him an obscure claim—he was less indigenous than the muskrats, but far more so than I was. "Sure," I told him, "go ahead."

All this had taken place on a bright, airy morning in late July or early August, with the kind of high sky that would make anybody think of haying. Henry said he was glad he'd stopped by, and that I'd see him again once the trapping season opened. I reached up, we shook hands, and he backed the truck down the driveway. His windshield caught the sun for a moment and blinded me and then, as the truck swung up into the yard to turn around, I could see through the glass what I had not been able to see before. He had a passenger—a little girl sitting in the middle of the seat, right at his elbow. She did not look in my direction at all, but stared at the dashboard with that look of vacancy and suspended animation that you see on the faces of children watching Saturday-morning cartoons. Henry grinned at me, waved goodbye, and the big truck went lumbering off.

That first meeting with Henry had been the summer before Elizabeth and Terri started school. Later, when they had become classmates and best friends, I learned that the girl I had seen in the truck was Stephanie, whom everybody called Tadpole. She was three years older than Terri, but that was a technicality.

*   *   *

Bowdoinham is a small, spread-out town. It tries to hold onto the idealized ethos of the New England village, but is in fact well on its way to becoming a bedroom community, a pucker-brush suburb. Like the state as a whole, it is full of outsiders moving in, old-timers dying out, and the uneasy sense of a lost distinctiveness.

The elementary school is the nearest thing to an agora that such a town has. Parents are separated by their backgrounds and expectations, and by the devious anxieties of people who feel that, in appearing to belong to the little unglamorous place they inhabit, they may misrepresent or compromise themselves. But children go to school, and it stands for the world. They make friends and enemies, and suddenly populate your household with unfamiliar names. It is as though you had sent them off as members and worshipers of a stable, self-sufficient Trinity consisting of Mama, Daddy, and themselves; and then had them return as rampant polytheists, blissfully rejoicing or wailing despairingly about the favors and sulks of capricious gods and goddesses named Tommy Blanchard, Vera Sedgely, Joanie Dinsmore, Nikki Toothacre, and Willie Billings. At school functions you would meet the parents of these entities, or, prodded by your child, would nervously call up Joan's or Nikki's mom, and arrange for that child to come over and play. And slowly, with no direct intention of doing so, you would find out about other families in the town—who they were and how they lived, how they regarded themselves and how they were regarded.

So we learned that Tadpole suffered from Down's syndrome. She was the first child of Henry and Debbie Delisle, born to them within a year of their marriage, when they themselves were just out of high school. Perhaps if they had had more education and experience they would have accepted the irremediable fact of their daughter's condition. As it was, they were mistrustful of the state and the school system and all the experts who came to help them and warn them and in some way to deprive them of the right to raise their daughter as they saw fit. Against every recommendation, they were determined to try to give Tadpole all the circumstances of an ordinary childhood.

When time came for Tadpole to go to school, Henry wrangled with the school board and the superintendent and the Department of Mental Health and Retardation. And finally everybody agreed that for as long as it didn't create any disturbance, Tadpole could go to school with Terri. Word of that sort of thing gets around, and some parents didn't like it, fearing that what Henry had gamed for his daughter would diminish the education and attention that their own children would receive. But I believe that most of us admired Henry and wished him well. He was his own man; in his battered old truck, with a tottering load of hay on it, or with Homer tethered to the head-board, he implied an old-fashioned resourcefulness and independence, which we could praise even if we couldn't emulate. It was heartening to see a man like that acting out of the best and simplest human impulse, and sticking to his guns, even if, in the long run, the case was hopeless.

And of course the case was hopeless, although at first it didn't appear to be. Tadpole was docile and affectionate, and in her first year and a half of school, she enjoyed an almost privileged status among her classmates. It was as though she was their mascot, like the wheezy old bulldog or jessed eagle you might find on the side-lines at a college football game. You would see a crowd of children fussing over her in the schoolyard, alternately courting her as though she were a potentate to be appeased, or babying her with bossy solicitude. Liz would report on all that Tadpole had done or said, as though she were a celebrity in whom we should take a communal pride. And we did take a kind of pride in her. Her being at the school with the other children seemed proof that humane flexibility, sympathy, and tolerance were still operative in this overgrown country. There was something quaint about it, something from the putative innocence of the past.

But by the end of the second grade, Liz was bringing home bad news. Tadpole had begun to balk at going to school, and would misbehave when she was there. She was bigger than her classmates and her truculence threatened them. They retaliated as children would, by teasing and persecution. She regressed, growing more withdrawn and morose, and would go through days of not speaking, or of only muttering to herself. Public opinion hardened. I don't think there were any petitions or formal proceedings to have Tadpole removed; it was just one of those sad things that had become plain and obvious. Henry and Debbie had no choice; they had to give in to the fact that confronted them every day. The next year, Tadpole and Terri were separated, and Tadpole was sent to school in Topsham, where there was a class for what the state calls Special Children.

When Terri would come over to play, she seemed untroubled by the change. She was as quick and inventive as ever. I did not know Henry well enough or see him often enough to speak to him about the matter, and hardly knew what I would or could have said. He got himself transferred to the night shift at the shipyard that fall, and he must have kept Tadpole out of the special class a good deal. I would regularly see the two of them together in the truck—usually first thing in the morning, when he'd just gotten off work. But he told me one morning, when he'd come to check the muskrat traps, that he had changed shifts purely to give himself more time for the wood-cutting, haying, trapping, ice-fishing, and hunting that seemed to be his natural vocations.

So on the September afternoon in question, Liz and I got into the car—none of the rest of the household had any interest in a dead moose—and drove over. It was nearly dark when we turned up into Henry's driveway. His garage lights were on. He had set up a work-table of planks and sawhorses along the rear wall; the moose was hanging by the neck squarely in the center of the garage. From the driveway, it looked like a shrine or a crèche—the brightly lit space, clean and spare as an Edward Hopper interior; Henry and four other men standing chatting; and, just behind them, the lynched moose. Terri came running out, excited as on Christmas morning, and took us in to see.

From the outside, the moose's head appeared to go right up through the low ceiling of the garage, but once inside I could see that, when he had built the garage, Henry had left out one four-by-eight ceiling panel, to give him access to the attic. He had put an eye bolt in a collar tie, centered above the opening, so that he could rig a hoist from it. It was a smart arrangement, enabling him to convert an ordinary two-car garage into an abattoir whenever he had a cow or pig or deer to slaughter. The moose he had shot was a cow, and she was a big animal, hanging with her head in the attic, her rump scarcely a foot above the concrete floor. A big animal but not, Henry said, a big moose: "She'll dress out about five-fifty. Just a heifer. She'd have calved next spring."

Henry introduced me to the other men—neighbors who had wandered over out of curiosity, and his cousin Paul, who had been his partner in the hunt.

We were somehow an uncomfortably self-conscious group; it was as though we were all trying to ignore something. Perhaps it was that Paul and Henry were still dressed in their stained and ragged hunting gear and were grubby and unshaven. The rest of us were in our ordinary street clothes, and only a few minutes ago were watching television or pottering around the house or having a drink and getting ready for supper. We had been in our familiar cocoons of routine and obligation, where the only world that matters is the human one. And now we were talking to men who were in another role, and we were abruptly confronting a large, dead animal, a thing from far beyond our lives.

I think it was more this awkwardness than aggression that made the man next to me, a bank manager new to town, speak the way he did: "Well, Henry. That's a weird damned animal. You sure it's not a camel?" Everybody laughed, but uneasily.

"Tell us about it," the man said. "How'd you bag the wily moose?"

Henry said there wasn't a whole lot to tell. The man asked him if he'd hired a guide. Henry said he hadn't.

"Well maybe you should have," the bank manager said. "If you had, you might have gotten yourself a bull. Then you'd have something to hang in your den."

Henry didn't answer. He got busy with a knife, whetting it against a butcher's steel. The man walked around the moose, looking at her appraisingly, as though she were an item in a yard sale. Then he said he had to get on back home, and left, and there was a general relaxing. Henry looked up.

Now he was going to tell us how you kill a moose, or how he had killed this one. None of us knew anything about moose hunting. The tradition of it had died out, and hunters—even very experienced ones like Henry and Paul—don't know moose in the way that they know deer. The hunt was limited to the upper third of the state, and a lot of people up there had set themselves up as moose guides, offering what was supposedly their deep-woods wisdom to anybody lucky enough to have a permit.

Henry snorted: "Hire a guide. You know what a moose guide is? He's a guy with a skidder, that's all. You go to his house and he'll take you out and leave you somewheres where he thinks there might be a moose, and charge you so much for that. Then you kill a moose and he'll charge you a arm and a leg to hook it up to the skidder and drag it out to your truck. So I go to this guy that's listed as a guide, and he explains it to me. And I say to him, 'Look. Don't tell me a word about where to find a moose. Now if I get one, what'll you charge to drag him out?' 'Hundred dollars for the first hour; fifty dollars per hour after that,' he says. See, they got you. Law don't let you kill a moose less than fifty yards from the road. So I says to him, 'You prorate that first hour?' 'Fifty dollar minimum,' he says to me: 'Take it or leave it.' Musta thought I was from Massachusetts. 'See you later,' I says. And that fifty dollar, hundred dollar shit ain't from the time he drives his skidder off his trailer into the woods. It's from the time he gets in his truck right there in his front yard."

Paul quietly removed himself from Henry's audience and went into the kitchen. It wasn't his story, and there was a lot of work still to do.

"We had topo maps, and I seen some good bogs. Day before the season opened we drove and scouted all day. I don't know much about moose, but I know a moose'll walk on a log road or a skidder track if he can, instead of bustin' through the bushes. About suppertime we see a cow cross the road ahead of us, and go down a skidder trail. We followed her down on foot. There was a bog in there at the end of the trail, about a quarter mile in off the road, and there she was, feeding. Her and another cow, too. That skidder trail was rough, but I figured we might be able to get the truck down it.

"Opening day it was raining. We parked a ways off and walked up to the skidder track and down to the bog. Got there before day. When it come day, one cow was there. I looked at her. She looked good, but not extra good. Animal like a moose got a lot of waste on 'em. Big bones, big body cavity—not as much meat as you'd think. That's what they tell me. And they told me when you see a cow, wait. It's rut, and a big bull might come along any time."

Paul came out from the house with his arms full—wrapping paper, freezer tape, a roll of builder's plastic. He spread the plastic over the table, and he didn't make any effort to be unobtrusive about it. But Henry was occupied by his story. It was like something he wanted to get off his chest or conscience. Maybe he just couldn't get over the strangeness of the moose.

"It ain't like a deer. A cow moose calls a bull. That's what they say and it's the truth. We watched her all day, and ever so often she'd set right down on her butt and beller, like a cow that ain't been milked. So we set there, too, and waited, but no bull showed. By dark she'd worked over to the other side of the bog. Shoot her there and you'd have to cut her up and pack her out."

Henry was standing in front of the moose. Her chin was elevated and her long-lashed eyes were closed. All of the things that had so splendidly adapted her to her world of boreal forest, bog, and swamp made her look grotesque here: the great hollow snout, the splayed feet and overlong, knob-kneed legs. In whatever consciousness she had had, it was still the Ice Age—she was incapable of grasping human purposes or adjusting to human proximity. Her death was almost the first ritual of civilization, yet she was in our present, suspended in the naked light of a suburban garage, and we could only stand, hands in pockets, as though it was something we did every day.

"So we come back the next day, a little earlier even, and I sent Paul around to the far side of the bog. This time I hear her walking in on that skidder track just before day, and she got out in the bog and bellered some more. We was going to give her 'til noon. I figured if a bull showed, he'd come up the track, too, and I could get him before he hit the bog.

"By noon she was all the way out in the middle of the bog again, but Paul stepped out of the bushes, easy, so's not to scare her too much. Took her the longest time even to notice him. Then she started trotting toward me, but she'd keep stopping to beller some more. It was almost like she was mad."

One of the men chuckled: "More like she was desperate, if you ask me. If she didn't call herself up a boyfriend pretty quick, she was a dead duck."

"Well. Anyway, Paul had to slog out after her, keep shooing her along. I wanted her to get all the way out on the trail, but she musta smelt me. Stopped about ten foot from the woods and started throwing her head around and acting jumpy, like she might bolt. So I shot her there.

"We had a little work with the chain saw to clear the skidder trail out wide enough for the truck. Then we backed in and put a rope around her and dragged her out to dry ground. Used a come-along to hoist her up on a tree limb and dressed her out right there. Then cranked her up some more, backed the truck under, and lowered her in. On the way out, we stopped by that guy's house. I went in and told him we wouldn't be needing his damn skidder this year."

The whole time Henry talked, Paul kept coming and going, bringing out knives, a cleaver, a meat saw, and a plastic tarp. Elizabeth and Terri had examined the moose and then gone inside. I had been worried about Elizabeth. She was at least as sentimental as the average ten-year-old about animals; at country fairs she would lean against the stalls and gaze with pure yearning at Suffolk sheep or Highland cattle and especially at horses of any description. But she and Terri had looked the moose over as though she were a display in a museum of natural history, something interesting but remote. They had walked around her, rubbed the coarse, stiff hair, and inspected the big cloven feet, and then gone about their business.

Now, as Henry finished his story, they returned, giggling. Terri was carrying a child's chair, and Liz looked from her to me, trying not to laugh. Terri ran up to the moose and slipped the chair under her rump, and then the two of them stood back and waited on our reaction.

It was comic relief or comic desecration. Because the moose's hindquarters were so near the floor, her hind legs were spread stiffly out in front of her. With the addition of the chair, you suddenly saw her in a human posture, or really in two human postures. From the waist down, she looked like a big man sprawled back on a low seat. Above the waist, she had the posture of a well-bred lady of the old school, her back very straight, her head aloof, and her whole figure suggesting a strenuous and anxious rectitude.

In the ready, makeshift way of country people, Henry had taken one of Debbie's old worn-out lace curtains with him, and when he had killed and cleaned the moose, he had pinned the curtain across the body cavity, to keep out debris and insects and to allow the air to circulate and cool the animal while he and Paul drove back home. The curtain was longer than it needed to be, and now Terri picked up one end of it, brought it like a diaper up between the moose's legs, wrapped it around the hips, and tucked it in, so that it would stay up. The effect was funny in a way I don't like to admit I saw—the garment looked like something between a pinafore and a tutu. It was as though the moose had decided, in some moment of splendid delusion, to take up tap dancing or ballet, and was now waiting uncomfortably to go on stage for her first recital.

Terri and Liz admired the moose. "She needs a hat," Terri pronounced, and they ducked into the house. What they came out with was better than a hat—a coronet of plastic flowers, left over from some beauty pageant or costume.

"Daddy, could you put this on her? She's too high for us."

She was too high for Henry, too, but he pulled the little chair from beneath the moose, then picked Terri up and set her on his shoulders. He stood on the chair and Terri, leaning out daringly, like a painter on a stepladder, managed to loop the coronet over one of the long ears, so that it hung lopsided. She slid down Henry to the ground, stepped back and dusted her hands together:

"There. That'll just have to do. I think Momma needs to see this. Maybe she'll lend us some mittens and a scarf. Let's go get her and Tadpole to come see."

"Terri, Paul and me got to get to work on that moose right now," Henry called after her, but she was already gone. The other two men who had come over to see the moose said they had to go, and left, one on foot and one in his car. Terri and Liz came back out with Debbie and Tadpole. Debbie looked at the moose and laughed. Terri was pleased.

"Don't you think she looks like a beauty queen, Mom? We could enter her in the Miss Bowdoinham contest."

"Well, I guess so." Debbie turned to Tadpole: "Look at Daddy's moose that he brought us, honey." Tadpole looked at it and walked over as though she wanted to touch it, but didn't. Her face had that puffy, numbed look of someone just wakened from a deep sleep, and her movements were slow and labored.

Debbie called over to Terri. "Now your Daddy and Paul have to start, and I've got to run buy some more freezer paper. You and Stephanie come with me, and we can let Liz get home for her supper."

Terri gave the moose a comradely whack on the rump: "Goodbye, moose. You're going in the freezer." Liz patted the moose, too, but more tentatively. Then they all trooped out.

I stood talking to Henry for a few minutes longer. He looked at the moose with her cockeyed halo and tried to make a joke of it. "If she'd been dressed that way this morning, maybe I'd have got a bull." But his laughter was awkward, apologetic. His remark about how little useable meat there really was on a moose, for all its great size, had not been lost on me, and yet I felt that it would be right to ask him for something, as a way of restoring to him a vestige of the old role of hunter as public benefactor, bringer home of the bacon. So I asked him if I could have some of the long hair from the nape of her neck, for trout flies.

"Sure thing," he said, all business. "Tell you what: I won't cut it off now—don't want no more loose hair than I can help when we go to skin her. But when she's done, I'll clip some off and drop it by, next time I'm down your way. You can count on it."

I thanked him and left. Liz was subdued as we drove back toward home. You might have asked an older child what she was thinking, but not Liz, not for a few years yet. Besides, I wasn't so certain what I was thinking just then: two scenes alternated in my mind. One was a recollection, back from the previous November, a morning when heavy frost had sparkled white as mica on the dead grass, and I had been driving to work. I saw Henry walking across a stubble field, a big fox slung over his shoulder. He held the fox by its hind legs; its tail, curved over and lying along its back, was luxuriant and soft as an ostrich plume, and it stirred lightly in the breeze. I felt some sadness for the dead beauty of the fox, but it was Henry I remembered. He ought to have looked like a mighty hunter before the Lord, holding the bounty of his skill and cunning and knowledge of the ways of wild animals in his hand. But he was walking with a shambling hesitation, to keep pace with the daughter clinging to his other hand and trudging glumly at his side, beyond any idea of triumph or happiness.

The other image was of something that had not happened yet. June would come again, and I would be up north fishing again—this time with a fly that would have, wrapped in tight spirals around the shank of the hook to imitate the segmented body of a nymph or mayfly, one or two strands of mane from Henry's moose. And I would look up from the water, almost dizzy with staring for so long at nothing but the tiny fly drifting in the current, and there they would be—maybe a cow and a calf—standing on the other bank, watching me watch them, trying to fathom it.

Shitdiggers, Mudflats, and the Worm Men of Maine

Bill Roorbach

H ard work," says Dicky Butts, and we haven't even started yet. "Get wet today," says Truman Lock. He pulls his graying beard, squints out over the bay. The blast of an offshore wind (strong enough to blow the boat and its no-lights trailer halfway into the oncoming lane as we made the drive over) is piling whitecaps, spraying their tops, bowing the trees around us, knocking my hat off my head, giving even the wormers pause.

Dicky says, "No fun today."

Walter—Truman's father—lets a long minute go by, says, "We do get some weather, Down East." He seems to know he's offering a cliché, works the rich inflections of his Maine twang extra hard: there's an observer here, myself, and no one (including me) knows exactly what the observer wants.

The night's rain has stopped and the cold front that caused it is finishing its push. The dirt parking area at the shore access on Ripley Neck is nearly empty—most of the wormers have decided to let this tide go—too much like March (here toward the last days of June)—too wild, too easy to stay in bed. "Not a climber in the lot," Truey says, one of a constant stream of plain observations. It'll take me fifty conversations with twenty wormdiggers before I figure out the obvious: a climber is a clammer. He means most of the usual guys aren't here today—clammers, crabbers, inside lobstermen, wormers—not even anybody picking weed. Just two cars in the lot—mature Subarus, both of them—no boat trailers.

We watch the tide. It will be a big one, Truey guesses, with the offshore wind blowing the bay empty. He's sitting at the wheel of his Chevy truck, Dicky at his side. Walter and I stand in the parking lot at their two windows. We all watch the bay. Low water is charted at 7:30 this morning. It's six now. We watch, and watch more. That's what we do, watch. No talking. Down on the mudflats a quarter-mile away a couple of men are bent low, visibly chopping at the mud with their worm hoes. "Bloods," Truey says.

"Those boys are blood wormers," Dicky says, deciding to pull me in a little, help me out here, whatever I'm up to. He's a stocky, good-looking man with a naked lady tattooed on one arm, a faded bird in a flower on the other. At thirty-three, he's the youngest of the team. He has a wide face and ought to look jolly, but he doesn't. Jolly you need to smile. He's taciturn and tough, burned and blown, his skin newly cooked over a deep spring tan, the creases of his neck white. He's got mud smears on the bill of his no-team baseball cap. You think maybe he's a little mean until he speaks and, yes, finally smiles, but it's a warm smile, not jolly at all in the wide face, a good father's smile, and you see how kindly he is, how helpful. This he wants to avoid showing. He pronounces the word *wormers*—names his profession—with softened r's and extra vowels, points out the bent men, says, "Ten cents a worm." Back to taciturn.

Ten chops, ten deep turns of the mud, a pause to pull a worm, ten more chops, drop a worm in the bucket. Ten chops bent over the heavy muck and those guys out there get a dime, a dime a worm, 100 weary chops to a dollar, 1,000 chops for ten bucks, 10,000 chops to make the tide pay.

"Those fellows are Garneys," Walter says. He knows every wormer in Washington County by sight, and probably most in the state. He's been at this forever. He wants me to know that a Garney is any digger from Beals Island, which is just over the bridge from Jonesport, a few miles east. He wants me to know that the Beals Island boys are known for working in bad weather, and for working low tide all the way up to the beach, staying in the mud longer than maybe is good for the worm population. But then, every wormer wants you to know that every other wormer is a fuckhead. I'm thinking of a certain group of Midcoast boys who told me how dumb and lazy the Down East boys are, including these very boys right here.

"Shitdiggers," Dicky spits. It sounds like genuine animosity, but if I said it I'd probably get a blood rake through the brain.

Truey pulls the muddy brim of his cap, patiently fills me in: "Sandworms, see, are but six cents, but it's faster getting. Those guys out there was here an hour before us. They'll be here an hour longer for their money, and rip the mud right to the weed line."

"It does take a toll on your back," Walter says dreamily, apropos of nothing in particular.

Oh, fuck. I'm here on a magazine assignment: get to know these guys, these peculiar wormers, these strugglers at the extreme end of our great economy, write a poignant piece about their miserable lives. But they don't seem miserable. Not as miserable as I am, for example, doing a job I'm really anxious about, inside a nascent career I'm really anxious about, a shaky career that has me saying yes to assignments like this, so many cents a word, really not the kind of thing I'm good at. For one thing, I'm feeling horribly guilty, stealing these guys' lives from them, worried sick what they'll think of their portraits when the magazine hits the racks in town. No one likes his own picture.

But here we are, all of us doing our work in this beautiful, dramatic place. Which is their place, one they know intimately, a place they know themselves to belong. They are their own economy, efficient, dependable, always bears, always bulls. Get to know them? They aren't going to let that happen unless I'm willing to work a couple of years alongside them, and probably not then. I've found Truey after an unbelievably long series of phone conversations with mistrustful Yankees, Truey the one wormer in all of Down East Maine who said, sure, sure, come along and worm.

"Bloodworms," Truey sighs, not with malice, exactly, but with the supercilious pride of a specialist: these fellows dig sandworms, and even if maybe they are less hardy, less appealing to fish, less marketable and so less valuable, they're easier to come by. He keeps looking me up and down. I smile too much, smile now.

This is not my first day worming. I had a day up Midcoast with a bunch of mean-spirited mo-fo's. Shitdiggers, for sure. The Midcoast boys abused me, rightfully so: what comes to them for talking to me? But more about them soon. Right now I'm Down East, anxious but hopeful. Months have passed since my Midcoast frolic without much progress on my story. My big break is slipping away. Truey and Dicky and Walter are my last chance. And a new strategy is in place: I haven't told them specifically about *Harper's*, only that I'm a professor at the University of Maine at Farmington, doing a kind of study of guys working, and that I'll write about them. All true. They maybe expected a pipe, a tweed jacket, elbow patches, a vaguely British accent. Instead they got me: UMF sweatshirt, long hair, guy basically their age, a *classic* summer dink and a flatlander to boot.

Truey looks me over thoroughly, maybe trying to think what will interest me. He nods in the direction of one of the Subarus in the empty parking lot: "That's Porky Bob. He's a climber, most generally, but they just ain't any steamers, not anymore. He'll be digging bloods today."

I'm rumpled and desperately bleary, slept poorly maybe three hours in the Blueberry Motel, the only motel open this time of year anywhere near, lone customer, windy night.

"They would used to get ten bushels," Walter says, "a whole pickup load on a tide. Now you're lucky with a plateful for supper." He looks pained and weary. "It's the pollution. It's the runoff from the blueberry highlands."

This does interest me. I'm nodding my head earnestly.

"Some say sewerage," Truey says.

"No," Walter says. "That's the lie. The clam, he likes the sewage. What he don't like is the sewage treatment."

"Many a wormer was once a climber," Truey says.

The three men leave me out now, rapid shoptalk. I hear it the way I hear Spanish: pick out words here and there, get the drift. They're speculating about the worm population at Pigeon Hill, which I know to be a beach up toward Hancock. They're bad-mouthing some climber. They're thinking the weather will clear. They're speculating about the take today. They're talking about urchins, near as I can tell, something spirited about sea urchins and the frukking Japanese. Walter would rather eat pussy than that stuff. But Jack Morrison made $2,800 in a day diving for 'em. And Truey's a certified diver. The rest sounds like daydreaming: all they need is scuba, an urchin boat (forty feet would do 'er), hot tanks for divers (the deep water in the Gulf of Maine is brutally cold in every season), some of that stuff is all, and you make $2,800 a day.

Without a word of transition, without a word at all, Truey is pulling his truck around in the ominously empty parking lot, listening all the while to some story Dicky is telling, then backing the Cox trailer smoothly and straight as a new ashen oar down the steep ramp to the bay. Walter plods down behind, thinking of something else, chewing a thumbnail. I march down after him, flopping in my new worming boots (the Down East salesman pronounced this *women* boots), anxious to be of use. But these aren't vacationers nervous at the winch of their thousand-buck trailer, this is Truey and Dicky knocking a scarred plank of junkyard lumber out from under the motor (a muddy Mercury 200, no messing around, a good old machine much reworked by Truey, who's a local stock-car racer, and Dicky, who's his mechanic): knock the plank, unhook the cable, let the boat hit the water, no splash. Now three of us are at the gunwales (I imitate every gesture they make, trying to be useful), waiting for Truey to park his mostly orange truck and return.

Dicky grins at me. "Gonna get wet," he says. He sees my thin sweatshirt and that I don't have a raincoat and yells up to Truey to bring what they got. He's so solicitous I stop worrying about the high wind. I stop thinking about the low-down, blood-worming, shit-digging Midcoast boys who laughed and left me stuck in the mud, laughed derisively and chopped across the mud away from me, giggling like middle-aged and tattooed twelve-year-olds, dunking worms in their buckets, dunking worms. I stop thinking about my deadline, two weeks past, stop worrying that my worming story is going to get killed. (In the end, okay, it did get killed, but me, I've got the experience of worming under my belt, my fat kill fee, and my own bloody worm rake, which will hang forevermore in the shed at my inland house.)

"This weather'll clear by noon," Walter says, watching the sky. He's built small and strong, is always preoccupied, always has a subject in mind and an informed, unexpected opinion. ("If them senators up in Washington was all women, we'd have our troubles solved.") He's not only a wormdigger but his wife's partner as a minor worm dealer. His own dad (recently dead of diabetes, from which Walter also suffers) was a wormer, too, one of the originals up in Wiscasset with worming legends Bill and Artie Wanser and Frank Hammond—the first guys in the business back when the war was over and life was sweet and anybody could be Ernest Hemingway—go sportfishing in the ocean—anybody anywhere in the world: customers.

Truey returns with an armless orange sweatshirt for me and a torn yellow slicker. "All we have extra," he says, with real concern. He's got muscles and the same demeanor as Dicky, and like Dicky he's warm and helpful and kind, all that just hiding behind a stern self-possession that you might read as distrust. But he's got a certain coldness to him, the bluff chill of the bad father. His cap says MRS. GIANT JIM'S STREET STOCK on it. Mrs. Giant Jim's Pizza, up on Route 1, is one of his racing sponsors. In Mrs. Giant Jim's they've got pictures of Truey in his lemon-yellow number five, holding the checkered flag after big wins at Bangor Speedway, never a smile for the camera.

I put the partial sweatshirt and ripped slicker on gratefully and the three wormers look at me a long time the way they've been looking at the tide: not much they can do about either, not much at all. We get in the boat, a twenty-one-foot aluminum camo-painted Quachita flat-bottom workboat full of worming stuff: four blood hoes, four sandworm hoes, three wormboxes, four buckets, several twisted blue gloves, one faded green one, three life preservers, first-aid kit.

We're off. Truey's the helmsman, Dicky beside him, both of them standing. Walter and I are on the middle seat facing forward, taking the spray.

I examine my women boots. Last time out, with the japing Midcoast boys, I wore my fly-fishing hip boots, which have thick felt soles for traction on mossy river rocks. The deep tidal mud up by Bar Harbor sucked them off my feet over and over again till they were gone. So now I've got better boots, the real thing, according to Walter (who has explained that they're "Number one in Maine"): tight-ankle LaCrosse hip waders. I've gotten them two sizes small to be sure of their snugness. I wonder if I should have tied strips of inner tube around the arches, as Walter also suggested, but I don't want to look like a total fucking dork. I start to tie and button the interior calf straps (a collar of eyes inside the boot below the knee that you tighten like shoelaces before you pull the thighs up), aware that Walter is too preoccupied to notice what I'm up to.

Dicky is staring. He says, "I myself personally prefer not to use the calf straps."

I say I don't want to get stuck in the mud, tell him the Midcoast story.

He and Truey grin at the picture of me floundering as the Midcoast boys leave me behind, especially the part where my ass is in the mud and I have to let go of my notebook and pen, losing them, then losing the boots. Har har har, then my new friends fall back into their default faces—pretty grim—let me finish tying the calves of my boots.

Dicky says, "If we go in you need to get them boots off pretty fast . . ."

"Ah," Truey says, "we ain't going in."

Walter isn't listening, is looking to where we are going. He points, says, "Some mud showing over there."

Truey says, "Benson Williams."

Dicky says, "Little Fred."

Truey says, "That fellow from Jackman."

These are people who have indeed "gone in." The tone isn't quite elegiac, but before I can ask for elaboration, Walter's telling Truey to slow down. There's a flotilla of lobster buoys, for one thing (which, to be sure, Truey has been missing expertly); for another, these waves will be big trouble if he gets the boat up planing. Truey nods with an irritated patience and you can see Walter has been giving him advice like this for a lifetime. Truey's forty, now. His dad is fifty-seven. Truey's name is actually Walter, too—Walter Lock III—but he was born on Harry Truman's birthday.

We are in the estuarine bay of the Harrington River, heading for Foster Island below Ray Point. I've gotten these names off of maps, for in the manner of most people deeply familiar with their surroundings, Walter and Truey and Dicky can't quite remember the names of the islands and spits and necks around us, only that good worming can be found on the flats that will appear here shortly. They venture several guesses, but can't agree on the names. Finally Walter says if you were to boat around the island you'd end up at Milbridge, the next town up the coast (up being toward Portland, which is a hundred miles south and west).

We're crashing over waves now. Truey and Dicky crouch a little, but stay on their feet in the stern. The old gas tank, less than a quarter full, bounces around back there. Walter kneels on the middle seat beside me. We all look resolutely forward. The spray is ice cold. I think of hackneyed Maine-coast paintings, proceed to compose one: five stripes of color—the gray plane of clouds, the green of the pines in the shore forest, the naked gray rocks, the brown rockweed exposed by the tide, water the gray of the sky but alive with whitecaps. We're the sole boat today; the scene is dramatic, timeless, lacks color, a Wyeth, which generation of Wyeth I'm not sure.

Our beeline has brought us across Harrington Bay to several hundred yards off Foster Island. Truey lifts the motor and we skim onto the mud. Again we sit and watch. You can see disturbed places in the exposed muck. "That is yesterday," Dicky says. "That is us." The wind is so strong I have to pull my San Francisco Giants cap down to my eyebrows, cock my head. I don't know why San Francisco—it's just a hat, but Dicky looks at the logo all day rather than in my eyes, asks me on the way home if it's a Chinese character on there.

"See them two?" Truey says. He's pointing out men I hadn't noticed, crouched men chopping at the mud much closer to shore. I don't at first see their boat, and ask how they got there.

"Canoe," Dicky says.

"Wouldn't be in a canoe today," Walter says. He hops out of the boat, overboard into the mud. From the bow he collects his sandworm hoe (what climbers might call a rake)—five claw-curved steel tines nineteen inches long, these welded onto a bar that is welded in turn onto a post that impales a wooden handle about nine inches long. The angle between handle and hoe is sharp; at work, one's knuckles are just behind the tines. Walter has shaped his handle to fit his stiffened fingers; the carving is artful: skin-smooth, oiled, comfortable. Next he hefts his wormbox, a homemade fiberglass case like a carpenter's box mixed with a budget cooler, fitted at top with the wooden handle from a broom. Attached to one end is a big old coffee can—a vessel for bloodworms, which sandwormers view as incidental, but which bring ten cents each—it's not like you're going to throw them away. He slides the box along the mud, leans forward, moves fast enough to keep from sinking beyond the point of suction. I study his style. He's a strong old guy, moves with grace through the mud.

"Watch him," Truey says, "he'll dig all around the mussel beds," this with a mix of affectionate pride and irritation at his dad's predictability. And sure enough, Walter is into the edges of the mussel bed, which is slowly coming exposed with the tide. He operates knee-deep in the muck, digging and stepping, moving his wormbox along beside him. Each big flip of mud seems to produce a worm. He holds them up one by one for me to see.

"Rattlesnake," Truey says, making fun, since Walter claims the mussel-bed worms are bigger.

"Tinker," Dicky says.

"Shitdigger," Truey taunts, and we all briefly laugh. I miss the switch back to grim, find myself laughing alone.

Walter slogs speedily off across the mud to the next mussel bed. Dicky and Truey and I wait. We wait a little more. Truey points out the bloodwormers again. "Man in the red is the fastest wormer Down

East," he says. "You watch him go." It's true, the man is chopping three strokes a second, stepping along the mud, a hundred yards ahead of his partner, hundreds of yards from his canoe.

"That fellow lost his son this spring," Dicky says. "Day pretty well like this."

We watch the man work. He does not straighten periodically as his partner does; he does not rest.

"Six hundred pounds of wrinkles," Truey says. "Boy and his partner. Was he twenty-one yet? Six hundred pounds of wrinkles in the bottom of their canoe. *Six hundred* pounds."

"Got turned by the wind," Dicky says. His own son is twelve, and for now Dicky gives him half the summer off. "The boy was not a swimmer. Though his partner made it all right."

"They should have went to college," Truey says. He's eyeing me closely, this professor, right here in his worm boat. Dicky, too, more subtly.

This is a test. I don't give a twitch, not a smile. I say, "That's a sad story."

We watch the bloodwormer, watch him digging like hell, plopping worms in his bucket, chopping the mud.

Dicky says, "College is not for everybody."

"True," I say.

I'm off the hook.

The wind has picked up. It's singing in my ears, watering my eyes. I'm thinking of the boy sinking in his boots. I ask what wrinkles are, exactly. Truey sighs, twirls his finger to draw the creature in the air, makes me to understand that wrinkles are those little spiral-shelled snails, what I have always called periwinkles. He says, "The Japanese eat 'em. I wouldn't go near 'em." You can't quite tell if he means the snails or the Japanese. His sons are babies, still, two and four, products of his third marriage.

"Nor is worming," Dicky says. Nor is it for everybody, he means.

We watch the sky, watch the tide, sit in the boat in the wind. No warning and the guys are overboard, grabbing their wormboxes and

hoes. Truey asks if I'm blooding or sanding. I say sanding—of course—
and they give me a hoe and a bucket. I pull my women boots up to my
thighs, tie the ties into my belt loops, and step overboard. I sink. I
step. I've got the bucket and the hoe. I sink, step, sink, step, suckingly
follow the men. Step, sink, looking for little round holes that signal
sandworm mud. When Dicky crouches to the task, I watch him. Strike
the tines full depth into the mud (nineteen inches!), two hands to
turn the heavy gray stuff, a quick grab to pick out the worms, one or
two or three to every dig in this spot. Good mud. Three or four digs,
then step.

"The trick is to keep moving," Truey says. The two of them are off,
leaving four-foot-wide swaths of turned mud behind them, digging,
digging, plucking worms, sliding the wormboxes—lean forward
steeply and step—dig right, dig left, dig middle, pluck worms, step.

I use two hands, grunt, and turn the mud. My back already hurts.
Two worms. I tug on one where it's escaping back into its hole in the
mud and it breaks, pull on the other more carefully and it comes
free—a foot long, orangey brown, cilia down its length, appearance of
a flattened and softened centipede, perhaps a half-inch in diameter,
diameter turning to width as the worm flattens trying to locomote
out of my hand. Dicky has given me his gloves, so I'm not worried
about the stingers hidden in the retracted head. I put the worm in my
bucket. *One.* Next chop and I note the tunnels the worms leave—
slightly discolored tubes in the mud. The worms can move very
quickly into the un-dug, disappear. You chop and grab. You don't wait
around. *Two.* You step. *Three.* I'm doing fine, not stuck, proud of my
new boots. Chop, two hands. The stuff is heavy. I'm glad I'm strong,
wish I were stronger, remember how I've bragged to Juliet that I'm in
great shape. *Four, five, six.*

"Those little digs'll hurt your back," Truey advises, kindly. He's
ten feet ahead of me already.

Dicky has walked to a new spot, far to my right. "Try to make it
all one scoop." He shows me, swoop, scoop, plops worms into his
bucket.

I make a big dig, do it right, turn a great chunk of mud, watch the hole grow wet, look in there for movement. I pull out an odd, long, flat worm that just keeps coming—three feet long, at a guess.

"Tapeworm," Truey says. He very nearly smiles, because tapeworms are ridiculous, useless.

I dig again, showing Truey every worm I turn, trying to get the sense of an acceptable size. The worms expand in length then quickly retract, so you can't really put it in inches. You just have to know. Truey okays a couple, shrugs at a third. The shrug is as negative as he'll get with me. Next worm is a blood. Truey turns back to his work: the tide is only low enough for two-and-a-half or three hours of digging this far out on the flat—you can't socialize. I examine the bloodworm, which is wholly different from a sandworm. No cilia, for one thing, and it's all pink translucence, smaller than a sand, more substantial than an earthworm, something deeply red beneath the surface of its skin. This one is smallish, not quite six inches, with a thickening at the head end, a bit of flattening at the tail. I roll it in my fingers. Abruptly, the head shoots out, a moist pink cylinder an inch long, ugly and sudden, un-benign, bulging and unfolding till the stingers show, four grasping needles in the circle of the nasty mouth. Walter has told me that if they get you in the webs between your fingers your whole hand'll blow right up. I haven't been worried till now—how bad could a worm bite be? Bad, is the answer. I let the worm grasp at the air a moment, then throw it in with the sandworms in my bucket—a mistake, as I will discover: the bloods bite the sandworms in half, making them worthless.

Step and dig, dig and step; my legs are growing exhausted, forty feet from the boat. The digging style Truey showed me seems to be saving my back, though. Dig and step. I've lost count of my take, but it looks like a lot in there—a crawling, wriggling, spiraling mass, sunken in the quart of seawater I've added to the mix. There's quite a bit of mud in there, too. Incredibly, I don't turn up a single clam. Incredibly, I forget about my assignment. My notebook never comes out of my pocket. I'm worming.

The wind is getting stronger yet, and colder, takes my San Francisco Giants cap. I lunge for it, fall in the mud, get the hat, put it dripping on my head, manage to stand by leaning hard on bucket with one hand, rake with the other. I wish for the sandy flats Walter has told me he used to work with his dad, up past Portland by George Bush's place, all along and up to Kennebunkport. You can't get near there now.

Step and dig. Dig and step. It's getting harder and harder to lift my feet. I keep needing to stand straight, but it's standing that gets you stuck. Suddenly, a mudhole boils in front of me. Before I can react, an eel pops out, leaps from his hole and into my face, struggles away, gets a few feet and pauses, gills gaping. I give a little scream of surprise.

"Oh, yes," Truey calls. He's farther away from me yet.

"Mud eel," Dicky shouts in the wind.

The seagulls descend, laughing. The eel slithers back in my direction.

"He's a meal," Truey shouts. He means the eel, for the seagulls.

I stop and watch the spectacle, seagulls, eel, the wind, the waves away off where the mud stops, the plane of dramatic clouds, the salty and sulfuric smell of the mud, the men working methodically away from me. I'm this close to having some sort of college-professor epiphany when I realize I've gazed too long. I'm stuck.

I look back at the boat—it's far. I look at Dicky and Truman and know I've got to get out on my own. I hear in my head the Midcoast boys' derisive laughter. I struggle. My mud muscles—some rare strands in the sides and tops of my thighs—are exhausted, can't do it. I pull with my hands on the lip of my right boot, get it to move a little. I pull on my left, but my foot leaves the boot and won't go back in. I remember Truey's story about Crawford Peacham's moronic son—how the dumb kid got stuck and they had to cut his boots off 'im. How the kid was covered with mud, mud in his nostrils, mud in his mouth, mud halfway up the frukkin' wazoo. I wriggle and pull and both socks are off inside the boots and both boots are stuck and I'm not connected to them except at the calves, where I'm firmly laced. I fall over, go up to my elbows in the mud, then very slowly up to my biceps. Both arms, both legs. Soon it'll be my face. Deadline two weeks gone. I'm sinking.

"He's stuck," Truey calls.

Dicky looks back, and just when you think the laughter should erupt the two of them are dropping their hoes and coming at me, almost racing. Truey gets there first and without a word pulls my arms out, stands me up, then puts his strong hands under my knees and yanks me free a leg at a time, oblivious of the gazes the blood-wormers downflat turn our way.

Dicky makes a forward-leaning race to the boat, pushes it over the mud in a mighty effort, brings it right up behind me so I can sit on the port gunwale. The two of them inspect me a moment, then go back to work without a tease of any kind. I sit in the boat a long time, getting my socks back on, getting my boots readjusted, resting my thighs and my back, getting the mud off my face. The whole time I keep my eye on a certain small hummock of mussels, watch it closely the way as a stock boy I used to watch the clock at the A&P, watch relieved as the hummock sinks in the returning tide.

"Did he quit?" Truey shouts over the wind.

"I think he quit," Dicky calls back. There's no doubt I better go back to work. I climb out of the boat, dig my way close around it in a big rectangle, afraid to move far from the safety of its gunwales. I chop and step and pluck and pull. It's like digging nickels out of the fetid mud, pennies. It's like freelance writing. Forget it.

Near Ellsworth, back in April, back when the deadline for my article was still months off, back before I'd found Truey and Walter and Dicky by telephone, back when I didn't know how many television stations and local papers and even *Yankee* Magazine had done stories on worming using the same Midcoast boys repeatedly, back when my ridiculous plan was to go out on the flats alone, hoping to meet fellow wormers, back then I drove down to a town near Ellsworth that I shall, with no great prejudice, call Wormville, drove all morning to pop into the town hall in this little coastal town—town hall being a well-kept colonial-era house—popped in, all fake confidence, all grins and swagger, to ask about a worming license.

"Who're you digging for?" the Wormville town clerk said, all smiles herself.

I faltered a little at the unexpected question, said, "Just digging?"

Now the town clerk was all frowns. She listened to my convoluted explanation of mission skeptically (UMF professor, writing about working men in Maine, meet the real guys out on the flats), but in the end she had to hand me a license application—all Maine residents are eligible—one form for all of the many Maine-coast commercial fisheries.

Later, over a lobster lunch at Ruth and Wimpy's incredible Lobster Shack, I would check off the box for marine worm digging, add my birthdate, height, and weight. Later still I'd cheerfully write a check for $43.00, cheerful because *Harper's* would pay (and pay for my worm rake, and various horrid motels, and maybe a dozen lobsters at Ruth and Wimpy's, at least that, even if the story got killed), cheerfully mail the whole thing off to the Department of Marine Resources in Augusta, which (as I would note with my newly acquired worm-digger's churlishness) isn't even on the coast. But right now, having provided me with all I needed to get started, the good town clerk of Wormville walked me to the town hall door and pointed across the street to one of the few other commercial buildings in town, a modern one-story affair with a pair of handsomely carved-and-painted wood signs: the first, Gulf of Maine Bait Company; the second, Gulf of Maine Wreath Company. She said, "Before you go drowning yourself on the flats you'll want to talk to Nelson Forrest," and was rid of me.

I walked over and was intercepted in the parking lot by Nelson Forrest himself, energetically on his way somewhere else. I rather nervously explained what I was after, using the whole professor bit, interested in the work, etc., still saying nothing about *Harper's*, or any national article. But here, finally, after two weeks of fruitless phone calls looking for sources, looking for reporterly access to the world of worming, I had someone live to talk to. Mr. Forrest seemed preoccupied, even a little annoyed, but once he got me in his office—thin paneling, tidy old desk, real oil paintings (appealingly amateur), smell of the sea, a phone, a fax—he leaned back in his chair, lit a cigarette, became voluble, answering questions I hadn't asked: "State law says the worms must be dug by hand." He's well tanned and much creased, his eyes blue as the sky over Cadillac Mountain on Mt. Desert Island (pronounced *dessert* as in deserter), which is due south, just across Frenchman Bay. To folks in Wiscasset, Wormville is Down East. To folks Down East, Wormville is Midcoast. Wiscasset might as well be Massachusetts.

Mr. Forrest stares intently at me, talks rapidly, explains the business, answering his own questions: "We pay ten cents a worm for bloods. Six cents for sands. Up in Wiscasset they're paying twelve cents, but they have less shipping cost." The diggers, whom Forrest carefully calls independent contractors, bring the worms to one of ten or fifteen dealers—places like Gulf of Maine Bait—for counting, starting about an hour after low water ("They'll stagger in for hours after that," he says, then corrects himself: "Well, not stagger, exactly"). On vinyl-covered tables the men (and a few women) count bloods rapidly into wooden trays of 250, then fill out a card:

250 BLOOD WORMS
dug and counted by:

Forrest also deals sandworms, but far fewer: "I hate sandworms; they're so frigging fragile. They'll die if you look at 'em." He transfers the worms to newspaper-and-seaweed-lined cardboard flats, where they rest in the walk-in cooler to wait for the worm van, a service provided by several independent shippers (Great Northern Seafood, for one example: "Worm Transit, Maine to Maryland"). Nelson's worms—3,000 to 15,000 a day—are driven to Logan Airport, and from there flown to points south (Maryland, Virginia, North Carolina), west (California, especially Sacramento) and east (Mediterranean France, Spain, and Italy) "It's a unique business. You tell people you sell worms . . . they look at you." The wholesale buyers are either distributors who service bait shops or the captains of fishing charters. The final price out there in the world—some guy fishing for sea bass or spot or weak-fish or flounder—is in the range of three to four dollars a dozen. Mr. Forrest nods proudly: "They do catch fish. See, they're two-thirds blood. Maybe it's the scent, we don't know." His competition, in his estimation, isn't other worm dealers, really, but twenty-four other ocean baits including eels, sea clams, herring, and squid. Of these, squid is probably the most effective, and, unlike worms, can be frozen for shipment, then frozen again by the fisherman after partial use. "Worms aren't the distributors' favorite," Mr. Forrest says. "They die, they're expensive . . . but they need 'em."

Terrible years, good years, the business seems to go on, though not like the old days. Nelson Forrest, who has never dug worms himself, wriggled into worming back in 1972—boom times. He shakes his head about the terrible years of the late eighties—tiny worms, and not many—won't venture a theory as to where the big ones went, though (like every cycle in business and nature), the sea-worm cycle does have its theorists. Pollution plays a role in many of these visions, overharvesting in others. Global warming gets a nod, and one strident wormer I talked to up near Wiscasset invoked Chernobyl (but oddly not the defunct Maine Yankee nuclear facility, which is right in Wiscasset's backyard). Some don't see doom, particularly, just the well-known fact that sea worms are unpredictable. Some years there are plenty of big ones, the kind the fishermen like; some years there just ain't. Nelson Forrest would like to see some conservation—maybe close the mud in winter, maybe think more about size limits. "It's a constant battle to keep the guys out of the little ones . . . and we don't buy on Sundays." He pauses, considers. "Though that's no conservation measure; the guys just refrigerate Sunday worms, bring 'em in Monday." Then he shakes his head, lights the fifth cigarette of our conversation. "When I started, I worried I'd be out of worms in ten years." He looks at me carefully, to see that I'm not missing the point, shakes his head again: "But we're running out of fish first. The fish are *gone*. Pollution, commercial overfishing, this frigging economy—they do destroy sportfishing." And where sportfishing goes, the wormers will go.

That afternoon there's a 2:30 tide, and Mr. Forrest sets me up with one of his crews, the group I have been calling the Midcoast boys, these fellows who, I'll later learn, are practically worming *poster* boys, they've been on TV so much. They love nothing more than razzing a guy with a tie and a microphone. The wormers know something most reporters won't admit: they're getting used. But torturing a reporter for a tide can make up for it, make time fly.

One of the crew, my guide, gets me to follow him in my own vehicle—sixty miles an hour on back roads to one Thompson Island. I watch his head turn at every sight of the water; he's checking the size of the tide, driving off the road. We park on the main drag into Bar Harbor, in front of an enormous fence that hides a gargantuan house.

After I've donned my fly-fishing boots in the face of my guide's skeptical impatience (but no warnings), he trots me past two no trespassing signs and through the summer-dink lawn, around a summer-dink gate, and past two more summer-dink property signs, then along an old lane through a quiet wood, shore pines and pin oaks, lots of poison ivy. Past the fifth and sixth no-trespassing signs we break into a little meadow that is on a point thrust into the Mount Desert Narrows. Trap Rock is in sight, and Thomas Island. Seals play out there. There's a strong onshore breeze, the sound of waves crashing, white sprays of foam thrown up on rocks out there. It's gorgeous.

In the cover of some scruffy pines and under yet another no-trespassing sign, three grim guys await. My guide offers no introductions. I pull out my little notebook filled with little questions to ask, but every one of them looks and sounds like it was written at four in the morning in the worst motel in Ellsworth. We all of us stand amongst boulders and birch trees and watch the tide, which for me means picking out a particular rock and keeping track of how wet it is.

I smile my rube's smile. "So what are your-all's names?"

Nothing.

"You. Hi. Where do you live?"

Nada.

"How much can a good wormer expect to make on the average tide?"

Silence.

"Ever get into fights over territory?"

Here we go. They all look at me. My guide says, "Old days you'd have a hell of a brawl. Now we see guys from Wiscasset or someplace, we might holler some."

"Tell 'em to *go the fuck* home," the next guy says, real fury.

My guide says, "Used to be you'd shoot holes in a guy's boat."

Another gently says, "Tires do get slashed. But some years the worms are one place and not another, and fellows travel."

"Where're *you* from?" the go-the-fuck-home guy says. Everyone looks at me closely.

Me, I don't say a thing, just look out at the tide.

"He's from the college," my guide says. "Farmington, up there."

"I thought only queers lived up that way!"

I'm supposed to defend Farmington, I guess. But I don't. What am I going to say? *Well, yes, we have some gay citizens, of course, about ten percent, I believe, something along those lines, same as Wormville, same as anywhere. Nice folks, our queers. Get used to it!*

We stand on the rocks. We watch the tide. The breeze itself feels tense, carries drops of rain. Where's the story? I don't say a word. The men around me stiffen.

Shoptalk saves the day. My guide says, "She gonna go out?"

The gentle man says, "Somewhat, I think." That onshore wind will keep the tide small.

The angry fellow says, "Probably under eight feet."

My guide: "Shit tide."

The angry fellow: "I'll give you ten bucks you bail out the bay."

They all snigger and have a look at me to see if I believe that's possible. I notice for the first time that the silent man is a young teen. He looks as if he feels sorry for me. I love him for that, gangly kid. He stands half behind the protection of his dad's back (his dad is the gentle one), holding a bloodworm hoe (six tines, nine inches long, short wooden handle), dangles it at the end of one limp arm, an empty joint-compound bucket dangled at the end of the other, the tools of the trade looking like mittens someone has pinned to his jacket.

"You like worming?" I ask him inanely.

"I'm just doing it so my dad don't get pissed off when I ask for *money*."

His dad doesn't laugh, stares the boy down.

Around a corner, on the rocky mud toward the mainland, a lone figure comes a-slogging, a stately, slow march through the muck, his bucket in one hand, hoe in the other. On shore he'd look weary; on firm land he'd look gimpy and stiff; on dry land he'd be another old salt spitting stories; but on the flats there's a grandeur about him. He pauses and looks at the mud, continues on, pauses and looks at the mud, stoops, begins to dig. His style is large, operatic: big strokes, very slowly made. He doesn't seem to be turning up many worms. "He's way inside," the angry man says.

"It's Binky Farmer," my guide says. "He's seventy-seven years old, that one."

"Way inside," the angry one repeats, but no one else seems to want to indict old Binky, whose only pension is a tide a day.

"Shoot him," the angry one says. "I mean it. Shoot him. It's the ethics of the thing."

My guide says, "It's not Binky who should be shot. It's these schoolteachers who come along in summah, trying to strike it rich during their taxpayer *vacation*."

All the boys turn subtly. Binky's off the spot. I'm back on. They eye me closely.

I pull out my pen, my little notebook, write down chunks of conversation, to remind everyone what I'm here for.

My guide looks on curiously, but no way he'll penetrate my handwriting. He offers a quote, is visibly pleased when I write it down: "We'll all need boats before long with all these no-trespassing signs."

"Fucking summer dinks," says the angry one. "Just try to keep me off this fucking point!" He swipes his rake in the air. "I been coming out here since I was *seven*." He swipes the rake in my direction again, for emphasis, ready to pop my summer-dink skull, find the worm within.

We watch the tide. It's going nowhere at all.

Five more wormers come into the meadow. No greetings, just nods, men who've known each other a long time. The new fellows take note of a stranger's presence, remain utterly silent, drift off to watch the tide from their own lookouts around the point. The rest of us watch the bay, watch the sky, watch old Binky as he straightens up, rests; we watch the seagulls, watch the island out there, watch as Binky goes back to work.

Suddenly, no word said, they're all rolling up their sleeves. Suddenly, the tide is right. I can't find my indicator rock—suddenly there are a million rocks. The new guys are off and moving through the mud. The father-and-son team hikes off across the meadow to the other side of the neck, disappears. I had hoped to work near them, in the warmth of their kindness. My guide and the angry fellow step over the seaweed-covered rocks and into the mud right in front of us. Resolutely I follow, uninvited. It may not be much of a tide, it may not be deep mud, but after a short twenty minutes, I'm stuck good.

The angry guy looks back, laughs, shouts something.

"What?" I shout.

"I said, You are a *queer!*"

"Leave him for the *tide*," my guide shouts. The two of them are laughing, hard, moving away from me.

"What?" I shout.

"Mud eel bite your *homo dick* off!" says the angry guy.

"What?" I shout.

My guide: "He won't get but four cents for that worm!"

Hor, hor, hor, hor, hor.

I'm alone. I struggle, still sinking. I drop my notebook, reach for it, lose my pen. I thrash after the notebook, quickly exhausted, then lose my hat, lose my sunglasses. I don't want to lose my Orvis wading boots, but after a struggle, I do lose them, abandon them there in the mud, socks, too. The notebook is the one thing I manage to recover, and with it stuffed in my shirt I crawl and slither and drag myself to a rock near shore, pull myself puffing up onto it, sit heavily, watch the wormers move out and away, chopping at the mud, warmed to their work, no thought of me in their heads.

"Fucking *queers!*" I shout. I'm reaching for an insult they might mind.

But they can't hear me. They're already hundreds of yards away in the wind, which comes at my face.

"Fucking *winter dinks!*"

They don't even turn their heads.

I drag myself rock to rock through the mud and to shore and slog my way back up the point through the yard of the summer mansion. All the no-trespassing signs have been torn down, torn to bits by those fellows who came after, strewn in bits everywhere along the way as if by some furious wind.

Dicky Butts's wife drives the town school bus, part-time. Health insurance? No way. Pension plan? Ha. They live in town, a quiet and genuine Maine place, a working town—no tourist facilities—just a village made of houses and trailers and shacks and sheds. Dicky's good little house is neatly kept, painted blue, on a small piece of an old family lot. His grandmother lives nearby, and his sister, too, and his mom and dad and his aunts and uncles and cousins and many a good friend. Their propinquity is his security, his insurance, his retirement plan.

Truey's house is on a corner of the property down by the road, next turn up from the worm shed. It's a small place, a ranch house, bedrooms in the basement. In the yard he's got an old army truck rebuilt to serve as a log skidder, huge tires draped with tractor chains—winter work. There are logs everywhere. Some cut, some tree length, all of them a season old, valuably waiting. Beside the skidder is his speedway trailer—high rack of worn racing slicks—leaning into the weather. The car itself, the estimable number five, is in a homebuilt garage, and in the garage is where you'll find Truey and Dicky, most high tides, mired in oil, changing engines, packing bearings, knocking out dents (of which in number five there are always plenty). Behind the garage in tall grass are a couple of car bodies—what's left of wrecks Truman and Dicky have used as parts for the racer. And there's kid stuff for the little boys—plenty of toys, a swing set, a play pool. Truey's wife is a nurse at the hospital in Calais, fifteen miles down Route 1. Her job provides the family with health insurance and a retirement plan. Her job also gives insurance of another kind: proof against bad worming.

Delores and Walter's house is at the top of a long, narrow lawn a couple of football fields up the hill from the road and the worm shed. It's newish, set back on the hill, modern lines, tall windows, peaked ceiling, furniture-showroom furniture. It's all very tidy, with an entire wall devoted to a wallpaper mountain scene, anything but the ocean.

It's well known, according to Walter, well known around the flats Down East, that Delores runs the Walter Lock Jr. Bait Company. He means he's damn proud of her business acumen, and not afraid to say so. Delores is tanned and short and built delicately around the ankles and knees, bigger and sturdier on top. She wears large, round eye-glasses, gives an occasional smile, looks closely at you as you speak, her bullshit detector set on stun. Walter says she's tough—she's the one to sell something—sell a car, sell a house, sell the worms ("If these senators up in Washington was just women," he says again, has said it five or six times since I've known him). There's a sign in her hand-some handwriting in the worm shed: "No more short counts. There will be no warning." I know it's her handwriting, because she's writ-ten me at the university, inviting me to come on back down, see the business end of things. It's her sense that I didn't quite get what I needed from the men, she wrote, in so many words, quite a few words. And today she's gone out of her way to answer all my ques-tions, even suggesting questions to ask. She knows I want some color for my write-up (she calls it), so she has told me that she and Walter tried a couple of winters in Florida, picking oranges (piecework, like worms), but lately it's been back to year-round Maine. As for Truey, Truey may seem like a tough guy, but Truey is her little love bunny.

While Walter and Truey are out on the flats, she's on the phone and watching the fax—getting orders from distributors and retailers all over, filling them. She shows me how everything works. Charts and graphs and order sheets. The volume of her sales gets translated into limits: if she's got orders for 10,000 bloodworms and 5,000 sandworms on a given day, that's as many as she'll buy from her diggers. A 500-worm limit means a digger can make no more than $50.00 that day, no matter how prolific the mud. Some families, the ones Delores likes, can get around the limits by bringing spouses and sons and daughters into the picture.

In the worming shed—the windowless cinderblock basement of a truck garage (the garage now converted to an apartment—the days when they could afford to run their own trucks are over)—she washes the counting trays, packs the worms. She hasn't stopped moving since I arrived. The worms go in the usual cardboard flats for the distributors, 125 sands or 250 bloods in a bed of seaweed. Also, increasingly, Delores makes a special fisherman's ten-pack for bait shops to sell, her own invention. A little maiden-hair seaweed, ten carefully counted worms to a small, clear, plastic bag, a twist tie, then into a partitioned shipping box, cardboard lined with styrofoam:

LIVE SEA WORMS. RUSH!

A lot of work, something she didn't have to do in the past.

It's impossible to talk to her when she's counting; she doesn't hear or see, waits till the little bag she's working on is completely and neatly packed. She doesn't move quickly, even though it's familiar work; rather, she's elegant with it, as if she were cooking a fancy French dish. Between ten-packs she gives a small shrug, a smile, talks a snippet of politics, a bit of worm theory, tells a quick story, offers a confession: "Back when we were paying two and three cents a worm, I'd kill 'em when they stung me. Now we're paying ten, I just pack the biters in like the rest." She likes her diggers loyal, she says, doesn't appreciate someone who's over limit trying to sell to other dealers, though she'll buy spare worms from almost anybody if she's got the orders.

Delores has two years of college, University of Southern Maine, thirty-some years back, cannot remember what major, did not get the degree. At this, I just shrug. For that, she likes me more. And I like her. She knows exactly who I am. She keeps me at her side, introduces me to everyone as a *scientist*. I don't correct her, and in some weird way my actual physical *stance* changes. The look on my face feels *scientific*. Even my questions change. I'm a new man. Give me a lab coat. I peer at the worms a whole new way, as if through some delicate instrument. For the first time among wormers I don't feel like an idiot. That's Delores.

In the hours after the tide, the wormers come in, quietly, tiredly, make their counts. There's no banter, no conversation, no braggadocio. The diggers just come in. There's Jordon LeMieux, whom Walter has called an ace blood digger. There's Spooky Nick, another ace, and Clarissa Larssen—the best woman wormer in Maine, in Walter's estimation. Squeak Snodgras comes in and counts his worms wordlessly, hands in his count slip, wordlessly leaves. There's a cool-looking teen boy, a hottie—Nike Air sneakers, T-shirt that says SLAM DUNK, inner-city haircut—standing by his long-haired and tattooed dad, and in the counting room at prom time the boy is attentive, engaged, watches carefully as Pop counts his allowance worm by worm into the tray. Another father stands beside his daughter, an athletic and serious young woman of sixteen—very, very pretty—with mud to her eyelashes. They count. No one talks, not even all the young guys— a dozen of them in their twenties (their muddy pants low on their hips, showing the cracks of their fannies: wormer's cleavage). No chatter. No high fives. Nothing but the counting, the exchanging of slips, this scientist watching. There are two guys with ponytails like mine (that is, scraggly), a bunch with tattoos, several apparent bodybuilders, a thin fellow with JESUS LOVES YOU on his sweatshirt. The wormers straggle in for a couple of hours, dumping their worms, counting them fast under fluorescent light, filling out their slips, collecting their cash or watching Delores put their counts in her book for a paycheck at the end of the week.

In a couple of months some of the boys will have to start blueberry picking up on the highlands; a few weeks past that some will go off logging. Some have skills like welding for whomever comes needing it; some will clean houses or leave town with construction crews or take temporary work at a mill. In December there's firewood chopping, even knickknack carving, and many an individual scheme. Then the new year: time to start thinking about the mud. Some guys will have to get out there in January—break the ice, dig the worms. Some will luxuriate till February. Some—the diggers with luck, or skills that match this year's needs, or spouses who work good jobs—some won't have to go out till March.

My first trip with the Down East boys proved a good one for them, Walter and Dicky both counting 1,500 sands—$90.00 each, plus enough bloods to carry the take over a hundred dollars for the tide. Truey, always a little more aggressive, got 1,650 sands that day. Dicky was kind enough to count my worms for me, and after culling me about fifty (too small, or diseased, or broken by the bloods I'd thrown in with them), my count for the tide was an unspectacular 155 worms. $9.30. The five killer bloods in there brought my payday up to $9.80. I refused the cash, but Delores refused my refusal, and so—after a spot of negotiating, and a suggestion by Dicky—I became a minor sponsor of Truey's big number five, glory of the Bangor Speedway.

Still trying, I make yet another worming trip, drive down from Farmington the night before a tide Truey thinks'll be a good one, eat a diner dinner, stay at the Blueberry Motel. It's a nice late low tide, and I sleep in, eat a big breakfast. Truey's broken a camshaft in the race Saturday night and wrecked his engine, so there's extra incentive for a big day for all of us. My boots are tight; I've been out on my own in the mud below Milbridge, practicing. I've bought myself a sandworm hoe. I have my own gloves, a proper shirt. I know the Harrington River mud now, and the Harrington River mud knows me. I'm ready to leave the ranks of professors, even scientists, ready to move up to shitdigger. The day is auspicious, the parking lot at Ripley Neck entirely full. Walter points out a Garney across the way, hovering in a workboat. "Spyglass," he says. "He'll sit there and wait to see where the real wormers go."

We cross the bay in good weather. The talk is briefly of cranberries: Walter has had a brainstorm: he'll dig a homemade bog in the woods up behind his house, grow cranberries. Dicky and Truey don't have much to say about that, then Truey invokes sea urchins, and they're off on that good subject again: $2,800 a day and you can go all winter. $2,800 a day, and you don't have to worry about the worm market drying up, and you don't have to cut wood, or make wreaths, or shovel snow or work blueberries. You just get in your diving gear, bring up the urchins, get your body heat back in the hot tank on the deck of your boat, dive and dive and dive again, get rich on the Japanese.

"It's a hard winter in this county," as Walter says. Here in June, the Down East boys are already thinking about ice.

That fucking spyglass Garney is going ashore in the neighborhood of some Milbridge boys. The sun is hot. Thunderheads are building up. You think of lightning, then you think of yourself plugged into the mud, the highest thing for hundreds of yards around, a lightning rod. Workboats are tooling every which way, and Truey and Dicky and Walter know everyone. "That fellow there is Minton Frawley. He went out to Arizona one winter and got himself in the movies. Did you see *Stir Crazy*? He's the guy looking up the girl's crotch in that bar scene."

"He's back worming," Dicky says.

"Scared of lightning," Truey says, meaning Frawley. "He'll run at the first boom-boom. Watch him."

"Winter does take a toll," Walter says, drifting on his own raft of thought. When we hit the mud, Walter gets in it, immediately marches to a big mussel flat, and begins to dig its borders. Dicky and Truey and I wait. Like most wormers, they like to watch the tide, size it up, have a chat. "Ask your daddy how many orders he's got," Dicky says. "I need some ambition."

He does look tired.

Truey just watches his father at work.

Dicky sizes up the tide, pretends a discouragement that looks real: "I don't think this is going to be a profitable day, Truey."

My deadline is long gone, my story's a kill, but here I am. The guys don't pay much attention to me anymore, negative or positive.

I'm up to about forty bucks in Truey's race car. Maybe one Saturday soon I'll go to the races, hang in the pit, a scientist, see, interested in speed. Maybe *Harper's* will like that story!

There's a rumble of thunder, not far distant. Truey smiles briefly at Dicky's joking, goes over the gunwales, gets himself ready to worm. Dicky reluctantly follows. I'm so reluctant I just sit in the boat and watch them start. More thunder.

"There he goes," Truey says. Sure enough, movie-star Frawley has turned his boat around and is heading back in.

Truey takes his shirt off, and you have to wonder if his naked-lady tattoo is by the same artist as Dicky's. It's the same woman, same colors, same thick lines. I climb into the mud. Today I plan to up my sponsorship of the glorious number five to serious partnership proportions. Today I want to dig like a Down East boy.

Truey is already at it, working hard.

Dicky can't seem to get started. "Help," he says. A plaintive joke. He doesn't feel like it today. In the end, though, he'll get 1,900 sandworms, 120 bloods: $126.00, a super tide. Truey will get 2,100 sands, 50 bloods. A money tide, a monster. Walter will do as well as Dicky. I will get 210 sandworms, zero bloods, working hard as I've ever worked, chopping and stomping and picking, legs sore as hell from previous outings, shoulders aching, mind blank, struggling in the mud, turning it, panting, mucking along, pulling worms: $12.60.

Truey hikes off far away across the mud. Later, when the tide comes up, we'll have to go pick him up. Walter is chopping away at some distant mussel mound. Dicky doesn't range too far, gradually gets his rhythm, digs faster and faster, coming into the worms. I never get a rhythm at all, stay close to the boat, trying to get a whole tide in, no breaks, no getting stuck. I know how to walk now, don't pause long enough to sink, but march forward, ever forward, chop left, chop middle, chop right, pulling worms from the mud. To me, they seem scarce today. To me, they seem terribly fragile. I break every third worm, miss a million that zip into their holes before I can get hold. The thunder booms a little closer.

Late in the tide, Dicky starts saying "Help," again, just kind of saying it out loud every twenty steps or so, groaning comically. He's found some good mud, is plunking worms into his box three and four at a dig. "Help," he moans, kidding around. Then he shouts: "Truey, let's quit." It's an old joke, and from across the flat Truman Lock gives Dicky the finger. Dicky excavates his way through the mud, pulling worms, pulling worms, dunking them in his box, saying "Help, Truey. Truey, help," a mantra for the dig. Then he bellows, loud as hell across the mud: *"Truey, get me outta here,"* and then he shouts it again.

The Past and the Present

from The Saltwater Farm and the Spleeny Yowun

Sanford Phippen

I don't remember ever using the actual front door to enter my grandparents' farmhouse. The door must have been open sometimes in the summers, as the enclosed porch door was; but year-round, everyone used the back sidedoor in the ell of the house. The main structure was a classic Cape Cod farmhouse, which downstairs featured the living room, master bedroom, a smaller bedroom, and part of the kitchen. The rest of the kitchen was in the ell along with the main shed, the wood shed, and the two-holer. Up over the sheds was an attic area used for storage and which also featured a playroom where my mother and her eleven brothers and sisters once played; and in my generation where my cousins and I also played.

The cow barn was not connected to the house. It stood a few yards from the back of the ell, and beside the barn were two more outbuildings, one in which Papa made barrels and one that served as a combination livery stable and horse barn. Nearer the house was the ice house and the milk room in which my grandfather and uncles stored the milk and eggs from their dairy and chicken operations. There were pig pens, hen houses, the smoke-house; and the largest building, which was a multi-door long garage where the tractor, truck, hay wagons, and other farm equipment were stored. Halfway down the backfield was the saw mill and way down the field was the ice pond where we used to go skating in the winters. Part of the back field was fenced in for the cows and bull. There were vegetable and strawberry gardens; and across from the enclosed porch, or southern side of the house, one could see the tops of the Mount Desert Island hills. Across the road from the farm proper was an old road that led down to the family property on the shore where we had our picnics and clambakes.

I was a little five-year-old towhead staying with grandparents one winter day when Grammie chopped the head off a chicken right in front of me, and because of my horror at this incident, she started calling me spleeny.

I used to love to curl up on the old couch in the kitchen by the stove and be looking at the *Saturday Evening Post*, *Life*, or assorted farm journals while Grammie was washing dishes, rinsing out milk bottles, or cooking. On that particular winter day, she told me, "We've got to go out to the hen house and get a chicken for dinner." I followed along behind her over the snow. She was carrying a pail of boiling water and a hatchet. I didn't know what was going to happen, but she made it seem, as usual, like fun.

Until the killing. She was struggling to hold the hen down on the chopping block with one hand while raising the hatchet high with the other. Being an expert, Grammie took off the head with one quick blow. And the headless chicken ran right at me, blood spewing all over the snow. I must have either cried out or just stood there looking shocked, for Grammie laughed at me.

"Don't be so spleeny, An-day!"

Finally, the chicken flopped down in the snow. Grammie retrieved the body and dumped it in the pail of boiling water. I'll never forget that sharp smell, or the sight of the bloody chicken's head lying in the snow.

To me, the farm was full of such scenes: sudden, violent, bloody death; the messy but beautiful birth of a calf; casual but also violent sex among the animals; manure and chicken shit underlying all. It was lively, earthy, and real. As a child growing up in such surroundings, I was alternately frightened and fascinated, never bored.

By 1950, Papa Warren was nearly eighty and Grammie was in her late sixties; and so the farm was in the control of two of my uncles, Oliver and Owen, then both divorced and living home. Oliver handled the milk business and Owen was in charge of the wood mill. The vegetable gardens were greatly reduced. Oliver and Owen did business with Jake Kaplan, a Jewish cattle dealer from Bangor, who seemed part of our family. Jake would drive down to the farm on Sunday afternoons in his Plymouth sedan. My uncles would sit out in the car with Jake, all of them with hats on, smoking and talking over their deals. Grammie would always bake Jake an apple pie, which he loved. There was a great deal of trust, respect, and affection between Jake and our family. We always benefited from his deals. In fact, it was Jake, years later, who tipped off Uncle Oliver about the good caretaking job the other side of Ellsworth that Oliver took, closing down the farm for good.

"Jake's smart, and a good man," Uncle Oliver told me.

One time Jake was carting away Buddy, an old sway-backed horse that I loved. I ran screaming down the driveway after Jake's old green Chevy truck that day until Jake stopped, rolled down the window, and looked at me. He seemed miles up.

"Jake! Where are ya taking Bud-day?" I asked, tears welling in my eyes.

"To the glue factory, kid!" he said and drove off.

As a youngster I remember gathering eggs, picking berries, picking string beans, picking and shelling peas, digging up dandelion greens, plucking feathers off the just-boiled chickens while squatting on the sawdust piles in the ice house, gathering lady's slippers from the woods and violets and forget-me-nots from the fields, and generally helping out my elders. "You be available now, and don't run off," my relatives would say.

My first big adult job was cleaning out the barn. I was about eleven and it was on summer mornings before The Milk Drive got underway. That was what my relatives called the daily delivery of milk, cream, and eggs about town in the old International pickup.

I'd step into the cow barn those mornings and there'd hang that hot, heavy smell in the close and dusty air that would hit me strong in the face. Even with the windows open, with the low ceilings, the piles of hay, and the dozen or more fat bossy bodies, it was a stifling and oppressive place. Nice and warm in the winter, however.

The walls were whitewashed and there would be thousands of flies everywhere. Uncle Oliver had rigged up an old radio, as well as a couple of electric lights in the barn, and it's a wonder none of us ever got electrocuted, standing around in the wet troughs, trying to turn up the radio so we could hear Johnny Desmond or Vaughn Monroe singing while we did the chores. If we didn't have our rubber boots on, we were always getting little shocks from both the radio and the lights, and every switch snapped and popped.

Papa named the cows after fairy-tale characters like Rapunzel, Snow White, and Rose Red. One of the bulls, I remember, he called Grimm. They'd be there all in their row, penned in their stalls with their huge, sad eyes looking at you, their ears and tails flapping at the flies, their bumpy heads bobbing up and down, their lower jaws and mouths chomping and chewing away at their continuous cud. And from behind, where I got to know them best, there was manure everywhere: caked on their legs and tails, on the water and milk pails, tools, floors, and walls. You couldn't even see out of the windows. All I had to do was to take a square-shaped shovel and scrape down the troughs behind the cows and pile the manure into a wheelbarrow and dump it out a back door, adding to the ever-growing pile half as high as the barn itself.

Grimm used to scare me when I was cleaning out the barn. I had to keep treading quietly by his pen to dump the manure; and it seems as if he'd always be on the verge of escape, snorting, raging, and butting against the wooden confines of his stall. My uncles had nailed reinforcement boards around and about the locked door, but it always seemed to me that the nails were loose and getting looser. I pictured the wild, red-eyed beast breaking out and butting me headfirst into the manure pile. As a small child, I once caught the bull and one of the cows when they were out in the pasture "doing the dirt," and I ran fast to tell Uncle Owen down in the saw mill that the cows were fighting. He looked out, and laughed, saying, "You look again, An-day! They ain't fightin'; they're propagatin'."

There were a number of mice and rats that used to live in the barn; but I didn't know who was scarier—the rodents or the wild cats that my uncles kept to keep down the rat population. The cats were gray and beautiful with yellow eyes and we yowuns used to try and capture them, but they were always too wild and would bite, scratch, and dig us whenever we tried to catch and pet them.

Of course, just as soon as I got done scraping the troughs, Rapunzel, Rose Red, Cinderella and Company would start plopping, drizzling, and exploding all over again. When I first started this job, I couldn't drink any milk for a week or so, for I would picture the milk all mixed together with the plop and pee and flies from the manure piles. I never did much milking of the cows, either. They and their teats nauseated me.

By the time I had the barn cleaned out, it would be time to go on The Milk Drive. Uncle Oliver and Ricky Rowe, a neighborhood boy two years my senior, would have the back of the International pickup all filled with crates of milk, eggs, and cream, the "homo" milk bottles had green cellophane tops, the pasteurized red, and the raw milk, which Uncle Oliver bottled himself from our cows, had just plain caps. The milk was in bottles then, but the cream came in half-pint cardboard conical-shaped containers and the eggs were in cardboard boxes.

"Did ya scrape that shit off the eggs?" Uncle Oliver would ask Ricky, his job while I scraped the barn. "They gotta look clean, ya know, for the summer people."

Uncle Oliver would fling a heavy canvas sheet over the back of the pickup—for there was no refrigeration—and off we'd go, jouncing along with the clank and jangle of the milk bottles in their metal crates, up one side of Taunton Peninsula and down the other, stopping at almost every house; for by the time I was growing up, Papa's dairy farm had little competition. Our milk carried the Hancock County Creamery labels and every afternoon Oliver would take the milk cans of our cows' milk to the Ellsworth creamery and return with the processed, bottled milk for the next day, which he'd store overnight in the "Milk Room," a small building with a few ice boxes in it connected to the ice house.

The Milk Drive was kind of fun. After a few trips I had memorized almost what everyone had or wanted each time. If they wanted more or something different, they'd usually leave a note in one of the empty bottles. Some customers would pay each time, while others would run up bills. According to Uncle Oliver, some never paid, including a few of the most prominent folks in town, but still Uncle Oliver delivered to them. All he'd say in explanation was "folks gotta have milk."

Summer people's places scared me the most. They were really foreign territory, even though I had been in many of them and had helped my relatives clean and care for them; but they weren't empty houses during the summer season. People were living in them and they were people I didn't know. And there was that difference between their cedar-shingled rusticity and the natives' year-round plain frame domiciles. There was a more worldly atmosphere and certain classiness to these coastal retreats. Down around the bay, with that beautiful, constant view of the Mount Desert Hills, they felt and smelled different. They were built rather close to one another, but inside the rooms facing the water seemed more open that our rooms at home without a view. Summer people's cars were apt to be foreign makes with foreign license plates. These people grew ferns and planted pretty gardens about their front doors and porches, and some of the more elaborate cottages sported water fountains, Japanese gardens, and statuary. There were tennis racquets, golf clubs, and sailboat equipment stacked in their sheds, garages, and entryways, items not readily found in my relatives' and neighbors' homes. These people were my betters and my parents' betters, or so I thought I understood. I wasn't to have a scene with them. They were our bread and butter, as we were their milk and eggs. I tried on every Milk Drive to catch a glimpse of some of them, and their kids, but most of them were asleep that early in the morning. If one ever did come face-to-face with them, one was to be pleasant, say little, always agree with them, act the dutiful servant. One could disagree and complain behind their backs and make fun of their strange ways and ideas, but never to their faces. This was the old established practice.

As the morning would wear on, Uncle Oliver tried to hurry Ricky and me up. "Goddamn it, boys. The milk's gonna turn sour," he'd say; or "Let's get the hell out of here before someone comes out and tries to talk to us."

All of my Warren aunts and uncles, and Sid, too, have this wild-eyed look. All twelve of them with their wounded and yet determined-looking faces with their red, horsey-faced English-Irish features. They always seemed to be looking beyond the here and now, never completely absorbed by the present or the task at hand. Most always good-humored, resigned to their fate, busy rushing about, they competed with each other, trying to top each other with the latest joke, a new purchase, a new job, new trip, new child. It got very irritating after a while, especially to all of us cousins, my brother and me. And yet, we, too, compete. Whenever the Warrens get together, they all talk at once.

Uncle Oliver and Aunt Eller were especially wild-eyed. They looked like they were always on the verge of running away from home or looked as if some monstrous eruption was beginning to evolve just beyond the person they were facing and they could only express their fear and excitement through their eyes. But while Oliver was very shy and quiet, never wanting to be noticed in his clandestine comings and goings, Aunt Eller was much more gregarious, liked having people visit and to dance, laugh, and drink with. Years after I worked for Uncle Oliver on The Milk Drive, he took the job as caretaker that Jake Kaplan had told him about; and when he left the farm for that job, Aunt Eller took over the Milk Drive.

One memorable time when I was home from college during the January break between semesters, I was with my lifelong pal Russell Barclay, who was also a student at the University of Maine, and we went on The Drive with Aunt Eller. The same International pickup, ten years older, and the same canvas sheet were still in use, but the atmosphere inside the cab was totally transformed thanks to Aunt Eller's ebullient spirit, especially in the company of young men. She had names for all the customers. One old lady living alone, she mysteriously termed "The Prostitute," while an old couple who had been married for many years she called "The Honeymooners," and a lady who had a number of children by various men she termed "The United Nations." A couple who never bought more than one quart of milk or half-pint of cream or a half-dozen eggs she called "The Misers."

That wintry day on The Drive, it was cold and icy, but still there were barking dogs with which to contend. At one stop Aunt Eller whipped off her slipper—she was wearing Uncle Fod's slippers—and waving it out the window on her side of the truck, yelled, "Hurry up, An-day! Run in that quart of skim to The Prostitute while I keep Rover busy."

By noon time, Aunt Eller stopped at the store and bought a six-pack of Narragansett for lunch. "You boys, being college men, don't want any milk to drink now, do ya? This is a cold day in January, and milk won't warm ya up as good as a beer."

Near the end of the day's Drive, we were feeling no pain, jouncing along in the broken-down seat of the rusted-out truck, when we came to the steep driveway to Ida Purdy's house. It was all icy.

As soon as we started up the incline, the back tires began to spin around. "Christ! Hold on, boys! Ya might have to get out and push! Old Ida's gotta get her cream. But I don't know . . . I'll wind 'er up and shift 'er down. Here goes nothin'!"

We jerked about, inching our way up the driveway, the back wheels spinning about eighty miles an hour, when all of a sudden Aunt Eller really floored her. The tailgate fell open, and about three or four crates of milk cartons and bottles went flying out the back and rolled down and splattered all over the driveway. A few dozen of them smashed or were crushed. The ice was covered with milk and eggs.

"Shit! There go the profits!" Eller said.

At least we had made it to Ida's front door. She came out, a little, old white-haired lady in a housecoat; and Eller hollered at her. "Whataya want, Ida? One-a-milk and one-a-eggs? Same as usual?"

"Nothing today," Ida said.

"How do ya like that, boys? The old bag's gone on the wagon just when we lost ours!"

It took a while for three of us to pick up the bottles, cartons, and pieces of glass, with old Ida tsk-tsking from her front door, clucking to herself, and saying things like, "Oh, isn't that too bad; that's too bad, dear, dear."

"I'll tell ya what, Ida," Eller said, "for the rest of the winter we gotta work out a signal system. When ya see me coming, a white hanky means come on up—unless it's icy like this again—and a red bandana or something equally flashy means go on by—OK?"

"Well, I guess so . . . "

"*I guess probably!*" Eller said. "I can't afford too many more stops like this one!"

As it turned out, there weren't many more stops left for The Milk Drive itself; for a few months after that icy incident, the old International pickup broke down for the last time. No one in the family wanted to invest in a new truck; and the county creamery had already taken over most of the routes with its own delivery trucks. So, after driving the milk for more than forty years by both horse and wagon and truck around Taunton, the Warren family was no longer in the dairy business. Aunt Eller went to work in a fish factory where she cut the heads off sardines and threw them at the tourists.

The saw mill was the only money-making operation still going down on the farm during the late sixties. I only worked there for Uncle Owen a little bit, when he needed me. The whir of that old rickety saw ripping and whining through the wood scared me even more than the summer people. It was like Robert Frost's poem, "Out, Out . . . " in which a boy working with such a saw gets his hand cut off and dies. My mother had once pointed out to me a man in Ellsworth with only one arm. She told me he was the only survivor from a grisly mill accident in which the saw blade got loose and cut through the men standing around. A couple of men were cut in two, or lost a few limbs, while the man she pointed out was lucky only to have lost the one arm. Every time that blade hit a knot in the wood, which I was helping to steady, I thought of that incident and the Frost poem. While I trusted Owen, I could see the blade flying loose and cutting my head off. I quit Uncle Owen and "The Wood-butchers," which is what my uncles had named the mill, for it just didn't seem safe.

Today, in Taunton Ferry, where there used to be a half-dozen busy farms like my grandparents', there are none. One doesn't wake up any more to the sound of wood being sawed, of roosters crowing and hens clucking, or any of the other farm noises of old. Fields have grown up, or been sold as house lots. When it used to be unique for anyone to commute to Ellsworth or Bangor for work, now it is unique for anyone to have any kind of job in Taunton Ferry.

Many of the old-time summer people have told me how years ago how much they enjoyed driving up to my grandparents' farm. They'd make the excuse that they were going to get an extra quart of milk, more cream or eggs; but they really loved visiting my grandparents, their children, and the farm.

"A remarkable family," one lady told me. "They were always so warm and welcoming, full of fun and good stories. It was like what we imagined farm life in Maine to be, only more so." What impressed this one woman especially was the story of how my grandparents finally had running water put in the house.

"The cows got sick," she said, "and it was decided to put running water in the barn for them; and only after that did they decide to put running water in the house, too, and that was only for a pump in the kitchen sink. Your grandparents thought of their animals before they thought of themselves. That fact made a great impression on me."

By the mid-sixties, Uncle Oliver had sold off most of the dairy and chicken business; and while still living in the family farmhouse, he was commuting to work in Ellsworth. By the late 1960s, when he was promised a place to stay at his work, he decided to close up the house and move. I was home from teaching at Christmas when I went down to see Uncle Oliver and take him a gift. It was only about four P.M., but dark; and when I knocked on the old side door in the ell of the house, I found it locked.

"Uncle Oliver?" I called.

"Who is it?" he called back.

"Andy."

"Just a minute." I heard him coming and then opening the locks, for there wasn't just one.

Entering the shed, I was momentarily surprised by the sight of about twenty-five cats, the wild barn cats, lapping out of dishes on the floor, their tails up in the air and their yellow eyes glowing in the half-light from the kitchen door. I followed my uncle into the kitchen where he had about four cauldrons of oatmeal bubbling on the stove.

"What are you doing, Uncle Oliver?"

"Tryin' to make friends with the cats so I can kill 'em!"

"Why?"

"I can't just leave 'em around here. There's nothing for 'em to eat any more. The milk's gone and the mice and the rats are gone, too. And now I'm going. They're too wild for pets."

Dana Hamlin, from *Temple*

George Dennison

Dana Hamlin

"Won't somebody help me. Help me. Won't somebody tell me what my trouble is. Won't somebody help me." Loud, chanted; a wailing yet droning tone desperate but boring, clear to everyone that there was no immediate emergency. Thin, wild-eyed, white-haired, powdery white skin, bluish cast to the skin of the thighs where her hospital gown had risen. A large doll on the tray of her wheelchair. She holds a diaper by one corner, trailing it on the floor, flapping it feebly toward whoever looks at her. This chanting broke in on us toward the end of the hour. It was eerie, broke my attention to Dana. I wheeled him out to the community room when I left and saw her. When I arrived, an hour earlier, she was quiet, was stroking the head of the doll that lay across the tray. She wasn't stroking it vaguely, but with firm contact and the kind of pause in the stroke that would serve to catch the baby's hair (if it had been a baby) and brush it away from the eyes.

Dana in the wheelchair, looking down, gathering his thoughts. One can see the huge function of energy. More is there than he can easily obtain for articulate memory—and if the whole thing can be energized, it will come out. That is what he seems to be trying to do.

To see the faculties dying, tissue dying, is to realize what a miraculous creation these sentient tissues are.

When I came to the nursing home yesterday: garish color TV, shrieking fat woman, palsied man making grotesque faces like a blow fish, "What can I do for you? What can, etc.?" rapidly—a scene of craziness and fragmentation, not age. Dana sane and rational in this madhouse of old age. Dana was sitting at the table (an empty table) in his wheelchair, sleeping, body collapsed inward on itself, his head dangling down like the head of a sunflower that has ripened and the frost has killed it, and now, on an upright stalk, the drooping head looks straight down, staring, full face into the earth. I talked to the cheerful young woman in the tiny cubicle of the office. She told me two o'clock would be a good time to talk with him. I drove around the Mosher Hill area, beautiful vistas, my fall feeling of nostalgia, *déjà vu*, and longing. A light rain—dry places on the road under the big trees.

The *cheerful, giving* character of the young women nurses.
"Can you bring me a glass of water?" "Sure can."—brisk, cheerful, comes almost at a run. This is by no means a common or much-encountered temperament, but it seems to me to be a rural and maybe a state of Maine temperament and I love it. Dana such a sweet *good* person. I wanted to caress his cheek, kiss him when I left—everything sweet and dear about age, all the power and fearsomeness taken away and that long experience of the world couched there almost as in an infant's body. I did pat his back; we are really strangers. And yet we began talking about Temple when I arrived. He didn't know me, didn't remember the two brief encounters we'd had. I appeared in his field of vision wanting to talk about Temple, and so he talked about Temple. The mere process of establishing where I lived resurrected the remembered places and turns of his milk route, and he began to talk—though with difficulty. Never asked my name, but wanted me to please repeat where it was I lived.

Dana answered questions that I hadn't yet put into words and that actually changed, or seemed to change, the drift of our talk. Like a child, I could believe in some sort of clairvoyance—so little static of self.

Dick Blodgett: "It's amazing he's still alive. He's been in more accidents and had more broken bones. Horses ran away with him, pulled him all over the place. And when they bulldozed the dump, once he backed up with a load of garbage and went right over."

Born 1880.

"I hauled milk for sixty years. That's a long time. I believe I've gone more miles on a milk route than any man in the world.

"The old creamery failed, so my dad went around to the farmers and asked if they'd let us haul their cream down to the North Turner creamery. They said they would. It was March. My dad took ill and my brother was shearing sheep, so Dad said to me, Would you rather haul milk or shear? and I said it didn't make any difference, both o' them was work. So that's when I started. I was sixteen years old."

When Dana said "both o' them was work," a light of wit came to his face—remarkable to see this. His sweet smile and a brightening of the watery left eye.

Handkerchief in his breast pocket. He extracts it with a certain effort and deliberation. He had already said to me, "I can only see out of this eye. This one here has cataracts. I could have had 'em taken off. Maybe I should've, but my sister did, and she had a bad time with it." Now he said, "My eyes water an awful lot." He held the handkerchief to his eye repeatedly, not dabbing, but holding it there, as if letting it soak up the fluid.

"When this leg gets better, I'll send for my crutches. My grandson has them. It would be easier for me to walk to the sitting room than turn these wheels."

About coming back. "We eat at around five, then pretty soon after, I start getting ready for bed. Yes, two o'clock is a good time."

Just before leaving, I explained to him why I had come in the first place. He said, "Well, I don't know what good I'll do, but I'll try to help." Seemed pleased.

I saw him at Temple's 175th anniversary party, sitting in his wheelchair in the back of the pickup truck. "My grandson laid two planks against the back o' the carriage and wheeled me right up. I could see everything. I sat just as close as I am to you to the tailgate of the carriage. More than a hundred people came by and talked to me."

I had seen him three years ago at the bank in Farmington, looking to the left and right with shy pleasure, a public figure, the oldest man, and so attractive in his pleased awareness of things that many did smile at him, so shy yet at ease—the grandfather of the town—anyone could greet him and he would greet anyone with a smile. Dipping into the little snap-purse, a leather pouch. His soft, button-up shoes, with their thin soles (like a dancer's slippers) were of the same vintage. He was walking well, and must have weighed twenty or thirty pounds more than he does now. He seems collapsed and desiccated. His arms are too weak to push the wheels of the wheelchair. His hands are misshapen, huge knuckles, fingers somewhat awry. They lie in his lap, a collection of bones in little bags of skin. He wears an old flannel shirt, checkered, and the dark green cotton work pants that farmers, mechanics, mill hands, woodcutters, etc. all wear around here. There is no meat on his shoulders or around his chest. Inside his shirt there is a cage of bones, and in that cage his heart is still beating. His hips seem wide and boney. His knees are boney, and there is nothing but bone between them and his hips, or between knees and feet. His neck is thin and weak, with loose seams and flaps of dusty soft skin; his head tilts forward. Bald, with a few dry strands of dead grass and broken spiderwebs this way and that, a little hair, cut short, above his ears. Pale, powdery, faintly speckled skin, a pale wart or cyst high in the middle of his forehead. Sunken temples. His ears seem large and protrude somewhat. Pale bristles of his eyebrows he scratches occasionally with his thumbnail, especially when he forgets something, and says, "Oh . . . it's funny . . . you know I can't always think of what I want to. Tell me again where you live." Prominent cheekbones, separated from his small, square jaw by deep creases and soft small folds of skin, his small nose, shrunken cartilage, a little button nose. Wide expressive mouth that smiles widely, upturned innocently at the corners like the smile of an introspective young child who is happy but does not grin. He talked for ten minutes or so, and then, "You know, I have some false teeth. I believe I could talk better if I put them in." He extracted them from the pocket of the flannel shirt where they were wedged behind a folded handkerchief, and with deliberate, somewhat tremulous movements fixed them (uppers) into place. "They drop out very easily now, so I keep them in my pocket. I lost two teeth out of them. I'm afraid of losing the whole thing." Said this with a brightening smile, attractive gentle humor. This was his first such sign of life. His voice is slow, hesitant, faint, but his sentences hang together, get finished, and go right ahead. So much effort goes into the mere act of talking, and of remembering, that often I thought he had lost the train of thought, or was even on the verge of nodding off into sleep—and though he did occasionally lose the thread, he surprised me again and again. "Mustache" of small, vertical wrinkles.

"I had four brothers, two sisters, and a mother and father—now I'm all that's left."

Dick Blodgett: "Dana's wife was the Sunday school teacher here in the Intervale. I went every Sunday. I was the only boy that did. (Laughs) Maybe that's why. She was a nice old lady."

Dana Hamlin II

They were playing beano when I came, a more rational scene. The woman with the doll was off to one end by herself, not playing— and in Dana's room two old men were in bed, one trembling. ("How are you today?" "I'm all right." "Are you cold?" "Yes. I'm cold."—she covers him.)

I talk with Leon about permission and advisability of taking Dana for a ride. He likes the idea. Terrible difficulty of doing anything—extracting his handkerchief from his breast pocket, wiping his nose. He asked me to open the drawer. I helped rummage for his glasses. He checked the case. "I can't see out of one eye so I just have the one lens. Hah! I've got a cataract on my right eye. If I'd've had my wits about me, I'd've had it taken off years ago, but my sister had that operation and it gave her a lot of trouble and that discouraged me."

Life is reduced to a few things; each one is difficult, and is done slowly with weak, trembling hands that are nothing but bone and tendon, knuckles, no meat, great hollows, great knobs, all speckled. Time goes very, very slowly. Is it easier to face death this way—so far off, an hour is like three hours, or like a day—a long time between breakfast and dinner?

Hard to pick him up to help him pee in a plastic bottle. No weight in his legs. Leon: "He weighs 135, but it's all concentrated in the top. He's top-heavy. How's your back; it won't be easy getting him in and out of the car."

His large ears, the bald skin of head so pale, ivory thin, without blood. Everything sunken, collapsed, drawing near to the bone.

In the bed next to his, an old man on his back, mouth open, tongue sharp in position of pain, pointed nose aimed at the ceiling—death soon.

Helping him pee. "Hand me that bottle there. Now stand behind me and lift me up." When this is written down, it reads like ordinary speech, but each word is an effort, and there are no gestures, and the blind eye is expressionless and the other recessed in a small triangular aperture under a bristly, heavy white eyebrow. It was a task for his trembling fingers to open his pants, a task to locate his penis and get it into the mouth of the receptacle. And actually I thought he *hadn't*, that he had missed and would wet himself. I didn't know what to do, didn't want to embarrass him, and a small wetting would be no great consequence. But actually he had succeeded. His penis was so shrunken that I had thought part was hidden, bent under the edge of the plastic jar.

He wasn't entirely easy about the idea of driving with me, doesn't really know who I am, though he does really know where I live. "You go down that dirt road and take a right over the stream. There was some buildings set right up in there. That was the other Waltonen—yes, John . . . ."

Wears the ubiquitous dark green cotton work pants, now many, many inches too large for him. A checked cotton work shirt, over that a dark gray, solid color, medium-weight cardigan sweater with black buttons. Brown corduroy bedroom slippers (he never leaves the wheelchair). Beside his bed are the old high-top shoes of soft, thin leather, thin soles, black, many eyelets for the laces. Another pair on a shelf in the closet. "Open that drawer"—a tone so gentle and so without ego that it doesn't even have the assertiveness of a request. In the drawer: a *National Geographic*, some Bible pamphlets, a modest clutter. "I put my false teeth in that plastic cup at night." He wanted me to put it on top of the little bureau.

"Hoist me up." (Wanted to change to better pants. Get his purse, his gray felt hat, his gray suit coat. His glasses. Already had his teeth.)

We had begun talking in the community room just after the beano game. The visiting women began to lead the group (a dozen) in hymns. My loud voice was probably a nuisance (Dana a bit deaf, not bad though). I wheeled him back to his room.

The gaiety, a *tormented* gaiety, wild, bright-eyed, demented, of the sloppily fat woman—shrill bursts of laughter, little screams. An old white-haired woman whose knees touched when she walked, went outside, waved to me childishly from a bench when I left.

Dana Hamlin III

Hunger for touch, like dying Jill, my dying mother—wants to kiss, be held. I saw this when Bob and Rita came to the car. He's fond of them, especially of Bob, who returns the affection, held Dana's hand, pressed his cheek to Dana's cheek, and Dana's face was *wreathed* (that word really fits: all that soft skin and those folds were lifted into arcs of smiles)—he nuzzled and kissed Bob's cheek. Same when Leon knelt at the front seat of the car, having helped me get Dana inside. Dana: "Aren't you coming?"

"I'd like to, but my boss would say no if I asked her. But I'd really like to. You'll have a good time." Dana's reactions were so ingenuous and childlike that there came a moment when Leon felt an uprush of affection and embraced Dana and pressed his cheek to Dana's cheek, and Dana kissed his cheek like a little boy who likes to be loved and is happy and loving.

Bob: "You've been having a look at Temple? How does it seem?"

Dana: "Well, it looks all right. I haven't seen any money floatin' around." ("Floatin'"—he really means like autumn leaves on the stream.)

Bob had pointed out a stand of white birch half a mile up the hill. His property line (Dana's old place) was there. Dana said, "You see those spruce right over the car there? That's where the corner is." The spruces were at the lower end of the birches, not a large stand. It was surprising that he could see so well out of that little triangle of one eye.

"How've you folks been? Have you been gettin' along? Well, that's good. It looks nice." ("We're trying to bring the fields back."—Rita)

"I'm doing poorly, but better than I was. I don't sleep so good nights, and there's pain in this knee I'm takin' some medicine for (foah). If I was younger I'd rather be out here. Do you know I woke up last night. I was dreamin', and in my dream I was tellin' them how old I was. (Laughs) Yes. In February 1979 I'll be 99. (Laughs) I'm 98 now." ("You've lived a long time, Dana. Not many people get to live that long.") "That's true. My son is doing poorly. He might not live as long as I" (and such is the Oedipus schmedipus complex, such is that universal rivalry, that Bob and Rita smiled, and Dana smiled).

He took us to the old creamery by the tracks in West Farmington, now a shell, falling apart. But the loading platform was still (mostly) standing. "There's the loadin' platform. We used to back the wagons right up to it. It was built in 1908. It belonged to the Turner Center creamery, then I think a company named Worrel took it over in 1918."

We drove on up the dead-end road above the creamery. "I think they made butter. They shipped the cream down to Turner on the railroad. Before the creamery was built we loaded it right into a boxcar. Used all kind o' tricks in the wintertime to keep it from freezin'. I used to put blankets over the cans, and kerosene lamps under the blankets." The road ended in a large sandpit. Tracks, creamery, sandpit, all close to the river.

He asked me to stop on the road above Varnum Pond. "I thought we could look at the pond a while. This used to be all clear. There was a big pasture here, and a set o' buildings right up in there." Couldn't see past the alders and scrubby woods.

He had pointed out to me—on the Intervale Road—where his younger brother had lived. "He's dead now."

"My younger brother and I used to cut ice here for the ice houses."

The other side of Slim's store. "This is where they used to stack the squares for the mill. There was a sawmill here. The squares was two by two and four foot long."

"Did you ever haul for Voter?"

"No . . . just once. He had a load of milk in his car, just like this, and he skidded on the ice. It's a pretty steep hill. Well, they asked me if they could transfer it to my wagon. . . .

"I made some money then, but it went."

The steep hill from Isalo's (Dick Blodgett's now) to Slim's store. "It was hard to get up in the winter if you had much of a load. For braking I used to use two wheel chains comin' down. I had my own team (pair) and sometimes my dad loaned me his."

Recognized Ted. "Anybody livin' in your old place up there? Anybody livin' at Doctor Little's?" (His milk route used to go up the Day Mountain Road, down past the Kennisons', down the long hill, over Temple Stream at Doc Little's. Then, "I used to go five miles beyond Docktuh Little's. I imagine if I was to take anybody up that way today, they wouldn't believe I could drive in so far.

"I used to set out at three in the afternoon, and my dad would meet me at three in the mornin'.

"There's the old pump house. Now the water line goes right down over in there. When we go back down (day-own) I'll show you where it comes out."

The milk route: "I had to start at three in the afternoon to get to the station at West Farmington by five in the morning. I suppose I'd rather work in the day, but the money was good.

"I was born in Temple. The house was in Temple and the stable was in Weld. Do you know Wilder Hill? Well, you go up over the top, and then down, and you come to a flat place. Do you know Alder

Brook? Well, it was down in there. But when I went to work haulin'
milk, my dad had the place on Center Hill, and I lived there until . . .
oh . . . I can't remember . . . oh, it's funny . . . what were we speaking
of? Oh, yes . . . well, that house on the Intervale, that was when I got
married. Nineteen-two it was. And I sold it in . . ."

(Leon: "Sometimes he talks at night, he hallucinates, I guess. He'll
call out: 'Now you watch the cows. I have to go away a while.' ") . . .

An Allagash Girlhood

Cathie Pelletier

My maternal ancestors, Bradfords and Diamonds, were among the Loyalists who left Boston after the American Revolution and went north to settle in Canada. It was the age of Wood, Wind, and Water and England needed white pine for the masts of her ships. There must have been excited talk in the public houses, or at church, or on the docks around Chaleur Bay about an abundance of virgin pine growing beyond the untouched hinterlands of the St. John River. In 1838, my great-great-great grandparents, Anna Diamond and John Gardner, were among those given grants to cut pine for the king's ships. Anna and two of her sisters left Campbellton, New Brunswick, with their husbands, and the notion of finding a new life in the wilderness. They traveled in pirogues, via a couple of rivers and portages, until they settled in what later became the town of Allagash, at the end of the road in northern Maine.

A few years later, another Diamond sister followed, along with her family, her possessions, and her best dreams. This was Lucinda Diamond, who had married George Moir. Lucinda and George are also my great-great-great grandparents. More settlers arrived with the next waves coming from New Brunswick and Nova Scotia, such as the O'Learys, Haffords, and McKinnons, also my ancestral grandparents. The first Franco name to put down lasting roots in Allagash came with my paternal great-grandfather, Nizaire Pelletier. Nizaire spoke only English, and he lived to be over a hundred years old. He died in 1924, but the homestead he built for his family is still being lived in today, the oldest building in Allagash. It was his son, my grandfather Tom, who ran the ferry across the Allagash River for thirty-seven years, until the first bridge was built. Grampie Tom, who married the French-speaking Edith Thibodeau from nearby St. Francis, also lived to be over a hundred years old. I may carry Nizaire's and Tom's surname as my own, but I am part of *all* these people, their joys as well as their tragedies.

It has to be the most difficult decision of a lifetime to leave behind all you know and love in the world. To achieve that, you need to put down long and sturdy roots. Maybe that's why northern Maine is calling me home, even though I've been living my life elsewhere for more than thirty years. I think Allagash is too deeply embedded in my genes for me to stay away forever. For me, it's always been about the land, that part of the world where I drew my first breath. I don't know the ocean, but the river is in my soul. I can't escape it, even if I wanted to. It runs like blood through all of my fiction. I was born in the house my father built on the bank of the St. John, that same river my ancestors used as their highway. It was an insular way of life back then. There was no such thing as "passing through town." Even today, once you leave the tarred road you're up against an ocean of trees, not water. Do you know that many people in southern Maine don't realize there's a town named Allagash? They think of it as *The Allagash Wilderness Waterway*. We were so isolated that, sometimes, it seemed as if everything important was happening somewhere else. We never even made the top of the map in most atlases. The northern tip of Maine is often set to one side, in its own box, like a sad hat that's gone out of style so no one wears it anymore.

I was still not twenty years old when I left Allagash to "live away." But I came back two or three times a year to see my family. And with each visit, I noticed the inevitable changes creeping in. While we couldn't go to the modern world, it was apparent the modern world had come to *us*. Old homesteads were disappearing just as satellite dishes were springing up. While I might have gone to Fort Kent once a month in my younger years, it seemed as if everyone suddenly had their own automobile. But cell phones and snowmobiles and cable TV can never take away the poetry of my youth.

What do I remember of my girlhood? When the memories come, they come like the river itself. They come rushing and sweeping, carrying along old dreams in their wake. They come like the seasons, those four trusted friends.

Summers. Tiny sweet strawberries. Plump blackberries. Burgundy raspberries. Hazelnuts. Big gardens full of peas and cucumbers and tomatoes, all things Mama could put up in Mason jars for winter. Sometimes we'd wake to see a moose standing in the garden, looking for something fresh and green to eat. I remember fireflies in the evening, so many and so bright they were small undulating ribbons atop the hay. But Daddy told me once that when *he* was a boy, there were so many fireflies on summer nights, back before pesticides and pole lights and progress, that it seemed as if the flats by the river were on fire. "When we were boys," Daddy said, "we'd run downhill to the bogan just to see the great blue herons scatter and fly up, dozens of them at a time."

You can't beat the smell of a clean river, or the wash left to dry on a clothesline near one. Mama used to bring her towels and sheets in off the line, before a summer rain hit us, and she'd hold them to my face and say, "Can you smell the river? Now doesn't that smell nice?"

Summers meant swimming in that river, even in those dangerous "Dog Days," when Sirius rose and set with the yellow sun. The river was our constant companion. It ran like a blue dream just beyond our back door and our back bedroom windows. Hot summer nights, we'd hear it rattling like the june bugs on our screens. But mostly, we never heard it at all, just as we don't hear our own hearts beat. Visitors to the house would say, "Did it rain hard last night?" and we'd smile and tell them, "That's the river. But we don't hear it anymore." We felt a pride in this. It meant we *knew* the river, we *knew* the land, for we lived in its heart just as it lived in ours.

The bad part of summer was all the bugs and the flies. Horseflies.

Blackflies. Mosquitoes. No-see-ums that we called midgets, but are really *midges*. When we sat out on the porch in the early evenings, we made "smokes" to shoo off blackflies. That's when you get a pail and set wood and twigs afire and then, when it's burning good, you cover it with green grass to make it smoke. During drier, hotter days, I would take an empty tin can and go up and down the shore, fighting off flies from morning until dusk as I rescued inch-long baby fish that were trapped in stagnant pools left behind by the receding river. It felt good to see them swim free again in the current. It was worth the fly bites.

I remember cutting hay one week for Daddy, food for the horses. This was the summer I was nine years old. All the men were working in the woods and he couldn't find anyone to do the job, so he asked me if I thought I could manage by myself. A tomboy, I ran both the tractor and the old-fashioned mower behind, having to stop the trac-tor at the end of each row in order to raise or lower the blade. The last field, come nightfall, Daddy helped me finish. I remember his silhou-ette as he sat on the tractor in front of me, outlined by a large, late-summer moon. I remember watching the last blades of hay as they fell away behind us, like the years that have passed since that night. Haying in the back field, with the light of the tractor and the moon. I may never feel as alive again as I did on that orange-moon night, helping my father cut hay.

When you grow up in the heart of such isolated country, before all those pole lights and porch lights, you understand what darkness really means. When there is no moon or stars, you see nothing but black in front of you. You walk slowly. You hear the animals, the wind, the crack of a twig beneath pine, a cricket's song. You listen to the night as it speaks to you. If you listen with your heart, you can hear the earth breathing.

Autumns. I remember cutting alders and attaching them at the top to form a point, and then using goldenrods to weave in and out of the trees until I had a perfect tee-pee. I remember boiling tea in an empty lard pail on the back ridge, that place where the maples run to pure scarlet and oak leaves are russet-brown. This was when I'd go with Daddy into the woods. Tea could never taste that good if you boiled it on the stove.

Mostly, when I think of autumns, I remember those potato harvests. This was when school was postponed for a month for kids to go "potato digging" with their parents. We were hired mostly by farmers around Limestone, not far from Caribou. Bedding and dishes and clothing were packed onto a pulp truck turned potato truck. We'd be gone for a month, leaving our house boarded up, its eyes black and sad, waiting for our return. My mother often cooked for the hundred or so pickers and workers, and Daddy was often field boss. The first day was exciting because we got to select a potato basket out of a mountain of new baskets, one that fit our age and size. We had new brown gloves. And we were assigned a ticket number and given sleek red tickets, one of which we'd stick on a barrel of potatoes once we'd picked it full. That's how tallies were kept as to who picked how many barrels. The ticket person would walk ahead of the potato truck that was being loaded with barrels. He or she would take the ticket before the barrel was hoisted up onto the truck by grapples for its ride to the potato house. At the end of the day, the numbers of barrels would be posted and we'd know for certain how many we had picked. Great pickers, with a great crop and a long section, could pick a hundred barrels and more a day, especially if "the picking was good." Our most fun was working for the farm run by my uncle, Bob O'Leary. This was Botto, Frolic & Wicks, a farm owned by men who lived somewhere in faraway New York. I always thought, with names like that, they might be three fat elves. We never once *saw* Botto, Frolic, or Wicks, but we knew they were big shots, wherever they were.

Each fall, Uncle Bob hired a crew of Indian pickers, Micmacs who came from the Gaspé Peninsula area, in New Brunswick. (And yes, we called them *Indians* then, which is what they called themselves.) We girls always had crushes on those handsome, dark-eyed Micmac boys. But there was segregation, even though we didn't realize back then that it existed. Indians lived in their own run-down buildings. Ours were run-down too, but we thought they were somehow better since, well, they weren't "the shacks where the Indians lived." They washed up in their own washroom, and they ate at separate tables in the dining room where my mother and Aunt Albertine served the food. The big hit song in 1962 was by Rex Allen and was titled, "Son, Don't Go Near the Indians." It was a godawful tale of scalping, and a young white boy falling in love with an Indian maiden he later learned was his sister, stolen and raised on the reservation. The refrain was "Son, don't go near the Indians, please stay away." I must have sung that song a thousand times on rides in the back of the pick-up to the cook shack, or in our sections as we picked potatoes. What must the *real* Indians have thought?

We slept in the rooms upstairs, over "the cook shack," as we called it. The pond behind the house was green with slime from the chemicals and sprays that were dumped there. After a week of getting up at dawn in the cold and picking potatoes until our backs broke, the romance was over. The next two or three weeks were just plain hard work. The baskets were heavy with caked mud and so were our gloves. The tickets were so fat and worn at the edges that they were difficult to stick onto barrels. But waking pre-dawn and hearing a heavy rain on the tin roof of the cook shack was heaven. There was no picking potatoes in the rain. By noon, the guys would be restless and so a good poker game would start up. I loved playing poker on those days. Fires would be cracking in the woodstoves as rain beat against the windows.

And then, when the harvest was over, coming back to Allagash with money in our pockets, following that blue river back home, was the best emotion in the world. These are highs I'll never feel again. The house would open its eyes once more and welcome us in. And Mama would throw open doors and windows to air out the place before she'd begin baking something good to eat. And we'd have green money to buy new clothes for school. One fall, I bought my first bicycle with money I earned myself. It was bright blue and cost $34.95. I felt as if I was made of liquid when I rode it, wind streaming through my hair. What freedom that was, to feel the earth falling away beneath my tires.

I remember Halloweens with haunting moons caught in the branches of spooky trees, and ghosts and goblins gathered at the graveyard gates, waiting for us to walk past. At school, we'd talk about that night for days, and when it arrived, we'd fill old pillow cases with the candy we were given. One Halloween, back in 1964, we were trick-or-treating with thick snow up to our knees. No one was ever afraid that someone might give us something to hurt us. The world today has turned scary, but it was a safe place back then. All we had to fear on Halloween nights was the headless lumberjack whose soul could never rest until he found his head again. We feared the wind in that clutch of spruce trees before we got to the safety of more houses. We feared not getting enough candy.

Before the first snowfall of the year, Daddy would back a big truck of hardwood blocks up to the cellar window above the house. He and my brothers would chop the blocks into firewood and it would be thrown through the cellar window and piled down there until tiers of it lined the walls. You could smell snow on the morning air. It was such an exciting time because it meant we were getting ready for winter. We were gearing up, and we were hunkering down. A child could sense from the adult world just how important this was. And when that winter wind came up from the river, she came with a true vengeance. So I always felt safe at moments like that, when the wood was being put up for winter. I knew someone was looking out for me. Daddy and Mama. They were keeping us safe from winter.

Winters. I remember big snowfalls, the sky so thick and heavy with flakes that all we could see were white, swirling moths, winging themselves downward. Snow can talk. On those coldest days of the year, it says "crunch," and "snap," and even "munch," as your boots eat it up. Other days it speaks with muted words, especially those warmer winter days when it's new and soft and a foot deep. Then it whispers with words like "swish" and "hush." There was so much snow that it would reach to our bedroom windows on the second floor. I remember sliding by the winter moon, our voices echoing out across the dark river. I can still hear the metallic sounds of skates on the bogan's ice, next to a pile of burning tires and wood slabs, as we skated our hearts out. The stars were so thick and shiny we could touch them if we stood on our tiptoes. Some Sunday mornings, Daddy would shout up the stairs, "There's crust!" This was a wonderful time, for it meant rain had frozen the top of the snow so that it was like a glass road. We could walk across fields and hills–sometimes glissade–atop four feet of snow.

Winters were long and white, with icicles so thick at their source they were a foot wide and sometimes six feet long. Newer houses, with good insulation, have now lost the art of making icicles. Nowadays, kids don't really know what icicles *are,* not the big ones. And they've never seen what Jack Frost can do to a windowpane, all those magnificent white ferns and spirals like lacy tumbleweeds. Does a modern kid still push the tip of his tongue on a frozen windowpane, letting it stick firmly? The trick is not to panic, just breathe warm breath so the frost will melt and your tongue will go free.

I always liked the smell of all that wood piled in tall rows in the basement. And wood chips all over the ground floor. And the feel of a real wood fire sending its heat up through the registers, up through the veins of the house. A hardwood heat is the kind of dry heat that goes straight to the marrow of your bones. And an old-fashioned register is the best place in the world to dry wet mittens coated with jangling beads of snow. But getting out of bed was always tough on winter mornings. Every country kid remembers how cold that morning floor felt to warm feet.

Mama made the house sing each Christmas with decorations and good things to eat. My earliest memory of Christmas Eve is of me sitting on the kitchen table as she made my ringlets. She was telling me that if I didn't go to bed, Santa wouldn't come visit. "Maybe he's close," Mama said. "Let's see." She opened the back door and by God, I remember to this day the clear and crisp sound of sleigh bells on the cold night air! I scrambled down from the table and ran as fast as I could for bed. Sleigh bells so close and so pure! Years later I was told that Mama had my brother take the garlows we had hanging in the basement, bells that came from a horse harness, and sneak around the house to ring them. I can still hear the sound of those bells as I write.

Sometimes, when the memories come, they come even faster than the river.

Spring. This is when the land wakes up. Finally, April would arrive and the river would break free of its ice and "run." Sheets and cakes twenty feet wide would come thundering along the banks. A continuous roar. When the river was open again and just swift water, we'd write our name and address on a piece of paper, roll it up and put it inside an empty mayonnaise jar. We'd tighten the cap and then hurl the jar out into the river. Our hope was that someone would find it "downriver" and write to us. Once, I got a letter from a young man in St. John, New Brunswick, several years after I'd thrown my last mayonnaise jar into the river. "I like girl and fast car," he wrote. I think I still have his letter.

Spring was rebirth after that long bitter winter. Adults would burn the hay fields while the snow was still at the edge of the woods. What an exciting time, with dusk coming on and the fields afire with an orange glow. They'd grow back so green it would hurt your eyes. It was only later that I began worrying about mice and insects dying in the flames. When I think of spring, I can hear the sound of icicles dripping and snow melting from the roof and eaves of the house. I can smell the wild cherry blossoms on the back ridge. I can hear all those warblers returning to tell us there really *was* a world out there, exotic and faraway. I remember slush and mud, until the earth finally dried itself out enough for a game of baseball before school ended for the year.

For some of us, childhood was a safe place to grow and learn and play. Sadly, it wasn't this way for all children. But I would go back, deep into the coils of the past, with Mama in the kitchen making donuts and biscuits and bread. I would go back to hearing Daddy playing his guitar downstairs on Sunday mornings, and singing "The Ballad of Will Rogers and Wiley Post," or "Come All You Texas Cowboys," or "Knoxville Girl." I would go back.

My parents left the family homestead to me, the only child of six to be born in that house. In the basement there are still jars on the shelf of fiddleheads, mustard pickles, beets, and rhubarb that Mama canned before she died. They are covered with dust, as if waiting. Memories are like this, too. They get dusty sometimes, but they still hang on, waiting for someone to come along and say, "Do you remember the time that old man from Fort Kent drove his car off the ferry and into the river?" And before you know it, the dust is gone and the past is as shiny as the day it was new.

These days, I'm pretty much a hermit, my computer the only link I need to the outside world. I want things to go slowly again. I want the boisterous sounds to disappear back into water slapping around river rocks, or june bugs on the evening screens. I want stillness.

Otherwise, how can I hear the ghosts when they whisper?

Autumn

Richard Russo

Though he never set foot in the state, my grandfather would have been a natural Mainer. When I was a boy, he was already in the autumn of his life, having survived two world wars, the Depression, and a daily existence too full of Duty (both secular and religious). Prematurely bald and rail thin from the malaria he'd contracted in the Philippines, he concluded that he would not live to be an old man. Or, more precisely, he believed that sixty *was* old. When he spoke of dying, as if it were something he meant to do next week, or the week after, as soon as things slowed down and he could get around to it, the idea filled me with terror, because I loved him and couldn't imagine the world without him, and the thought that a man could contemplate his own mortality with such perfect equanimity seemed perverse to a boy my age. Worse, my grandfather's reasoning was impossible to follow. On the one hand, he seemed to believe that what life called for was constant vigilance. If you didn't pay attention and plan ahead, when the winter came you'd run out of coal and freeze, or you'd run out of food and starve, or run out of money and have to go naked. On the other hand, he cheerfully conceded that something along these lines might just happen anyway, whether you paid attention or not, because winter always had a few tricks up its sleeve that you'd be lucky to anticipate. As I say, he'd have made a great Mainer.

In Maine, at least midcoast, where I live, the first leaves start to turn in mid-August. This is a sobering sight, one that calls to mind the white, hooded figure in N. C. Wyeth's *A Winter*. He's already stalking us, and probably has been all summer long. In Maine, winter is reality, summer a lovely illusion, and those first August-orange leaves are a reminder of this hard truth. After Labor Day, all's fair, but when the temperature's in the eighties and the days are still long enough for my wife and me to take our walks after dinner instead of before, this notice is hard to swallow. Just as sixty is too soon to be resigned to death, the third week in August is too soon to be reminded of approaching winter, especially with some of Maine's finer pleasures on our doorstep.

Come September, the tourists that have clogged the streets of every village from Kittery to Bar Harbor will head home, taking with them their car alarms and cell phones and digital cameras and hi-tech baby strollers and hip-hop CDs. The sleek sailing vessels will tack away, their propellers snagging lobster pots in their hasty departure, returning our harbors to the lumbering, boxy fishing boats and the men who work the water year-round. After Labor Day we can walk into any restaurant on the coast without a reservation. The price of lobster drops and tiny rural farm stands groan under the weight of real tomatoes and corn. Nearby you'll find a battered scale for weighing what you've put into secondhand supermarket bags, and also a wooden box containing coins and dollar bills from which it is expected that you will make honest change. And yet such seeming Keatsian abundance is also largely an illusion. Yes, the gourd doth swell in Maine and the trees do bend with apples under the maturing sun, but Maine's rocky soil will never feed the world. The tomatoes will disappear with the first frost, the one right around the corner, leaving only a few killer zucchini, good mostly for jokes and compost. No, in Maine you won't find autumn sitting careless on the granary floor, her hair soft-lifted by the winnowing wind, drowsed by the fume of poppies. By mid-September the wind off the Atlantic is both earnest and portentous, making Mainers more watchful than drowsy. Did we put in enough wood? Did we ever complete the form sent to us by our heating-oil company back in June, locking in the price? How long does antifreeze retain its potency? we wonder, knowing we can't afford to be wrong. Winter is coming and not even the proximity of L.L. Bean, with its bumper crop of Gortex and Thinsulate and fleece and scratchy wool, is all that reassuring.

Autumn, as my grandfather understood, is the season of paradox. When the leaves turn, when the physical world is at its most heart-breakingly beautiful, what we are witnessing, purely and simply, is death. In the autumn of his life, my grandfather loved the fall, loved the smell of burning leaves. He took as perfectly natural the fact that wood smoke penetrated his emphysema-diminished lungs more deeply and satisfyingly than even the pure oxygen from the tank that stood at attention behind his green armchair, the chair where, after a life of worrying that he'd run out of fuel or food or money, he would run out of air.

I, like my grandfather, am both a worrier and a lover of autumn. It is the time of year, at least in Maine, when those of us inclined to worry find our inclinations most validated by nature. (One is a fool to worry in summer; by winter it's too late.) Each October for the last several years, my daughters and I have climbed nearby Mount Megunti-cook, which overlooks the ragged midcoast. From the cliffs at the top, the village where we live sits almost directly below. If the sun is bright and the sky cloudless—and such a day will always be available in mid-October—the reflection of light off the ocean can be almost painful, its shimmer musically surreal. Toss in a couple of schooners under full sail, just barely identifiable for what they are from such a height, a vast carpet of peak foliage extending as far as the eye can see, and a plain white church steeple or two, and a middle-aged man with two smart, beautiful college-bound daughters just might—despite his hereditary inclinations—find himself guilty of optimism. On such an afternoon, lying back on the warm rocks, my sweat from the climb drying in the crisp air, I could almost be convinced that nature just might reverse itself this year and head back in the other direction to-ward summer, of which we Mainers never quite get our fill. Almost.

But of course the late-afternoon trek down the mountain is darker, the leaves underfoot not so much beautiful as wet and treach-erous. Somewhere along the path the air turns from cool and crisp to chill and clammy, and in that moment something pivots on its fulcrum and it occurs to a man like my grandfather—and, yes, a man like me—that now would be a good time to make a show of competence: to service the furnace, to make sure the chimney flue hasn't rusted shut, to check that the gutters are not clogged with leaves. Time to find the lamps and the bottles of clear oil we'll need when the ice storm comes and we're again without electricity. And batteries.

By the time we reach the bottom of the trail and emerge from the woods into the flat, empty campground, I've made a mental list. It's a partial one at best, and like my grandfather I'm smart enough to know that what I'll end up needing most probably isn't on it, but by worrying, I've already fulfilled my first autumnal duty. Worry is not competence, but we make do with the former since the latter may reside only in our imaginations—or in summer, when it's not really needed.

My Mexico

Monica Wood

In Mexico, Maine, where I grew up, you could not find a single Mexican. Originally named in sympathy with the Mexican revolutionists, my hometown retained not a shred of solidarity by the time I came along, unless you counted an aged jar of Tabasco sauce in the door of somebody's fridge. The only Spanish anybody knew derived from a scratched 45 of Doris Day singing *Que Sera Sera*.

In third grade, when I discovered that the wide world included a country called Mexico, I spent several befuzzled days wondering why it had named itself after us. Sister Germaine adjusted my perspective with a pulldown map on which the country of Mexico assumed a shapely, pepper-red presence and its puny namesake did not appear at all.

In high summer, when tourists in paneled station wagons caravanned down Main Street on their way to someplace else, hankies pressed comically to their noses against the mill's smelly effluvia, we kids liked to sit on the concrete stoop of Nery's Market and play License Plate. Sucking on blue Popsicles, we observed the procession of vehicles carrying strangers we'd never glimpse again, and accumulated points for every out-of-state plate. No one ever stopped to look around or buy anything, though once in a while a woman (always a woman, with the smiley red lips all women had then) popped out of a parked but still-running car to ask directions we could not provide, or to take our picture. I was the one in the smudgy tee shirt bought in Niagara Falls by my priest uncle, who loved to travel. Or maybe that was my little sister, or my bigger sister, or one of our friends; who could tell one kid from the next? The tourist lady arranged us to her liking and plunked onto one of our heads a straw hat she'd bought somewhere else in Maine (Norway? South Paris?). We dutifully smiled when she asked us to, imagining ourselves being admired many months hence by strangers passing a photo album around a Pennsylvanian parlor.

The tourist lady's presumption didn't rankle, not even when she found us insufficiently accessorized. Driving through the middle of nowhere in the early sixties, repelled by the stench of paper being made, she had spotted a posse of sun-burnished children with home-cut hair and thought: *Oh, I must get that.* Then she wound her way out of town, fiddling with her camera and eyeing the brightening hills until, an hour later, approaching the Rangeley Lakes if she'd been heading north or the White Mountains if heading west, she cocked her head and asked her husband at the wheel: *Why Mexico, do you think? I should have asked those kids.*

Not that we could have enlightened her. What did we know (licking the wood-tasting dregs of the Popsicles for which we'd pooled our coins) about the Mexican Revolution? The only Mexico we knew was this one, ours, with its single main street, our fathers across the river there, toiling inside an omnipresent brick-and-steel complex that shot great, gorgeous steam clouds into the sky so steadily that we couldn't tell where mill left off and sky began.

The first death is the one you mourn forever. My first was my father, and, as he himself might have said, it was a real corker. That loss—a sudden, stinging, inconceivable insult—remains so keenly engraved, so hard-glinting in its smallest detail, that it cleaves my childhood memories into a knife-clean "before" and "after."

The morning of my father's death begins like all other mornings: my mother stirring oatmeal at the stove, a cat twining round her legs, her parakeet jabbering on her shoulder. My oldest sister, Anne, who teaches at the high school, is at work already; and my father, who got up at five-thirty for first shift, is toiling somewhere in the spongy air of the wood room. Or so we believe. Betty and Cathy and I, our hair mashed from sleep, rouse ourselves after Mum's second or third call. Cathy and I attend St. Theresa's—second grade and fourth grade, respectively—a French Catholic school that we can see, over the rooftop of my best friend's house on Brown Street, from our third-floor kitchen window.

Below us, on the second floor, come the muted morning sounds from the Hickeys: that's Norma leaving for work at the power company. Her mother, the only one-armed person I know, opens her door to pick up the morning paper and snap it open in a nimble abracadabra, one of her most enthralling sleight-of-one-hand feats.

Below that, on the first floor, our Lithuanian landlady begins her daily cooking of cabbage and root vegetables that smell more or less like the mill. The ancient Mortuses speak halting English, charge us seven dollars a week in rent, and engage in an intermittent but escalating skirmish with Mum over whether or not we girls should be allowed to bring our friends up to visit. *Too much stairs*, they say, which could mean almost anything.

Mexico is full of buildings like ours, triple-decker apartment buildings with open stairways on the back side and three stacked porches attached to the front. We call them blocks. In the Mortus block, where we live, the three apartments are identically laid out—four rooms and a screened porch—but each has a separate, and separately revelatory, air of foreignness. The Mortus apartment, densely furnished, emanates a steamy, overdraped blurriness that I still associate, perhaps inaccurately, with all Lithuanian households. The Hickeys' floor, occupied by two big and tidy women, seems like a trick, its scrubbed interior latitudes magically expanded. Every time I enter, I think of the Popeye cartoon in which Olive Oyl peers into a small tent and finds the inside of the Taj Mahal. Our top floor, full of girls and mateless socks and hair doodads and schoolbooks and cats and winter jackets and molted feathers, operates on the same principle, in reverse: when you open our door, the physical world shrinks.

In this filled-to-brimming place on the morning of my father's

death, the parakeet perches on my oatmeal bowl, his scaly feet grip-
ping the rim. He pecks at my breakfast, spattering gruel, gibbering
words gleaned from my mother's patient repetitions. He can also sing
and dance, but not now; Mum wants us at school on time and so far it
doesn't look promising. Cathy appears, wearing half of her school uniform—the starched white blouse—and a slip. I'm half dressed, too, in
opposite: army-green skirt and pajama top. My mother presses our
clothes in stages, so that is how we put them on. Outside, the morning radiates the particular cool of April. Betty comes last to eat, but no
one hurries her. She's mentally disabled (we said "retarded" back then)
and gets to stay home with Mum, lucky girl. We dawdle over orange
juice as Cathy, against orders, places the parakeet on a pencil to see if
he'll do a spin; it's his best trick and kills the room every time. This is
how mornings go, a tango of getting ready, each girl a separate challenge, Mum alternately shooshing us and making us sit, sit, sit to eat.

I'm the slow eater. The "absent-minded" one. The writer, in other
words. I watch out the window—with my adult, writer's eyes now—but
nothing looks different. Dad is already dead, but we don't know this
yet, can't imagine this. When I look out the window—then or now—
all I see is Mexico, my Mexico, the only Mexico that matters.

Across the way: the Velushes' gloomy windows and creepy, tan-
gled garden, a source of ever-evolving speculation. What abides
there? Fairies? Devils? Across from them, the Gagnons: We play with
their girls and have a crush on Mrs. Gagnon with her down-the-back
ripple of auburn hair. Mr. Gagnon, rarely glimpsed, works in the
woods. Cathy and I help Mrs. Gagnon with the piecework she brings
home from the shoe shop in Wilton, stitching shoes in a chatty
round robin, a scene of feminine collusion that will turn up in a
novel forty years later. Cattycorner from the Gagnons are the
O'Neills, cousins of ours on Mum's side, and then the Yarnishes,
their driveway patrolled by a disgruntled crow who calls "Hi, Joe! Hi,
Joe!" all day long in a tone belying welcome. He bit Betty on the leg
once. After that, the Dons, the Downses, the Witases, the Fourniers,
kids at every stop. Most of us attend St. Theresa's together; some
can't speak to their grandmothers except in a strenuous pastiche of

mispronounced words and family sign language. Most of us have parents or grandparents who came from foreign climes—French Canada and the Maritime Provinces, Italy, Lithuania, Ireland—and the rest of the neighborhood fills out with Fleurys and Gallants and Lavorgnas and Desjardinses and Vaillancourts and Arsenaults and Nailises and Flahertys, a census that repeats itself to the town line and across the bridge to Rumford, the mill's official home.

To the tourist lady we probably all looked the same: white kids in similar clothes, children of millworkers and housewives, oblivious of the wider world. What she didn't see, because she didn't stay, was that, like the trick tent in the Popeye cartoon, when you opened doors you found surprise. In our household, we had boiled dinner every Sunday. We had a picture of Pope John and President John and the Sacred Heart of Jesus hung over the couch. My brother—the frontman in a band called the Fabulous Impacts (they performed in matching shiny-green jackets)—came on Sundays with his wife and babies and guitar to sing the rockabilly songs we knew from the radio. At my grandfather's on Mexico Avenue we listened to ballads from Ireland, long, lugubrious story-songs, often about death and dismemberment.

At my friend Denise's they ate *tourtières* and sang comic French songs about family entanglements; reconstructing all the verses required a minimum of five bouffanted aunties. At Denise's you had to say please and thank you, you had to remove your shoes, and you had to obey Mr. Vaillancourt, a sweet, taciturn man who reminded me of a tame bear.

I had another friend, Janet, who lived atop her parents' tavern on the riverfront. There we listened to Top 40 songs on the downstairs jukebox. We ate bar food that we took upstairs, out of eyeshot of the regulars—those bleary, distant men, some soft and fleshy, marshmallowed onto the barstools at three in the afternoon; others so thin they appeared to be constructed from artfully twisted coat hangers. The Fortins called their place Tarry-a-While, and people did.

In church we sang exquisite, haunting, four-part *Tantum Ergos* from the choir loft. We prayed high mass in Latin. We began each school day by greeting our teacher with a singsong "*Bonjooour, ma soeur!*" and reciting the Lord's Prayer or a Hail Mary in French. For my family, all this French represented a cultural compromise: as non-Franco kids, Cathy and I were a minority, having begun our school life at St. Athanasius in Rumford with the "Irish nuns," switching schools only after the town discontinued its bus service.

In other words, we were not all the same.

Willa Cather famously observed that a writer acquires most of her material before the age of fifteen, years that determine whether the work will be poor and thin or rich and fine. The material in my town was rich and fine indeed. Out of our front doors walked future writers and actors and playwrights and singers and musicians, our art informed by a thousand twining strands.

The boy who found my father grew up to be an opera singer of no small reputation. Back then he was just another kid in town, whose mother taught piano; a teenager on his way to school who executed a disbelieving double-take when he passed the saggy row of rental garages on Mexico Avenue. The sight of my father lying in front of the garage door, cap knocked off his head, lunch pail spilled at his feet, must surely endure in his memory. I have met this grown-up boy on several occasions, have heard him sing, too—but only once. His tenor is rich and soaring and heartcrushingly beautiful, and to me every note sounds like that morning.

The other key player in the morning drama is Mr. Cray, our town constable, coming up the driveway as I dawdle over my oatmeal, watching idly out the window. Mr. Cray, florid and heavyset like my father, moving with my father's hefty step, the first dissonant note of the day. I squint down three stories. "Mum, Mr. Cray is here."

Here is where the memory of any morning turns into the memory of that singular morning. "Mum, Mr. Cray is here." My mother bursts into song. Or so it seems, on this morning in which nothing is as it seems. *Ohhh*, my mother sings. *Ohhh*. For a moment—before the first stir of alarm, a tiny knot of suspicion struggling up through my esophagus—I assume that Mum's keening will be shortly explained, will become a clear and ordinary droplet in the blizzard of information that makes up any childhood. Her hands fly to her face, she whirls around to face the door, egress blocked by a laundry basket and ironing board that she threads her way around. We're confused now, and getting scared. As we listen to Mr. Cray's footfalls on the stairs—a sound exactly like my father coming home from work—the morning acquires a pitiless momentum, embodied in Mr. Cray's inexorable progress. He bypasses the Mortuses on the first floor, keeps going; bypasses the Hickeys on the second floor, keeps going; and finally stops outside our door, which my mother flings open, crying out, "He's dead, isn't he?"

Who? Who does she mean? Big Mr. Cray, as formless and crumpled-looking as a pile of warm sheets, fills up our tiny front hall. A strange commotion arises there. I begin walking backwards, something we do sometimes for fun. Backwards, retreating from the noise surfacing from my mother's throat, backwards into our bedroom, backwards, trying to reverse time. Betty waits there, sitting on the bed, alarmed but uncomprehending, her eyes pale as dimes. Cathy— the bravest, the one who takes nothing at face value—stands her ground in the kitchen, where the morning will take on the shellac of permanence and become the museum piece we will all come back to again and again, seeing something new each time in this preserved, precious thing. At last, Cathy barrels into our room, crying, "Daddy's dead!" She's the announcer, the town crier, the loud one. And she's blubbering loudly now, drowning out the disquieting sounds in the kitchen. Her uniform sash divides the white of her blouse, but her skirt still hasn't made it from the ironing board. She's got a hairbrush stuck in her hair. "Daddy's dead!" she announces again, understanding it all of a piece, accepting a grief she will never quite get over. I cry, too, of course—instantly, violently—but my reaction feels less like grief (though how can I tell, having known none before this?) and more like the involuntary reaction to a physical blow, that helpless empty space between the blow and the pain. Betty looks at us both for a long moment, receiving the information at last, then she, too, cries.

My mother will explain to us later that she dreamed it—three nights running, she dreamed that my fifty-seven-year-old father dropped dead on his way to work. She will wonder aloud whether she offered Mr. Cray any relief or comfort when she met him at the door already forming the words he dreaded to utter. All that was left for him was to say yes.

My father, like most people, must have applied a kind of rhythm to the ordinary day. I followed that rhythm in my mind many times after that morning: his feet hitting the floor upon waking, the morning ablutions, the door clicking shut behind him, the three downward flights. Possibly he stopped to pet the Mortuses' cat, Tootsie (like all men in our family, Dad was a cat man), before stepping into our vacant driveway, where cars were not allowed. Perhaps he was in pain; I hope not. Even so, his last mortal moments are swaddled by the familiar. It's cold, but the air contains the coming spring. He leaves us, turns right at the Dohertys onto Gleason Street, passes the O'Neills, the Gagnons, the Velushes, turns right again at the Caliendos onto Mexico Avenue until he reaches another driveway with six attached garages at the end, each bay just barely big enough to fit one car. He was a farmer on Prince Edward Island, Canada, and at times deeply misses the red, furrowed fields and his siblings who remain, but the farm could never give him what he found here: steady, decent, good-paying work. He found his wife here, had five children over twenty years. His youngest is eight and a half; his oldest is twenty-eight. In eight years he will retire. What does he intend to do then, this man who has never taken a vacation or owned a house? Extended trips back to the island, perhaps, or long, pleasant days here, in summer at least, tilling the borrowed plot he tends in his father-in-law's yard just a few houses up the street from where he stands now, possibly short of breath, at six o'clock in the morning, the beginning of an ordinary day. *Here we go*, people say at these moments of familiar repetition, the day's momentum released with the turn of a key or the punch of a time card or, in my father's case, the fitting of his hand around the handle of a rented door. The door clangs upward. *Here—*. And he's gone. I hope there was a moment of anticipation. A sense of a new kind of beginning.

The rest of that morning, after my father's implausibly permanent departure, fills with arrivals. My sister is called back from the high school. My brother is called back from the mill. My priest uncle, who will oversee the funeral, is called back from his parish. By four in the afternoon we can barely close the fridge for all the casseroles and have literally run out of places to sit.

Late in the day, a final visitor arrives: a well-dressed stranger in a tie, his hair white and neatly combed, his face grave with sympathy. My mother is sitting in the kitchen, same chair into which she collapsed hours ago after Mr. Cray said his yes. A silver pin glints from the stranger's shirt pocket: *Oxford Paper Company*. "The Oxford," we call it; my father made his living there, and my friends' fathers, and my brother, and my friends' brothers, and my grandfather, and my friends' grandfathers. This man, who looks like Don Ameche, my father's favorite actor, is the mill manager. My mother, who has not risen from her chair all day, rises for him.

He stays only a few moments—charged, bright, layered moments that contain almost everything I will ever know. They are moments in which I feel both enthralled and confused, honored and ashamed. Because I'm a child, these moments arrive unsorted; I am not yet a writer; I do not yet think through the written word. And so I can only observe and wonder: An important man has come to see my mother; he resembles an actor; his condolences tip a scale that I did not know existed; his visit infuses an incongruous little trill into the muted dusk of our grief. The mill manager's presence elevates my father's importance; this much is clear. Which means this man is more important than my father. And that my father cannot be, as I so long have thought, the most important man in the world. These teetering intuitions provide my first, feeble inklings about social class and its myriad contradictions, its necessity in times of trauma, its cool, dispassionate lessons about who we are and where we are in the world.

The day of my father's death ends, for me, a few weeks later, after I've begun to perceive another, related, equally subtle perception: my mother's widowhood shames her. With the loss of her husband has come another, less tangible one—the loss of our appearance as a family whole. Gone is the illusion of bounty, the sustaining tableau of a man with a lunch pail leaving 16 Worthley Avenue every morning and returning to that same address every night. We are changed. We are less. My mother doesn't say this, but it's in the air, and I live in dread that some stranger will ask me, as people do back then, "What does your father do?" I live in dread of the answer. I can't say the word "dead."

Or so I thought. Learning to write is to learn that anything—anything in the world—can be made bearable. My sister gives me a new word, my first writer's word. "You can say, 'deceased,'" she tells me. My sister, my own future English teacher, instructing me already: "You say, 'deceased.'"

Deceased. The word takes on the palliative properties of a mill manager's visit. It provides the necessary distance from the thing it describes. It offers me a way out of my own part of the story, providing a solid place from which to observe the rest. Which is the writer's job.

A few weeks after that, in a postscript to the day, comes another present, another gift from my sister. A diary. It is blue, with a fake-leather cover and pickable lock. It contains three hundred sixty-five glossy, lined, blank, waiting pages. I fill it up.

My writer's material arrived in a day built of layers and layers of human endeavor that I have been sorting through ever since. That long, complicated day of my father's death—fed by the shock of loss, the consolations of family, the comforts of place, the confusions of class and station, and a burgeoning awareness of the power of words—lives on in everything I write.

When I blow into town these days, I sometimes feel like the red-lipped tourist lady from forty years ago, trying in vain to see the place whole. Unlike her, I stop and linger, often for days, for I have two families here now: my own family of origin, plus the one I married into. Though I've lived in Portland for thirty years, Mexico is still home. Everything that ever happened to me—everything worth writing about—happened here. Mexico will always be the place where my father died, where the Yarnishes' crow hollered down the street all day, where we began every school morning with a loud *bonjour*, where we helped our neighbor sew shoes for an industry that finally moved overseas, where we watched strangers in car after car drive past us, through us, checking their wristwatches or folding crinkled maps, road-weary and unseeing and aimed elsewhere.

Big Jim

Robert Kimber

In the summer of 1955, the year my father quit his job with the Bankers Trust Company in New York City and bought Big Jim Pond Camps, the year, that is, when my father took a flier and did what he had always wanted to do, which was own and run a hunting and fishing camp in Maine, he discovered after just a couple of months at Big Jim that substantial as the place may have looked to the casual eye, it was as tender and vulnerable as a new-born baby, in need of constant coddling and attention if it were not to succumb to the heat, humidity, rot, rust, and decay of Maine summers, the crushing weight of winter snows, the rank growth of alders that kept marching, marching against this tiny beachhead of cleared land, threatening to engulf it if they were not constantly beaten back.

Take the main lodge, two stories high, built of full logs, nobody knew when exactly, but a long time ago, around the turn of the century. Downstairs: one big, open room, forty by twenty-two feet, the guests' dining room. Upstairs: eight little bedrooms, supposedly for the help, but so stifling hot in the summer and icy cold in the fall that neither my parents nor any previous owners had ever asked a cook or waitress to occupy one of those rooms. Then, sticking out the back, an addition that housed the kitchen and sticking out the side of the kitchen, the back dining room, where the owners and the help ate.

This whole gangling structure perched on a narrow shelf of land between the water and the hill that rose steeply behind it and every other building at Big Jim. All eight guest cabins, also built of full logs, stood within just a few footsteps of the shore. If that potbelly of a hill had ever added a few inches to its girth, it would have pushed Big Jim's lodge, camps, shower house, ice house, woodshed—every last stick—out into the pond.

Rain and snowmelt poured down the hill in the spring, soaking the soil, rotting the camps' underpinnings, tilting them ever so slightly year after year toward the water. Don Yeaton, Big Jim's year-round caretaker, and I crawled under the lodge, drove blocks and shims between sagging foundation posts and the joists to keep the floor from bouncing up and down like a trampoline. We replaced rotting posts and sill logs, first in Camp Four, then in Seven, then Three, then Eight, then started all over again.

The roofs were covered with green roofing felt. Pine needles collected on them, held the moisture, rotted the felt, which expanded with the heat, contracted with the cold, pulled at the nails that held it down. We climbed up on the roofs with gallon cans of black roofing tar, smeared the leaks, hoped the black goo would hold this roof together until next year, when we'd get around to laying a fresh layer of green roofing felt.

I tried to convince Don and my father that the camps needed standing-seam metal roofing or—second best—asphalt shingles, something permanent, or good for twenty years anyhow. But Big Jim didn't have either a lot of time or a lot of money. Green roofing felt was a lot cheaper, a lot quicker and easier to lay.

I realize now that the impermanence of those roofs was just right for Jim Pond. Big Jim's camps were, after all, *camps,* temporary dwellings, not as permanent as a house, not as impermanent as a tent, but somewhere in between. You make camp, and you break camp. Camps are not forever, much as I may have thought they were.

That first summer and the next and the next one after that I worked with Don at Big Jim, then over the next decade a few more summers plus a couple of autumns and winters, too. Don had gone to work washing dishes in a lumber camp when he was twelve. He'd been just about everything a man could be, both in the woods and out: lumberjack, river hog, teamster, guide, game warden, millwright, truck driver, dozer operator, plumber, rigger, mechanic. During Prohibition, he'd hauled packloads of bootleg whiskey across the Canadian line to a rendezvous point he kept mum to the end of his days. At forty-two he enlisted in the Navy, was assigned to the Seabees, and built airfields in the South Pacific. He had come to Big Jim when he got out of the Navy in 1946 and stayed on ever since.

Like my father and like the century, Don was fifty-five years old; his hair was graying, his square-jawed face permanently tanned and creased from a lifetime of sun and wind. A handsome old devil, but dressed in a white shirt, he looked, he said, like a crow in a milk can. He walked at a steady, mile-gobbling gait, never pushing, never puffing, never tiring, rocking slightly side to side, a metronome ticking off the miles. Game wardens and bootleggers learn how to pace themselves. He went on occasional benders but knew how to pace them, too, indulging only at slack times, only after hunting season was over at the end of November and before it was time to reopen for ice-out and the first spring fishing in May.

That Don was something of an old rascal made him all the more appealing in my eyes. I got his life history only in hints and tag ends, never enough to make a coherent story.

"There was times when I was drivin' truck," he told me, "when I'd stop for a drink, and when I come out again, I'd be so drunk I'd see three roads in the headlights instead of one. I'm not proud of that, but it's the truth."

Married twice, divorced twice. He never went into the details, but did sum up the essential point in very few words. "There's many a man has left a good woman to marry a slut," he said. "I ought to know. I done it myself."

End of story.

The hardest thing he had ever done in his life, he said, was visit the widow of one of his Seabee buddies to give her a few snapshots he had of her husband and tell her, as best he could, how her husband had died.

I loved Don Yeaton. I trotted around at his heels, a happy puppy. In me, he had the ideal right-hand man, an apprentice eager to learn and equipped with the nearly inexhaustible energy of a twenty-year-old college kid. I wanted to know everything he knew, do everything he could do, hunt deer, build log cabins, trap beaver, maybe even go on an occasional bender.

Don was Big Jim's genius loci. Owners could come and go, but without Don, the place would falter, stagger, and die. There would be no firewood to burn. No truck, tractor, chainsaw, generator, or outboard motor would run; no toilet would flush; no shower would shower. Without Don, we wouldn't have had a shower at all. He built the shower house the first year he was there, a neat little full-log building with Big Jim's traditional green roof. In back, partitioned off from the two shower stalls, he concocted a Rube Goldberg hot-water system out of an old wood heater stove and a boiler he salvaged from the Stratton dump.

Every Wednesday evening and on Saturdays when we worked only half a day, Don went in to Stratton to visit his lady friend, Virginia. Before he left, he visited the shower house. He went in still wearing his dungarees, a faded green Dickies work shirt, and his old Navy fatigue cap turned cockeyed on his head, the bill of it sticking out over his right ear. He came out again scrubbed and combed, outfitted in clean khakis and a sport shirt.

"Shower's the only fit way for a man to take a bath," he said.

I understood him to mean that a man shouldn't settle into a tub and sit there in his own muck. A man needed to stand under a cleansing downpour, preferably warm, and sluice his grime on down.

All Big Jim's necessities and luxuries Don provided.

Unless our guests had unusually keen eyes, they saw nothing of Big Jim's flaws. They saw instead a Maine sporting camp looking just the way a Maine sporting camp was supposed to look: cozy, woodsy, but with a touch of rustic elegance about it, too. The lodge stood at the far right of the yard, with the camps strung out to the left of it, a mother merganser with her ducklings trailing obediently behind. The two peeled spruce posts supporting the gable roof over the front porch of the lodge, bleached nearly white by the weather, looked almost Doric and added a classical note to the place. For all our clientele knew, the underpinnings of the camps were as unshakeable as Gibraltar, the roofs tight as the tightest drum. Ask any of our guests, and they would say that Big Jim offered not just the image of solid comfort but the reality. In their experience, the floors under their feet didn't as much as quiver. Not once, even in the most ferocious, wind-driven downpours, did a drop of water seep through onto their heads or pillows.

On the screened-in porches, Big Jim's guests could settle into a rocking chair at five in the afternoon, safe from the blackflies, and sip their gin and tonics as the wind began to die over the water, promising a perfect evening for trolling. They could take in the glory of the pond stretching out in front of them about a mile across, Norway Point off to the right, named for the stand of Norway pine on it, and straight across, where the Northwest and Northeast Inlet streams came down out of the hills, the island, round and domed and densely covered with spruce and fir.

Rolling away on every side, hills upon hills: Jim Pond Mountain, Farm Hill with that big rock slide on it, Antler Hill just to the left of it and quite a bit higher, and beyond them, on and on, all around Big Jim in every direction, hills and mountains, ponds, lakes, rivers, brooks, some with names, many without: Kibby Mountain and Snow Mountain, Pickle Hill and Picked Chicken Hill; Hathan Bog and Spencer Bog and Hay Bog Brook; Big Island and Round Mountain ponds and Felker and Baker and Douglas ponds; Spencer Stream and Kibby Stream; the Moose River and the Dead River.

Not the wilds by any means but timberland, forests that had been cut before and would be cut again. Still, peaks enough to climb, ridges enough to run, valleys enough to explore, waterways enough to fish to keep a man going a long time and, in the middle of it all, Jim Pond Township itself, much of it uncut since the 1920s, the loggers' old winter roads only a network of footpaths now that Don and I swamped out and blazed fresh each year for hikers in the summer, hunters in the fall.

Big Jim Pond lies about a mile and a quarter east of the Dead River's North Branch. Maine Highway 27 runs west of the river, parallel to it, and often in sight of it on its twenty-five-mile route from the tiny village of Eustis to the Canadian line. In 1955 there was no bridge across the North Branch that connected with any road leading to Big Jim Pond Camps. That lack of a road connection with the outside world meant that everybody and everything that came into camp had to travel a complicated path. Our guests drove down a narrow woods track to our parking area and boat landing on the west bank of the river. There, they called into camp on a crank telephone (five short rings was our number), most likely got my mother, Jean Kimber, who would be in earshot of the kitchen phone and who would then dispatch either my father, Frank Kimber, or Don or me, whoever was handiest, to climb into the Model A Ford beach wagon and go pick them up.

The call could just as well be from the grocery wholesaler who delivered cartons of canned peas, corn, carrots, beets, peaches, and pears, quarters of beef and pork, slabs of bacon and tubs of lard to the boat landing, or from the guy who brought the bottles of propane that lit the gas lamps in the kitchen and fueled the ancient gas stove the cook could resort to if he needed some quick heat and the wood range was already tied up. All this stuff, plus an endless procession of five-gallon cans of gasoline to keep Big Jim's machinery running— even the washing machine was powered by a little one-cylinder, lawn-mower-size gas engine—plus toilet paper and typewriter ribbons and postage stamps, every last toothpick or pencil crossed the North Branch in our ferry, a big green scow hitched to an endless rope that ran through pulleys anchored to trees on either side of the river.

All that fuss—having to haul all our supplies across the river and then into camp in the Model A, having to do the same with our guests and their gear, then having to do it all in reverse again when they left after a week or two—was a price both we and our clientele gladly paid because the North Branch of the Dead River was Big Jim's moat. On its far side, you parked the overstuffed plenitude of your bulgy Buick sedan. On this side, you climbed aboard the lean austerity of our 1932 Model A beach wagon, a vehicle never matched for elegance before or since, the body and doors all wood, all painted green, the roof built like a canoe with light ribs and planking covered with heavy canvas painted black, no glass in the windows, wide open to breeze and sun: a rolling verandah, a motorized surrey with no fringe on top.

Over there, you left the *Ed Sullivan Show* and the House Un-American Activities Committee behind to set off over here on a road that wasn't a road at all but a buckboard track on which the Model A Ford had replaced the buckboard. Big Jim in 1955 was still halfway between horses and horsepower, not caught up with—no, not overwhelmed by—a world ten years after Hiroshima. This road-not-a-road was a mile-long bower, the canopy of red and sugar maples shading us, keeping the soil cool and damp and hard in the two tracks under the beach wagon's wheels. No dust ever rose here, even in the driest of summers. On this side of the river, we had most of Jim Pond Township to ourselves, six miles by six of woods where no bulldozer blade had cut through the forest floor. Over here, time ran slower than it did on the other side of the North Branch, and even if you had never been to Jim Pond before, you knew, just minutes into your passage through that leafy tunnel, that you were heading for a place that would prove an oasis for the eye and heart and soul.

Don, my father, and I each had our dreams for Big Jim. Not that any of us ever talked about them. Real men didn't talk about their dreams, but I knew all three of us had them anyway.

Mine, a pipe dream. I dreamed Big Jim would live forever. If no young man believes he will ever die, no young man believes the world he has been born into and fallen in love with will die, either. I expected that Big Jim's moat would never be bridged, that the trails that had once been loggers' winter roads would not become logging roads again, that the lease the owner of Jim Pond Township granted my father each year would continue to be granted year after year, on into perpetuity. I had still not experienced, on my own hide, change and the fragility of human arrangements.

My father's dream: To hold his own, to break even or at least even enough that he could hang on here, to keep waking up every morning in his camp set back on the hill a little ways and look out, over the roof of the lodge, onto the water and the hills beyond, to go out in his Rangeley boat any evening he liked after supper and troll for togue and landlocked salmon or, on windstill nights, to cast a fly to rising trout. To never, ever again climb aboard the 7:23 that had carried him every morning from our commuter town in New Jersey to Hoboken, to never again work from nine to five in the real estate division of the Bankers Trust Company, where he had dealt with deeds and mortgage papers all day. He had his dream, a good part of it anyway, and dreamed only of keeping it.

Don's dreams became projects. If you indulged in dreams alone, you had nothing to show for it. If you indulged in projects, you had a shower house, running water and flush toilets in all the camps, a root cellar dug into the hill, shored up with timbers and planking and equipped with two sets of tightly fitting, insulated doors. It could be forty below outside, but inside you could keep carton upon carton of canned goods, jars of pickles and fruit juices, barrels of potatoes and carrots and beets, and nothing would freeze.

In that first summer, which was a time for Don and his new boss to feel each other out, he didn't push hard. He eased my father into the idea of projects.

"You know, Frank," Don had said one night after supper, "I think it'd be worth our time to add a screened-in porch to that little house-keeping camp over in the cove. It's awful miserable havin' to cook and eat inside a stuffy little camp in hot weather. If we screen in the deck that's already there, folks can sit outside in the cool of the evenin' and enjoy their supper. Make the place a lot more comfortable."

It just so happened that sometime in the spring, before my parents had even arrived at camp, Don had cut and peeled the fir we would need for the corner posts and rails of that porch and for the plates and rafters of its roof, so the work went quickly. In three days we were done, a mini-project completed, not a full-scale construction job, just an upgrading, an improvement, but something new nonetheless; something that hadn't been there before was there now. We swept the porch clean, raked up the sawdust and wood chips, picked up the scrap ends of screening and roofing felt, gathered our tools and put them in the boat, stepped back to admire our handiwork.

"There, by the bejesus," Don said, and we climbed into the boat and headed back to camp for supper.

We had to spend most of our time, of course, not on projects but on the relentless, routine work that kept Big Jim functioning: the woodpile, for instance. Big Jim cooked and baked on a wood range, so even in the summer I hauled wheelbarrow loads of wood from the big drying shed back of the ice house to the kitchen woodbox twice a day. But come fall, especially the final weeks of deer season in late November, the demand for firewood increased five, six, tenfold. The hunters in each guest camp kept a fire going from the time they came in at dusk until bedtime, which might not come until a poker game finally broke up at midnight. The huge heater stove in the main dining room had to be roaring by five in the morning if the place was going to be warm enough to keep coffee from freezing in the hunters' cups at breakfast. When the season closed at the end of November and my parents went south to a house they had built in Daytona Beach, Don moved into their camp for the winter—the roomiest camp at Jim Pond and the only one, apart from the main lodge, with a kitchen—and he needed enough wood for both heat and cooking to see him through until May.

All told, Big Jim gobbled up twenty or twenty-five cord a year, wood that we felled, dragged into the wood yard with a 1940 Cletrac crawler tractor, then bucked up with a brutishly heavy old Homelite chainsaw. Any stick that cracked open easily, neat slabs popping off it with one whack of the axe, we split small enough to fit into the cookstove fireboxes. Any lumpy, knotty, twisty-grained stick that didn't yield instantly would wind up in one of the big, boxy heater stoves. When the pile of wood got so high we couldn't see over it, we'd load as much of it onto our 1939 Chevy truck as the body would hold, haul it into the camp yard, pile it in the drying shed that was open to the air on all four sides, then go back for another load and another until all of it was in. Then we cut some more.

Every morning after we had driven the Chevy out to the wood yard, Don would say, "Well, Robert,"—he always called me "Robert," which he pronounced something like "Rahbut"—"it don't look as anybody's done a goddamn thing out here while we was gone."

Nobody had, and we would set to it for another day.

Young and green as I was, I thought twitching whole trees out of the woods with the Cletrac and working them up into a small mountain of sweet, clean stove billets that shone in the sun was just plain fun, though I had sense enough not to say so.

Don, who was neither young nor green, did not emote about the work, either. He just did it the same way that he walked, neither hurrying nor dawdling, just doing what needed to be done at a steady pace, knowing that the next jag of wood to fell and buck and split and pile would be there this afternoon if we didn't get to it this morning, tomorrow if we didn't get to it today.

In spare moments during the workday—before breakfast in the morning, during the hour lunch break, after our five-o'clock supper in the evening—I fit in all the little jobs a chore boy would have done if we had had one. I tended to all our guests' needs. I made sure their cabins were supplied with firewood, kindling, and old newspapers for tinder. First thing in the morning, I built a fire for Mrs. Fyte, who suffered from arthritis, so she wouldn't have to get up in a damp, cold camp. I took a bucket of hot water to Mr. Reese, who, unlike most of Big Jim's male guests, wanted to shave every day. If it had rained during the night, I bailed out our fleet of Rangeley boats tied up at the dock, waiting there for their passengers like patient horses at the hitching rack of a saloon. I checked the bait traps and filled bait buckets for anyone who wanted to troll shiners. If Mr. Thorpe wanted to cast a fly on the river in the evening, I drove him down there in the

Model A, pulled a canoe off the rack at the boat landing, and paddled him to the best pools upstream and down. If both Mr. and Mrs. Thorpe decided the next day that they wanted to visit the homestead museum of the famous opera diva Lilian Nordica, who was born and raised in Farmington, I again drove the Model A down to the river and ferried them across, and when they came back after dark in the evening and called on the phone to be picked up, I picked them up, all with a smile I didn't even have to fake.

At noon, just before lunch, when Don and I came back from the woods dripping sweat, I ducked into the dank, delicious coolness of the ice house, where Don had stored, under a thick blanket of insulating sawdust, the hundred and fifty blocks of ice he had cut out of the pond in February. I scraped away the sawdust and horsed two or three of those blocks onto a wheelbarrow, carted them around to the back side of the kitchen, lugged them up a set of stairs onto a small landing, and slid them into the ice compartment of the walk-in icebox that kept Big Jim's quarters of beef and pork, its milk and butter and eggs and cheese, from souring and spoiling. At cocktail time in the late afternoon, I revisited the ice house and lopped a breadbox-sized hunk of ice off one of those big blocks. In the kitchen, I washed the ice, attacked it with an ice pick, and then delivered little wooden buckets full of chipped ice to all the occupied camps.

Big Jim ran on wood and water, fire and ice.

By the time I got back to Big Jim in the June of our second summer, Don had convinced my father that what the camps had been lacking for their entire history was a lounge. Don had planted that seed back in early September the previous summer when we had nobody in camp for a few days and my father and mother, Don and I were sitting in the red Adirondack chairs on the porch of the main lodge pretending we were our own guests lazing out there enjoying the absence of bugs and the bright, clean air with a nip of fall in it.

"Somethin' me and Otho never got 'round to was buildin' a lounge onto the west end of the dinin' room," he said. "An afternoon like this one's perfect for sittin' out here, but in a few weeks with cold fall rains comin' on, it sure would be nice to be able to just walk into a room next door with a fire goin' in the stove and some books and magazines to gawk at."

Otho Record had owned and run the camps from sometime in the late thirties until he sold to Wayne and Peggy, the young couple who had lasted only two years and who had sold in turn to my father. Over the several years my father had come to Big Jim as a guest, he had gotten to know and like Otho, so Otho's opinion added some extra weight to Don's own.

"Well," my father said, "Otho spoke often about wanting to do that, but what with building the bathrooms onto the camps and running the water to them and all the other things you and he did in those years, it's no wonder you didn't get around to it."

"Could have a poker table in there, too," Don added. "Now the boys have to crowd into one camp or another for a game. No question, Frank. It'd add a lot to the place."

"Let's see how things pan out this year and what kind of season we're likely to have next year," my father said. "I agree that some kind of space here in the lodge for people to get together in after a meal would be a nice thing to have."

Don, I was sure, had carried the day.

And indeed our project in that second summer was cutting and peeling camp logs so they could dry for a year and be ready to build with in our third summer. In the winter, Don had scouted out and marked about forty tall, straight fir a foot and more at the butt, also some smaller ones for floor joists and rafters. Just a week after I arrived in June, we went out after those trees with two axes, a two-man crosscut saw, and two spuds.

"Aren't you going to take the chainsaw?" I asked.

"Don't want to horse that brute around all day," Don said, which was his way of saying he preferred to cut those trees by hand: no ear-splitting racket, just the sweet sound of a sharp axe chunking out a notch, the steady rhythm of the saw rippling back and forth, spitting sawdust out of the kerf. We felled two trees, then split up to limb them and peel the bark.

You trim off every branch close to the trunk, getting rid of as many lumps at this first stage of the game as you can. Then you run the corner of the spud lengthwise down the trunk, slicing through the bark so you can tuck the front of the curved blade into that cut and start rolling the bark off, first down one side, then the other. When you're done, you have a snake lying out straight as a string and glistening gold in the sun, shed skin lying in tatters on either side. But in no time at all, the sap that imparts that sheen to a freshly peeled softwood will dry out and leave the log still clean and fresh, but without the glow that seems to be an emanation from the heart of the wood. No matter how clean the logs are when the camp is finished or whatever preservative or stain you might buy to protect them, they will never again look the way they did in those first few minutes; and if anyone should ever find a way to keep that glow from fading, we would have a building material fit for the City of God.

As it was, Don and I had building material quite fit enough for a lounge at Big Jim Pond Camps, a pile of logs dragged into the camp yard with the Cletrac and stacked up on skids to keep them out of the muck and snowmelt of the next spring. And when, in our third summer, we had gotten ahead enough on the woodpile and put new roofing paper on two camps, we dug the post holes for the foundation of the lounge, set the posts, and laid the three stringers that would carry the floor joists.

There are any number of ways you can build a log camp, but in Don's universe the only right way was to notch the bottoms of the logs at the corners so that each new log straddled the one below it. Any rainwater that got driven into the joint could not collect there to rot the wood but would roll off the rounded surface.

Not all projects required the right way. For the shower house and the bathroom additions on the camps, Don and Otho had used the much quicker and easier method of setting corner posts on the sill logs, cutting the logs for the walls square at the ends to fit snugly between the posts, then spiking them into the posts. But this lounge was a different story, a showpiece. It had to have some class. And then, though Don never said so, he probably saw it as his swansong project. He was fifty-seven; Big Jim wasn't likely to need another new building in his time, so this one should be a masterpiece.

Building with logs isn't what you'd call fine woodworking, but we came as close to that standard as axes would let us get. We scribed the exact shape each notch should have onto the log with a compass, rolled the log up, then took turns, first Don, then me, carving the notches out with the axe and hewing off any lumps or curves in the log that kept it from settling down snugly on the one below it. We might roll a log back up three, four, five times to shave off just a little more wood along the length of it or to clean the notch out so that it fit the log below tightly.

When Don was satisfied, he'd grin and say, "Just the cock for dolly," and we'd spike that log in place.

In late September we finished the lounge, the floor varnished and gleaming, a couple of bookshelves built onto the wall just inside the entrance from the dining room, a Franklin stove in the far corner, a green sofa against the back wall with end tables for drinks and magazines at either end, a big hooked rug on the floor, a couple of rocking chairs, a view of the pond from a picture window we concocted out of three big sliding windows Don had salvaged from the wrecking of an old hotel in Lewiston, and, in the middle of the room, a snazzy octagonal poker table, complete with a green felt playing surface and little sunken compartments in front of each of the eight players' stations for chips, drinks, and ashtrays.

The weekend after the lounge was finished and furnished, Don brought Virginia into camp late Saturday afternoon for a little celebration. The fall foliage was at its peak, the maples across the pond flaring up red and orange against the green of the softwoods; fair-weather clouds scurried across a blue sky.

I'd built a little fire in the Franklin stove and opened the doors up, as much for atmosphere as for warmth. We settled into the green couch and the rockers, my father and mother, Don and Virginia, and me, and made fairly short work of a fifth of Canadian Club, classy booze my father had bought a couple of weeks ago at the state store in Farmington and tucked away specially for this occasion.

Sitting in this room built of clean logs, its rafters and roof boards overhead still so new they seemed to rain light down on us, I let my head drift off on the fumes of that good whiskey, picturing a future I thought all but assured. In it, all five of us would keep gathering in this room Don had been itching to build for years. Don would keep going out to see Virginia every Wednesday evening and Saturday noon; they'd keep dancing at many another hunters' ball—how many more I couldn't guess, but many more. What the practical arrangements might be to make all that possible, I did not trouble my woozy head about.

"Fall is so beautiful," Virginia said. "Just look out there. I love the fall, but it's so sad, too, because you know what's coming right behind it."

The other project going on in the summer of 1957 was not ours. It was the bridge across the North Branch and the bulldozed road that would run a mile downstream from the bridge to meet up with our buckboard road.

That year, the new road went no farther. The jobber built a small camp at the junction of the new road and the buckboard road, and that winter two men with horses cut birch that a mill in Dixfield would turn into spools for the Coats and Clark thread company.

We had to admit the new road had its advantages. Our guests could drive themselves into camp and drive themselves back out again. We could drive our Mercury station wagon to Stratton or Farmington, load it up with groceries, hardware, roofing paper, gas cans, anything and everything, and drive the stuff right to Big Jim's back door. Delivery trucks could drive in, too. We soon had, up on the hill back of the kitchen and next to the guides' camp, one of those huge propane tanks that looks like half an airliner fuselage. Never again would Don and I horse hundred-pound gas bottles into the green scow at the river, then into the Chevy truck or, in the winter, haul them in behind us one at a time like sleds.

Once we had hewn the rafters for the lounge and were ready to put on the roof boards, a truck from Jordan Lumber in Kingfield drove right down to the porch of the main lodge, and we had our roofing boards delivered within twenty yards of their final resting place. A week later, when the roof was up and papered, the same truck came back again with the finish boards for the floor.

Now who in his right mind could complain about that?

My college years were over; my ten *Wanderjahre* just beginning: drafted in 1958 for two years, stationed in Germany, graduate school, a teaching job in Berlin. I didn't get back to Jim Pond for an extended stay until the summer of 1968. In the few visits I'd been able to make in the previous decade, I could see the continuing changes the road was bringing to both the camps and the surrounding territory.

That it made life easier at Big Jim any fool could see. Because the Fotters' grocery store in Stratton was only a twelve-mile drive door to door now, my parents could make frequent, easy runs to buy perishables there and no longer needed all the cold-storage space the big walk-in icebox had provided. Two used gas refrigerators my father was able to pick up and the propane tank that could be refilled at a moment's notice took care of the camp's refrigeration needs, also relieving Don of cutting and storing ice in the winter. His only winter responsibility now was to keep the roofs shoveled clear of snow so they wouldn't cave in. The ice house, with its insulating sawdust, was obsolete; so too was our old cantankerous sawmill now that we could get lumber delivered right to pond's edge. The sawmill had all but disappeared, the shed roof caved in and the timber framing rotted out from under the tracks and the log carriage. Young poplar was springing up in and around the wreckage.

And of course the bulldozer had continued on its march, following many of Big Jim's hiking trails, making wide gravel roads of them and extending the reach of the road network. Hunters and fishermen could stay in Stratton or Eustis and in an hour's drive or less reach parts of Jim Pond Township that would have been inaccessible before the bridge and roads went in. Big Jim's clientele shrank. Because more and more people could easily get into more and more of the area, fewer felt the need to stay at a sporting camp on the township. Also, many guests who had been coming to camp year after year were aging and dropping off Big Jim's mailing list. In my father's first years at camp, he had hired a cook for the entire season, May through November. Now he and my mother did the cooking and waiting on tables, only hiring a woman to help with kitchen and cabin chores if business turned out a little better than expected.

He and Don were both sixty-eight, far from decrepit but sixty-eight nonetheless. Don allowed as he was slowing down. Come deer season, he still guided hunters from dawn to dusk, some old customers he had guided for years on end and who remained loyal to him and to Big Jim, but now, instead of sitting up with his party for a few drinks in the evening, he headed straight for the guides' camp and bed the minute he finished his supper.

Virginia, who had worked for the local telephone company as an operator in the Stratton office all the years we had known her, had been offered a better job in the company's headquarters in North Anson and had moved there.

The next two years I spent teaching in the Boston area, where Rita and I met and married. In the summer of 1971, we moved to Maine, not to Jim Pond but to Temple, a small town near Farmington. We had bought an old farm with a rickety house on it that demanded all our time to make livable for the coming winter. Our weekend trips to Jim Pond were few.

In late July my father called us to say the main lodge and the ice house right next to it had burned to the ground. Don, sleeping in the guide's camp right behind the lodge, had wakened to the flames and raced out to Eustis to summon the state forest service tank trucks. The forest service team had come in as quickly as they could, but by the time they arrived, the buildings were already a total loss. All the firemen could do was wet down the guides' camp and Camp Two, both of which were quite near the blaze, and prevent the fire from spreading into the grass and trees.

The only explanation for the fire anyone ever came up with was spontaneous combustion in that great mound of old sawdust in the ice house. The conditions were ideal: some dampness left over from the melted ice, just enough air for oxidation. Once we had stopped storing ice, we should have shoveled that sawdust out, carted it off down one of the new logging roads, and thrown it to the winds. But none of us had thought to do that.

Two summers later, the family company that had owned Jim Pond Township for generations sold it. The new corporate owner didn't want a commercial camp on the land and would not renew my father's lease for the next season.

Oddly enough, or perhaps not oddly at all, this sudden end to Big Jim Pond Camps did not hit any of us as a catastrophe. My father and Don were both seventy-three. Big Jim was about the same age, and, by the time the township was sold, the camps had long since ceased to be a going business. My parents had come up from Florida later and later each spring and left a little earlier each fall. The only clients who came, even before the fire, were few and far between, mostly old friends for whom Big Jim remained an oasis for the soul and who were content simply to be there. Once the lodge had burned, Big Jim was just where my parents spent their summers, where Don continued to live, and where a handful of couples might turn up in the course of the season for a few days.

My father sold off everything movable on the place—boats, motors, the stoves and furniture in the camps. Friends of mine in need of housing but with little money took down three of the cabins, numbering the logs as they worked, carted them away on lumber trucks, then reassembled the cabins on their own plots of land. You make camp and break camp, and sometimes somebody else makes camp again.

With the exception of the owners' camp, the remaining buildings were bulldozed and burned. Now, thirty-five years later, the alders have taken over the camp yard.

My father had owned and run Big Jim Pond Camps for eighteen years. I suppose, from most perspectives, his venture at Jim Pond was a failure, even a crazy enterprise from the word go. How could a man who had worked in real-estate law for much of his life buy a place where he owned a set of buildings but not the land underneath them, where the fate of the business hung on the annual renewal of his lease?

Well, the lease always had been renewed year after year, decade after decade. My father had been more than willing to go in on those terms. Life was not forever, and if Big Jim wasn't either, too bad. Four, seven, eleven, or however many years doing what he wanted wasn't so bad a deal. As it turned out, he got eighteen.

I never thought of my father as an adventuresome man, but he had been brave enough to take the chance he took. He had also managed his assets just carefully enough to get him to the end of his days. He died at eighty-one, felled by a heart attack in his Daytona Beach house. He and my mother must have been living on not much more than their Social Security checks. His bank account was down to only a few dollars. He owned only the house, its furnishings, and his car.

Don had died shortly before my father, in a house in Eustis where his mother had lived out her last years and that he had inherited from her. The newspaper report of his death said he had been trying to repair a gas heater and it had exploded on him, that he had been found lying face down on a heating grill. But Tommy Lamont, who worked for the state forest service in Eustis, told me when I saw him a couple of months later that the newspaper report was wrong: Don, too, had died of a heart attack.

"He was a good man," Tommy said—somewhat defensively, I thought—as if he knew, as I did, that whatever Don's failings had been, they were as nothing compared to his goodness, and that nowhere near enough people knew how good he had been, that all they saw in him was an old ne'er-do-well woodsman with a woodsman's persistent hankering for whiskey.

My father may have owned Jim Pond Camps, but the only one of us who had truly earned the right to call Big Jim his own—because it was his work that kept the place from falling down, his work that brought in the wood and the ice and kept the roofs from caving in year after year when my parents weren't there and I wasn't there and he was the only person there, holding this small part of the world up on his shoulders—that only person was Don.

His funeral in Farmington was a routine affair. He was a veteran; a flag draped his coffin; a few older men whom I didn't know but who I assumed were there from the V.F.W. attended. So did Virginia, who had come over from North Anson.

The minister, clearly called in on a rotation basis, knew Don not at all and went through his rote service: "O death, where is thy sting? O grave, where is thy victory?" And that was that.

I'm never quick on the uptake. I always think, long after the opportunity has gone by, of the clever argument or quick-witted response I should have thought of in a discussion days earlier. I knew at the time that this service for Don cheated him, did him no honor or justice at all. But I could find no words to speak at the moment, so Rita and I left and went home, and when I said to her what a sad, empty fiasco that had been, she said, "Don would have laughed."

Maybe. Laughed or snorted.

But whatever he would have done, he was Big Jim. He still is. And these words are just some of the words I couldn't find to say for him that day.

Once More to the Lake

E. B. White

One summer, along about 1904, my father rented a camp on a lake in Maine and took us all there for the month of August. We all got ringworm from some kittens and had to rub Pond's Extract on our arms and legs night and morning, and my father rolled over in a canoe with all his clothes on; but outside of that the vacation was a success, and from then on none of us ever thought there was any place in the world like that lake in Maine. We returned summer after summer—always on August 1 for one month. I have since become a saltwater man, but sometimes in summer there are days when the restlessness of the tides and the fearful cold of the sea water and the incessant wind that blows across the afternoon and into the evening make me wish for the placidity of a lake in the woods. A few weeks ago this feeling got so strong I bought myself a couple of bass hooks and a spinner and returned to the lake where we used to go, for a week's fishing and to revisit old haunts.

I took along my son, who had never had any fresh water up his nose and who had seen lily pads only from train windows. On the journey over to the lake I began to wonder what it would be like. I wondered how time would have marred this unique, this holy spot— the coves and streams, the hills that the sun set behind, the camps and the paths behind the camps. I was sure that the tarred road would have found it out, and I wondered in what other ways it would be desolated. It is strange how much you can remember about places like that once you allow your mind to return into the grooves that lead back. You remember one thing, and that suddenly reminds you of another thing. I guess I remembered clearest of all the early mornings, when the lake was cool and motionless, remembered how the bedroom smelled of the lumber it was made of and of the wet woods whose scent entered through the screen. The partitions in the camp were thin and did not extend clear to the top of the rooms, and as I was always the first up I would dress softly so as not to wake the others, and sneak out into the sweet outdoors and start out in the canoe, keeping close along the shore in the long shadows of the pines. I remembered being very careful never to rub my paddle against the gunwale for fear of disturbing the stillness of the cathedral.

The lake had not been what you would call a wild lake. There were cottages sprinkled around the shores, and it was in farming country, although the shores of the lake were quite heavily wooded. Some of the cottages were owned by nearby farmers, and you would live at the shore and eat your meals at the farmhouse. That's what our family did. But although it wasn't wild, it was a fairly large and undisturbed lake and there were places in it that, to a child at least, seemed infinitely remote and primeval.

I was right about the tar: it led to within half a mile of the shore. But when I got back there, with my boy, and we settled into a camp near a farmhouse and into the kind of summertime I had known, I could tell that it was going to be pretty much the same as it had been before—I knew it, lying in bed the first morning, smelling the bedroom, and hearing the boy sneak quietly out and go off along the shore in a boat. I began to sustain the illusion that he was I, and therefore, by simple transposition, that I was my father. This sensation persisted, kept cropping up all the time we were there. It was not an entirely new feeling, but in this setting it grew much stronger. I seemed to be living a dual existence. I would be in the middle of some simple act, I would be picking up a bait box or laying down a table fork, or I would be saying something, and suddenly it would be not I but my father who was saying the words or making the gesture. It gave me a creepy sensation.

We went fishing the first morning. I felt the same damp moss covering the worms in the bait can, and saw the dragonfly alight on the tip of my rod as it hovered a few inches from the surface of the water. It was the arrival of this fly that convinced me beyond any doubt that everything was as it always had been, that the years were a mirage and there had been no years. The small waves were the same, chucking the rowboat under the chin as we fished at anchor, and the boat was the same boat, the same color green and the ribs broken in the same places, and under the floorboards the same freshwater leavings and debris—the dead hellgrammite, the wisps of moss, the rusty discarded fishhook, the dried blood from yesterday's catch. We stared silently at the tips of our rods, at the dragonflies that came and went. I lowered the tip of mine into the water, tentatively, pensively dislodging the fly, which darted two feet away, poised, darted two feet back, and came to rest again a little farther up the rod. There had been no years between the ducking of this dragonfly and the other one—the one that was part of memory. I looked at the boy, who was silently watching his fly, and it was my hands that held his rod, my eyes watching. I felt dizzy and didn't know which rod I was at the end of.

We caught two bass, hauling them in briskly as though they were mackerel, pulling them over the side of the boat in a businesslike manner without any landing net, and stunning them with a blow on the back of the head. When we got back for a swim before lunch, the lake was exactly where we had left it, the same number of inches from the dock, and there was only the merest suggestion of a breeze. This seemed an utterly enchanted sea, this lake you could leave to its own devices for a few hours and come back to, and find that it had not stirred, this constant and trustworthy body of water. In the shallows, the dark, watersoaked sticks and twigs, smooth and old, were undulating in clusters on the bottom against the clean ribbed sand, and the track of the mussel was plain. A school of minnows swam by, each minnow with its small individual shadow, doubling the attendance, so clear and sharp in the sunlight. Some of the other campers were in swimming, along the shore, one of them with a cake of soap, and the water felt thin and clear and unsubstantial. Over the years there had been this person with the cake of soap, this cultist, and here he was. There had been no years.

Up to the farmhouse to dinner through the teeming, dusty field, the road under our sneakers was only a two-track road. The middle track was missing, the one with the marks of the hooves and the splotches of dried, flaky manure. There had always been three tracks to choose from in choosing which track to walk in; now the choice was narrowed down to two. For a moment I missed terribly the middle alternative. But the way led past the tennis court, and something about the way it lay there in the sun reassured me; the tape had loosened along the backline, the alleys were green with plantains and other weeds, and the net (installed in June and removed in September) sagged in the dry noon, and the whole place steamed with midday heat and hunger and emptiness. There was a choice of pie for dessert, and one was blueberry and one was apple, and the waitresses were the same country girls, there having been no passage of time, only the illusion of it as in a dropped curtain—the waitresses were still fifteen; their hair had been washed, that was the only difference—they had been to the movies and seen the pretty girls with the clean hair.

Summertime, oh summertime, pattern of life indelible, the fadeproof lake, the woods unshatterable, the pasture with the sweetfern and the juniper forever and ever, summer without end; this was the background, and the life along the shore was the design, the cottages with their innocent and tranquil design, their tiny docks with the flagpole and the American flag floating against the white clouds in the blue sky, the little paths over the roots of the trees leading from camp to camp and the paths leading back to the outhouses and the can of lime for sprinkling, and at the souvenir counters at the store the miniature birch-bark canoes and the postcards that showed things looking a little better than they looked. This was the American family at play, escaping the city heat and wondering whether the newcomers in the camp at the head of the cove were "common" or "nice," wondering whether it was true that the people who drove up for Sunday dinner at the farmhouse were turned away because there wasn't enough chicken.

It seemed to me, as I kept remembering all this, that those times and those summers had been infinitely precious and worth saving. There had been jollity and peace and goodness. The arriving (at the beginning of August) had been so big a business in itself, at the railway station, the farm wagon drawn up, the first smell of the pine-laden air, the first glimpse of the smiling farmer, and the great importance of the trunks and your father's enormous authority in such matters, and the feel of the wagon under you for the long ten-mile haul, and at the top of the last long hill catching the first view of the lake after eleven months of not seeing this cherished body of water. The shouts and cries of the other campers when they saw you, and the trunks to be unpacked, to give up their rich burden. (Arriving was less exciting nowadays, when you sneaked up in your car and parked it under a tree near the camp and took out the bags and in five minutes it was all over, no fuss, no loud wonderful fuss about trunks.)

Peace and goodness and jollity. The only thing that was wrong now, really, was the sound of the place, an unfamiliar nervous sound of the outboard motors. This was the note that jarred, the one thing that would sometimes break the illusion and set the years moving. In those other summertimes all motors were inboard; and when they were at a little distance, the noise they made was a sedative, an ingredient of summer sleep. They were one-cylinder and two-cylinder engines, and some were make-and-break and some were jump-spark, but they all made a sleepy sound across the lake. The one-lungers throbbed and fluttered, and the twin-cylinder ones purred and purred, and that was a quiet sound too. But now the campers all had outboards. In the daytime, in the hot mornings, these motors made a petulant, irritable sound; at night, in the still evening when the afterglow lit the water, they whined about one's ears like mosquitoes. My boy loved our rented outboard, and his great desire to achieve single-handed mastery over it, and authority, and he soon learned the trick of choking it a little (but not too much), and the adjustment of the needle valve. Watching him I would remember the things you could

228 E. B. White

do with the old one-cylinder engine with the heavy flywheel, how you could have it eating out of your hand if you got really close to it spiritually. Motor boats in those days didn't have clutches, and you would make a landing by shutting off the motor at the proper time and coasting in with a dead rudder. But there was a way of reversing them, if you learned the trick, by cutting the switch and putting it on again exactly on the final dying revolution of the flywheel, so that it would kick back against compression and begin reversing. Approaching a dock in a strong following breeze, it was difficult to slow up sufficiently by the ordinary coasting method, and if a boy felt he had complete mastery over his motor, he was tempted to keep it running beyond its time and then reverse it a few feet from the dock. It took a cool nerve, because if you threw the switch a twentieth of a second too soon you would catch the flywheel when it still had speed enough to go up past center, and the boat would leap ahead, charging bull-fashion at the dock.

We had a good week at the camp. The bass were biting well and the sun shone endlessly, day after day. We would be tired at night and lie down in the accumulated heat of the little bedrooms after the long hot day and the breeze would stir almost imperceptibly outside and the smell of the swamp drift in through the rusty screens. Sleep would come easily and in the morning the red squirrel would be on the roof, tapping out his gay routine. I kept remembering everything, lying in bed in the mornings—the small steamboat that had a long rounded stern like the lip of a Ubangi, and how quietly she ran on the moonlight sails, when the older boys played their mandolins and the girls sang and we ate doughnuts dipped in sugar, and how sweet the music was on the water in the shining night, and what it had felt like to think about girls then. After breakfast we would go up to the store and the things were in the same place—the minnows in a bottle, the plugs and spinners disarranged and pawed over by the youngsters from the boys' camp, the fig newtons and the Beeman's gum. Outside, the road was tarred and cars stood in front of the store. Inside, all was just as it had always been, except there was more Coca-Cola and not so much Moxie and root beer and birch beer and sarsaparilla.

We would walk out with a bottle of pop apiece and sometimes the pop would backfire up our noses and hurt. We explored the streams, quietly, where the turtles slid off the sunny logs and dug their way into the soft bottom; and we lay on the town wharf and fed worms to the tame bass. Everywhere we went I had trouble making out which was I, the one walking at my side, the one walking in my pants.

One afternoon while we were there at that lake a thunderstorm came up. It was like the revival of an old melodrama that I had seen long ago with childish awe. The second-act climax of the drama of the electrical disturbance over a lake in America had not changed in any important respect. This was the big scene, still the big scene. The whole thing was so familiar, the first feeling of oppression and heat and a general air around camp of not wanting to go very far away. In midafternoon (it was all the same) a curious darkening of the sky, and a lull in everything that had made life tick; and then the way the boats suddenly swung the other way at their moorings with the coming of a breeze out of the new quarter, and the premonitory rumble. Then the kettle drum, then the snare, then the bass drum and cymbals, then crackling light against the dark, and the gods grinning and licking their chops in the hills. Afterward the calm, the rain steadily rustling in the calm lake, the return of light and hope and spirits, and the campers running out in joy and relief to go swimming in the rain, their bright cries perpetuating the deathless joke about how they were getting simply drenched, and the children screaming with delight at the new sensation of bathing in the rain, and the joke about getting drenched linking the generations in a strong indestructible chain. And the comedian who waded in carrying an umbrella.

When the others went swimming my son said he was going in, too. He pulled his dripping trunks from the line where they had hung all through the shower, and wrung them out. Languidly, and with no thought of going in, I watched him, his hard little body, skinny and bare, saw him wince slightly as he pulled up around his vitals the small, soggy, icy garment. As he buckled the swollen belt, suddenly my groin felt the chill of death.

Affirmations

Logging Truck

Carolyn Chute

O l' beast! Ol' thing of dread. Godzilla of the hills. We hear you. Thing of thunder! Hark! Come down aching, groaning with your bounty . . . ship of my people . . . ol' thing. Thing of worship. Holy. Holy. Holy. Smeared. Hot. And dented. Red temple. Green temple. Bronze brown. Poor man's debt. Rich man's debt. You don't come easy. In the kingdom of grim weather, in the kingdom of great wood, in the kingdom of durable men, metal is supreme.

They've got you built with big lights on the loader now . . . new idea . . . so men can work all night, the grim feeler, the oversized halting grasp, reaching on and on and on and on throughout the hours to make another load, to make another twenty loads, another fifty loads, another hundred loads, another thousand. How many loads to make a payment to the company? How many to replace your busted springs? Ol' thing, you want to lay down and die, don't you . . . every moving metal part preplanned to seize, to implode, to ruin. Ol' thing of dread. Ol' heartbeat. Ol' bread 'n' butter. Axis of the earth. No laying down yet! It is not finished. What is your wish? Another motor? Another two transmissions? More tires? Oh, tricky, smoky, stuttering goddamn bastard, you. No laying down yet! But soon. Soon. When it is really the finish. No trees. No men. No bills.

The World from Bellevue Street

Gerry Boyle

Even in winter the downtown streets of Camden are full of hunched red-faced tourists, holding their hats to their heads as they inspect the wares of the shops: paintings of sailboats and farmhouses, tea cozies with chickadees, salt and pepper shakers in the forms of rosy but inexplicably bright-eyed Maine lobsters.

If you live in Maine, Camden is one of the places you take guests who have been cooped up too long in your house. There are "Maine" things to see there—the bay, the harbor, the view from Mt. Battie—and you can always find something to buy and something else to eat.

That's what we did with our company one winter afternoon, coming in out of the cold to a lunch of clam chowder, hot and thick. After the chowder had thawed us from the inside out, we finished our coffee and headed home. Driving west out of town into the setting sun, we traversed the tree-lined roads that lead back to the other Maine, from whence we had come.

And in a day or two, when the visitors had returned south, I drove over to one of the places I go to regain my bearings—Bellevue Street in Winslow.

Winslow is in central Maine, across the Kennebec River from Waterville. It used to boast a bustling paper mill and a high school where the Black Raiders sports teams were a force to be reckoned with. The Black Raiders still win, but the mill is closed, and if there was little obvious reason for tourists to visit the town before, now there's virtually none.

I don't know why I take such satisfaction in keeping this corner of Maine for myself. I started doing it nearly thirty years ago, slipping in here on what I thought was a temporary visa and soon deciding to apply for central Maine citizenship. Now my adopted county is Kennebec. If I ever have doubts about the wisdom of my decision, places like Bellevue Street sweep them away like the ice chunks that float downriver each spring.

Bellevue Street is a side street shaped like a wide letter U. Both ends poke out across from St. John Catholic Church, which is one of the anchors of the community today, but probably was even more so when the mills in Winslow and Waterville were running full tilt. Back then Winslow and Waterville were populated mostly by French-speaking immigrants from Quebec, many of whom manned paper machines and looms and, when their shifts were over, walked home to places like Bellevue Street.

On the longer stretch of the street there are houses on only one side. They're tenements mostly, with wooden staircases on the outside walls, glassed-in porches, a single-family house or two mixed in. The houses have seen better days, and when I stopped last time, there was stuff piled on porches, beside front steps: a cockeyed gas grill, broken easy chairs dusted with snow, bicycles whose riders had grown up and moved on, unidentifiable objects shrouded in blue tarps—the way you store things when you don't have room indoors, where the houses stand shoulder to shoulder.

Across the street is a small, grassy area with two aluminum benches. They face the edge of a bluff, its steep slope bristling with sumac, like a barricade set out to keep marauders at bay. The sumac is low and doesn't obstruct the "bellevue," which includes Bay Street, with its riverfront businesses, a stretch of the Kennebec River, the brick-walled mills on the far shore, the streets of Waterville laid out like one of those miniature villages people set up under Christmas trees. The vista is marked by steeples: churches (Protestant and Catholic, built in that order), the Colby College library and chapel atop Mayflower Hill.

Sometimes as I sit on the bench atop the bluff, my gaze is drawn to these distant landmarks. Other times it's pulled closer: traffic moving on Bay Street, people walking in and out of the Tropical Sunsations tanning parlor, cars lining up at the drive-thru of Dunkin' Donuts, the delivery guy leaving Car Quest auto parts. Until a couple of years ago, if you were on the bench first thing in the morning, you could watch clients coming to the methodone clinic. The clinic—frequently criticized by local police as a potential threat to public safety—has since moved out of town.

There is only one business on Bay Street that relates even nominally to waterfront and that's the Lobster Trap restaurant. The Lobster Trap has tables out on a deck that overlooks the river and the former Hathaway Shirt Co. factory on the Waterville side. The lobsters come from the coast, of course, but they could come from the lowest, salty reaches of the Kennebec, below Bath some forty miles away. I like to think of the river tumbling over Ticonic Falls (the view to the right from Bellevue Street), rolling south through Augusta, Gardiner, the wide expanse of Merrymeeting Bay, then battling the incoming tide in the guts above Bath, to complete itself with a flourish by Popham Beach.

Above Bellevue Street, the mighty Kennebec travels almost incognito, though, rolling past the mills, pooling above the hydro-electric plant with its art-deco windows, recruiting the waters of the Sebasticook River at the confluence to my left. But it's the same river that once functioned as a highway to and from the coast, used for centuries by native tribes and just once by Benedict Arnold on his ill-fated mission to conquer Quebec City. I remember a fellow a few years ago who, for a hundred-dollar barroom bet, went over the rapids at spring high water in a kid's raft. He survived to collect on his bet, but local rescuers, who dispatched all sorts of equipment in anticipation of his demise, billed him for their time so the enterprise was a net loss.

Today these reaches of the Kennebec draw striper fishermen, kayakers, and bald eagles, which range up and down the river year round. You can spot the eagles from Bellevue Street, flapping easily on their six feet of wing, rising to cross the bridges, circling back over busy Bay Street, never in any sort of rush. There is a timeless patience to the eagles and to the river itself, cleaned up since its industrial days. It's as if the Kennebec knows it's the reason these communities exist, that it will be here long after they are not. The communities themselves remain self-reliant, through good times and through bad, a little insular, maybe, but confident in their ability to survive.

Sitting on my bench, I've often considered the stoic independence that is part of the appeal of this part of Maine. I think of the many, many people I wrote about in the *Morning Sentinel* over the years. As I scan the rooftop, I can even pick out, at least roughly, where some of them lived. An old man in Waterville's South End, for instance, who brought me into his kitchen to tell me about what it had been like when his neighborhood was all French-speaking. He went to the refrigerator and got us both beers: Miller High Life, even though it was ten o'clock in the morning.

I recall, too, migrant workers from Guatemala, living in a furniture-less apartment, ten men to a room. A kid in a tiny apartment, flanked by her karate trophies, her proud mother beaming. Murder scenes—I remember three off the top of my head—where crowds gathered, somber faces illuminated by the police cars' flashing blue lights.

There was a woman, middle-aged and anonymous, who walked every day to her father's grave in the Grove Street cemetery—marked by tall trees from my vantage point on Bellevue Street. After I wrote about her visits in the newspaper, she sent me a letter on flowered paper. She said it was the first time anyone had written anything about her father. He deserved to be remembered, she said, not for any grand public accomplishments, but because he was a good man.

He never would have asked to be recognized, not in the way our culture seems to demand these days. If we can't get fifteen minutes of fame, we'll take fifteen seconds. A ballgame on TV inevitably includes people waving at the camera. We define ourselves by who knows about us, who admires us for whatever reason, and too often we design our lives with that celebrity in mind. If you live a good life and no one hears about it, is it still a good life?

This is the sort of question that comes to mind when I sit on the benches on Bellevue Street looking down at this corner of the world.

To my left, in the distance, is Fort Halifax, historic but largely unheralded. The fort was built on the sandy point where the Sebasticook flows into the Kennebec, a favorite stopping place for the Native Americans who plied the rivers, and for the English, who built a fort and trading post in 1754. A single blockhouse survived until the spring of 1987, when the rivers flooded and swept away the blockhouse (along with several entire houses on nearby Lithgow Street). The houses were never found, but someone did locate several of the hand-hewn beams from the blockhouse miles down river. They hauled them back and built a new blockhouse around them. It stands on the shore of the Sebasticook just across from Bee's Snack Bar, which overhangs the river and, remarkably, withstood the roaring waters. After the flood receded, they put a sign on the diner above the window at the high-water mark. Someone left out a letter so the sign says, "We surived the 87 Flood." The sign still hangs there, uncorrected. After all, you know what they meant.

Now all fixed up, Fort Halifax Park is a hopping place in the summer. Thousands of people come for fireworks on the Fourth of July. There is a big bandstand there now, too, and musical acts appear regularly. I stopped last year and there was an Elvis impersonator. In his jumpsuit and sunglasses, he was a pretty close likeness, handsome and a good singer, too. He did one Elvis hit after another, pointing to the members of his invisible band (actually a karaoke machine) and working up quite a lather. At the end of each number he wiped his brow with his scarf and then tossed it to someone in the audience, which was small in number but long on enthusiasm. Most of the people in the crowd were women who had been young when Elvis was. They grabbed for the sweaty scarves and, laughing, pretended to swoon.

It makes me smile to think of it, but I don't want anyone to think I'm poking fun. It would be an easy thing to be cynical about, and I suppose the same could be said about a lot of what I've described here. But this is my Maine, as it is for all the people who live here. It's a place where parents have sacrificed for their children, many of whom have moved away. It's a place where people go about their business and don't expect a public pat on the back. It's a place of natural beauty that doesn't usually make the guidebooks.

And it's a place newcomers discover and some, like me, find that it gets under their skin. But it isn't at all like Camden, and people who read this and come to visit may be disappointed.

Or maybe they'd get it, appreciate the beautiful Kennebec, the steepled town, the view that is like a slice of history. Perhaps they'd understand that if one considers the panorama from the bluff carefully enough, the community opens up like one of those prehistoric middens they've cut in half and exhibited at the Maine State Museum.

Much as I love the view from Bellevue Street, I know there are other places, like Camden, that may appeal more to the visitors who want to see "Maine." Yes, the chowder is good there, but for us, it's a long drive home.

The Ogre and I

Elaine Ford

I'm not sure why he befriended me. Clayton Smith was a fixture of the church and community, a Mainer born and bred, as his forebears had been for six generations. I was from away, a newcomer to the state, and the best part of thirty years younger than he. In 1985, soon after my husband and I moved to Milbridge, a small coastal town in Washington County, I began to attend services at the Congregational Church. Inexorably I became drawn into the life of the church—Clayton's church. For a time the venerable deacon observed me singing in the choir and helping out at bean suppers, and he must have decided I was all right.

In 1985 Clayton was a balding man with a florid face and a bulldog set to his jaw, of modest height, his build best described as portly. Gold-rimmed spectacles rested on a nose that managed to be hooked and stumpy at the same time. He always came to church in a suit and tie, and he came every week, sitting in a front pew—perhaps so he could hear the sermon better, perhaps to serve as a role model for more frivolous parishioners, who tended to bunch up in the rear. He favored suspenders, sometimes striped, and in summer a poplin bucket hat with a brim.

No question about it, Clayton's severe expression scared people off. Words that leap to their lips when recalling him all these years later are "gruff," "disapproving," "crusty." I too found him intimidating. For some reason, though, Clayton began to converse with me at coffee hour, greeted me in an amiable way when we happened to meet in the post office, and, the following August, mentioned that if my husband and I cared for wild blueberries, they could be had for the picking out on his land. At the time I didn't realize how astonishing an invitation this was from a man as private about his home and property as Clayton. I suspect that in his old age he was not sorry to have a few friends who hadn't long ago pegged him as a curmudgeonly stubborn old tightwad.

Clayton Smith was born in 1911 in Machias, the shiretown of Washington County, less than fifty miles from the Canadian border, and spent his boyhood there. His father worked as a sawyer in a lumberyard. For well over a century Clayton's ancestors had felled and hauled and processed trees in Washington County; his great-great-grandfather, Turner Smith, a lumberman, had been born in Machias in 1799. Working with wood was as natural to Clayton as his unapologetic Maine accent. However, he determined not to content himself with the lumber business as a means of earning a living. At the age of nineteen he earned a teaching certificate from Washington State Normal School, the earliest incarnation of the University of Maine at Machias, right there in his hometown. The following year he married Vonette Chipman, one of three daughters of a lobster fisherman. She'd grown up in Milbridge, thirty miles to the south on Route 1.

"Von was a Chipman," Clayton told me, after we'd come to know each other, his pride wrestling down his modesty. "And a Strout on her mother's side." In Milbridge that means something: Strouts settled in the area before 1794; Chipmans and Strouts from the town fought in the Civil War. In 2008 the phonebook listed eight Chipman and seventeen Strout families in Milbridge alone, with many more scattered throughout the county.

Clayton's first teaching job was in the town of his wife's birth. Subsequently he taught in Rockport, Hallowell, Farmingdale, Manchester, Old Town, and Bangor. Along the way he acquired B.A. and master's degrees from the University of Maine, as well as four sons. He was a selectman in Farmingdale and a member of the 96th Maine State Legislature. Not surprisingly, among the courses he taught was shop. I can picture him admonishing his woodworking students: "Measure nine times and cut once."

When Clayton retired from teaching in 1972 he purchased a tract of land on the Kansas Road in Milbridge. The Kansas Road is located as far inland as is possible in a coastal Maine town, hence, perhaps, the road's name, which evokes cornfields rather than tides. A more colorful explanation, given to me by a town historian, has to do with the era known as Bleeding Kansas, in the 1850s, when the territory was riven by violent disagreement over whether Kansas should be admitted to the union as a free or slave state. Since the rural Maine road's inhabitants were constantly squabbling—no doubt about more mundane issues than slavery—other citizens began to refer to it as the "Kansas" road, a battleground where hotheads were forever at each other's throats, and the name stuck. Whether that story is apocryphal or not, Clayton enjoyed presenting himself as the Old Man of the Kansas Road.

Having built his house with his own hands, he was more than a little proud of it: a boxy white no-nonsense structure with spacious garage, everything kept up in spiffy condition. The house sat on the top of a rise, his acres sloping down through wild blueberry fields to the Narraguagus River. His vegetable garden was enormous. In the tough clay he cultivated jungle-like stands of rhubarb, dozens of tomato plants, beans both pole and bush, several varieties of potatoes, sweet corn, peas, wildly enthusiastic raspberry canes, cantaloupes, pumpkins the size of boulders. He refused to run a hose out to his crops. Maybe his instincts told him that watering, like certain other issues of life and death, was God's bailiwick and gardeners best not interfere with His plan. "Waterin'," he liked to say, "makes for shallow roots." I suspect that in his heart he believed the same was true of human beings.

Taking him up on his invitation, my husband and I often picked blueberries in Clayton's fields, with his blessing. The first time we squatted among the bushes with our plastic containers he came down from his house to pass the time of day. "Those berries, I don't spray 'em," he remarked. "Infested with maggots, ya know." Arthur and I looked at each other. Was this a test? Were we silly people from away who would pass up free provisions out of squeamishness—or not? Well, if wild blueberries are small, we figured, their maggots are a whole lot smaller, invisible to our eyes, and we took quarts of the fruit home anyway. I guess we passed his examination.

Though forbidding of mien, Clayton wasn't a loner, and he always found plenty to do with his time. He was a Shriner and a Mason, holding offices with imposing titles like District Deputy Grand Master and Assistant Grand Lecturer. In Milbridge he was an active member of the Pleiades Lodge on Bridge Street, across from the church. Especially in the winter, when he couldn't garden, he spent much of his time making wooden toys: trains of various sizes, boats, pull-toys, all brightly painted in primary colors. One day he invited me on a tour of his home shop, where he had every sort of carpentry tool, from a table saw down to delicate coping saws and baby clamps. "My wife used to do all the painting," he explained, some wistfulness in his voice. "After Von passed, had to do it myself."

Clayton constructed each toy to last for generations. Among my favorite possessions are a two-tier pie carrier and a downscaled clam roller in which I stow my caps and mittens; these are the only items I recall Clayton producing that weren't intended for kids. Over the years hundreds of Clayton's donated toys, pie carriers, and clam rollers were sold at the church women's summer fair, earning considerable money for worthy purposes. H.O.M.E., a grassroots organization in Orland that provides skills for low-income people to help them climb out of poverty, also received bushels of his toys to sell in its store. He supported charities that don't offer handouts, but instead encourage the poor and disadvantaged to become self-sufficient. One Sunday morning he stood up in church and delivered an impassioned speech in favor of Heifer Project, another such enterprise, this one in aid of ragged peasants in foreign lands. His vegetables may have thirsted after rain, but he couldn't abide the idea of people sitting around aimlessly, waiting for their luck to turn.

In the words of a longtime parishioner, "Clayton was not afraid to give you his opinion." Females, for example, shouldn't be deacons;

it wasn't fitting for them to be serving communion. Another venerable member of the congregation, a woman Maine-born and raised, just like Clayton, says, "He was—what do you call it? A chauvinist." When he held the office of church moderator he ran a tight ship, according to the clerk who served under him; he had no patience for idle tongue-wagging in council meetings and would cut a blabber off in mid-sentence. He viewed with disdain a good many of the laws and regulations concocted by the federal government and Augusta, especially those involving taxes. He didn't hesitate to tell you how to compose a chowder or a berry pie, and he was expert at both himself. Nobody made biscuits like Clayton's. On one memorable occasion he prepared fish chowder and biscuits for an entire church supper, insisting on doing every bit of the work single-handed. When the meal was over, one of the church women, no mean cook herself, ventured into the kitchen to inquire how in the world he'd got the haddock to hold together that way instead of disintegrating into the soup. He revealed his secret: "Lay the fillets out on wax paper, salt em good, and let em set awhile before they go in the pot." She went home and tried it, and it worked.

I didn't know his wife, Von. I have only a fleeting memory of a frail and wispy old lady; she died in 1986, just months after we moved to town. I'm told she was a fine quilter who taught the church women the craft, beginning their tradition of turning out a group-effort quilt every year to raffle off for the church coffers. Like her husband Von was meticulous, and like him, she believed there was only one way to do something: the right way, her way. Though her insistence was quietly expressed, I have to wonder whether her opinions and her husband's didn't occasionally collide. A few months before he died Clayton participated in a Maine Humor Night at the church. The story he chose to read was about a couple who quarrel over something absurd and don't speak to one another for eight years, communicating only through their cat, Calvin Coolidge. Of course it all comes right in the end. Whether the choice of story gives us any insight into Clayton's marriage I wouldn't dare guess, but the union lasted for more than a half century, and as a widower he spoke of Von with great affection.

For a Christmas Eve service in 1988 I wrote a play, an updating of the nativity story set in Maine, and persuaded Clayton to act in it. His role—a star turn—was that of Smitty, a diner counterman who's tight with his money, suspicious of the government and strangers, reluctant to let hippie tourists spend the night in his nice clean barn. He played the part with masterly comic timing and a stage presence he'd no doubt acquired in his years of teaching. Thanking him after the service, I half apologized for the all-too-recognizable role I'd stuffed him into. "Oh, I knew right off the bat I was typecast," he said without cracking a smile.

Even odder than my friendship with Clayton was the one between Clayton and the minister, Earl Lowell. The men grew close after Von died and Earl's wife, seized by a women's-liberation impulse inexplicable to the congregation, tossed her gentle husband out of the house and sued for divorce. Earl and Clayton were a strange match: the dig-in-your-heels deacon, who'd seldom if ever left the state of Maine, and the Brooklyn-born, easy-going doctor of divinity, a former dean at a community college in upstate New York, who'd retired to Milbridge and then got un-retired in a hurry because the parish needed a preacher. These newly minted bachelors made the rounds of public suppers and all-you-can-eat fish fries from one end of the county to the other, probably more night life than they'd had in their two lives combined up until then.

Around 1987 Clayton sold Earl, at below market value, a parcel of land across from his house on the Kansas Road, and the congregation—including Clayton, of course—commenced to helping their minister build a house on the lot. I think the understanding between the two men, whether stated or not, was that Earl would keep an eye on Clayton in his declining years. However, there was a hitch: Earl, though a much younger man, declined before Clayton. Doctors found a malignant tumor lodged against Earl's pelvic bone, and he endured surgery and months of chemotherapy before returning to live in his not-quite-finished house across the road from Clayton's. Earl emerged from his ordeal with a terrible limp and a dire prognosis, but in spite of the odds everyone hoped for the best. And then one day Clayton shocked us all by announcing that he'd made up his mind to sell his house and move to Belfast to live with one of his married sons. The friendship between the men faltered. I don't know the precise grievances on either side, but my guess is that abandonment was the kernel of it, Earl angry at Clayton for fixing to move away, and Clayton angry at Earl for fixing to die. Several years after both had, in fact, died, I wrote a story that used this situation. What follows is a scene from the story, de-fictionalized. Clayton is holding a garage sale, and Earl, who's interested in a set of bunk beds Clayton advertised, decides to walk across the road and look them over. Curious to find out what's up with Clayton, I tag along.

Clayton had moved his truck and tractor-mower out of the garage and set up boards and sawhorses inside. On the planks, in heaps and stacks and boxes, were all manner of household goods. Dozens of canning jars, the kind with glass lids that clamp on. His wife, Von, had been noted for the quality of her preserves, and she'd apparently assembled quite a stock of jars. Pairs of rubberized boots in various sizes and stages of decay. Three or four toasters. Ancient electrical tools with frayed cords: Who knew when one might come in handy. Two bedroom dresser lamps, milk glass painted with roses, pink ruffled shades. At the back of the garage, in a lawn chair, presiding over the dispersal of the earthly remains of his whole past life, sat Clayton, glowering.

"Well, Clayton," I said, "this is a surprise."

"Guess you don't read the paper."

"Not the yard sale ads." I picked up a dented aluminum six-cup percolator and peered underneath. "You didn't put any prices on, Clayton?"

He grunted. "Make me an offer."

Oh no, I wasn't going to play that game. Offer too much and he'd think you a fool. Offer too little and he'd take it as an insult. I set down the coffee pot and began to examine some Christmas tree ornaments in a flimsy box stamped Made in Occupied Japan. "So you're really going to move," I said. Meanwhile, Earl had put on a pair of

hunting boots and was stomping around in them. He spotted someone he knew on the lawn and went traipsing out of the garage,
rawhide laces trailing behind. "Didn't you tell me the only way you'd
leave this house would be in a pine box?"

"Those ornaments are antique," Clayton said.

Nineteen Forty-six? If that's antique so am I. "How much do you
want for them?"

"How much are they worth to you?"

Oh, well, why not let him think me a fool? "How does seven dollars sound?" I said, figuring that was the absolute tops he could expect for them in his garage.

"Eight," Clayton said.

"Seven-fifty."

"Done." As I was counting singles out of my wallet, Earl came
limping back into the garage, the rawhide laces dragging on the concrete. They'd collected some twigs and a shriveled leaf.

"Those boots suit you?" Clayton asked.

"A little snug," Earl said.

"That's because they're stiff. Nobody's been wearin' 'em lately."

Forty years or so, I thought.

"You walk around in 'em, they loosen right up."

Or he could always lop his toes off.

The bunk bed parts, boards of varying widths and lengths, leaned
against a wall of the garage. If it hadn't been for the scuffed blue
paint on them, you'd have thought they were just a bunch of old
planks stacked together for no particular reason. The mattresses must
long since have been hauled to the dump. Clayton noticed Earl eyeing
the planks and said, "You interested in those beds?"

Right away I saw that Earl wasn't going to play games with Çlay-
ton; in fact, the idea would never enter his mind. They were friends,
buddies. Eating partners. Companions in misery. Those are the kind
of people you're above-board with. "Sure am," Earl said.

From the depths of the lawn chair Clayton said, "Make me an
offer." It was so dim in that garage you couldn't see the expression
on his face.

I stopped breathing, sensing that something awful was about to happen.

"Fifty dollars," Earl said heartily. Generously, or so he must have believed.

Clayton scrunched down farther into the lawn chair. "Made those bunk beds," he said in a voice you could hardly hear. Nevertheless, a summer person inspecting one of the frilly-shaded lamps swiveled her head to catch what he was saying. "For my boys."

"I know," Earl said, his face bright and cheery. "It's good they'll be put to use again."

"I don't accept your offer," Clayton said, dropping each word like a wad of biscuit dough.

"Fifty dollars, and not a penny less."

Oh my God, I thought. Earl must think Clayton's angry because he offered too much! I wanted to sprint over and drag Earl out of the garage, but three long planks balanced on sawhorses and loaded with possessions intervened.

Slowly Clayton rose out of the lawn chair, like a backhoe out of a bog. The inner corners of his eyes almost met and his wattles quivered. "I do not. Accept. Your offer," he said.

I gripped the box stamped Made in Occupied Japan. One or two ornaments crunched in the box.

On his way out of town Clayton left the bunk bed pieces, painted like new, propped up against Earl's bulkhead door: a gift or apology. He thought he'd left the Kansas Road and Washington County for good. But Clayton's house didn't attract a buyer, because, to the surprise of no one, he'd put way too high a price on it. The value for him—the work he'd invested in building and maintaining it, the shelter he'd provided for his family, the connection with the land and his roots—didn't jibe with the number of dollars that some retiree from New Jersey would be willing to fork over. No waterfront to speak of, just the stony Narraguagus below a few acres of scrubby bushes and woods, and a plain house, after all. But Clayton was incapable of seeing the situation through New Jersey eyes. For a while he stewed in

Belfast, worrying that his property was going to wrack and ruin in the hands of those numb realty people and soon wouldn't be worth a thin dime. Then he came back and camped out in his all-but-empty house, hiring and firing a succession of hapless real estate agents, living in the company of ghosts. I'm certain more than money pulled him home. Only after he'd died, and his heirs were free to strike a more realistic deal, did the house finally sell.

In the last year of his life Clayton knew he had a brain aneurism; it could blow at any time, and that would be that. He revealed this circumstance to me in his usual matter-of-fact way and I asked in alarm, "Isn't there something they can do?"

No, he replied, but it doesn't matter. "I've made my peace."

Clayton E. Smith died June 8, 1991, at the age of 80.

Winter, from *Northern Farm*

Henry Beston

O ur house stands above a pond, a rolling slope of old fields leading down to the tumble and jumble of rocks that make the shore. We do not see the whole pond, but only a kind of comfortable bay some two miles long and perhaps a mile or so across. To the south lies a country road, a wooded vale, and a great farm above on a hill; across and to the east are woods again and then a more rural scene of farms and open land. It is the north, and as I set down these words the whole country lies quiescent in the cup of winter's hand.

Last night, coming in from the barn, I stood awhile in the moonlight, looking down toward the pond in winter solitude. Because this year winds have swept the surface clean of early snows, the light of the high and wintry moon glowed palely upwards again from a somber, even a black, fixity of ice. Nothing could have seemed more frozen to stone, more a part of universal silence.

All about me, too, seemed still, field and faraway stand of pines lying frozen in the motionless air to the same moonlit absence of all sound. Had I paused but a moment and then closed the door behind me, I probably would have spoken of the silence of the night. But I lingered a longish while, and lingering found that the seeming stillness was but the interval between the shuddering, the mysterious outcrying, of the frozen pond. For the pond was hollow with sound, as it is sometimes when the nights are bitter and the ice is free from snow.

It is the voice of solid ice one hears and not the wail and crash and goblin sighing of moving ice floes such as one hears on the wintry St. Lawrence below the Isle of Orleans. The sounds made by the pond are sounds of power moving in bondage, of force constrained within a force and going where it can. The ice is taking up, settling, expanding, and cracking across, though there is not a sign of all this either from the hill above or from the shore.

What I first heard was a kind of abrupt, disembodied groan. It came from the pond—and from nowhere. An interval of silence followed, perhaps a half note or a whole note long. Then across, again from below, again disembodied, a long, booming, and hollow utterance, and then again a groan.

Again and again came the sounds; the night was still yet never still. Curiously enough, I had heard nothing while busy in the barn. Now, I heard. Neither faint nor heavy-loud, yet each one distinct and audible, the murmurs rose and ended and began again in the night. Sometimes there was a sort of hollow oboe sound, and sometimes a groan with a delicate undertone of thunder.

As I stood listening to the ice below, I became aware that I was really listening to the whole pond. There are miles of ice to the north and a shore of coves and bays, and all this ice was eloquent under the moon. Now east, now west, now from some far inlet, now from the cove hidden in the pines, the pond cried out in its strange and hollow tongue.

The nearer sounds were, of course, the louder, but even those in the distance were strangely clear. And save for this sound of ice, there seemed no other sound in all the world.

Just as I turned to go in, there came from below one curious and sinister crack that ran off into a sound like the whine of a giant whip of steel lashed through the moonlit air.

My old friends and neighbors, Howard and Agnes Rollins, used to tell me that the ice often spoke and groaned before a big storm. I must watch the glass and the wind and the northeast.

[To David McCord]

We have had a first snow. It came at nightfall and was more sleet than snow, clicking at the panes like witches' fingernails, and volleying against the sides of the woodshed and the long, peaked roof in wild outbursts of wilder sound. Twice in the night, the inner house all still, the darkened world without all one vast fury, I got up to replenish the stoves—a figure in a red dressing gown going from one bed of coals to another, popping in generous billets to burn the rest of the night, and discretely tending to draughts and closing iron doors, fitting back lids. The next night, all stars and cold and lonely wildness, we had a fine show of Northern Lights over the new snow. By daylight, such a sifted whiteness brings out all the rusts and russets in a winter landscape. It was a day without birds.

It is the full midwinter, the season of snow, ear-tingling cold, and skies into whose blue the earth reflects back its own intensity of light. It is not heat but light that is returning to the world, and so glittering is the morning air and so cloudless the sky that the sun rolls up over the eastern woods like a sudden miracle of radiant gold, borrowing no red from the lower atmosphere.

No sound is more characteristic of this leafless time than the cries of blue jays from the nearer woods and the trees and buildings of the farm. Again and again, when I am busy out of doors, I hear that single screaming call across the wilderness of snow. I hear it just as the austere shadows of winter are coming to life with the sunrise, I hear it, and hear it answered, through the bright hollow of high noon. There is as yet no touch of spring in the note; it is the familiar harsh call and nothing more. Yet to us on the farms it is music, for it means that life in the air, daring, vigorous, and even jocular, is sharing the winter with us, and has not fled from us before the deep bitterness of cold.

I rarely see or hear them during January. But with February and the return of the light comes the flash of blue, and a first salute to the earth and the sun reborn.

The secret of snow is the beauty of the curve. In no other manifestation of Nature is the curve revealed in an almost abstract purity as a part of the visible mystery and splendor of the world. What I think of, as I set down these lines, is the intense and almost glowing line that a great dune of snow lifts against the blue radiance of the morning after a storm, that high, clear, and incomparable crest that is mathematics and magic, snow and the wind. How many times have I paused to stare at such a summit when I have found it barring my way at a turn of the unploughed country road! It is when winds are strong, temperatures low, and the snow almost powder-dry that you will see such monuments of winter at their best. Dunes of sand obey the same complex of laws, but the heavier sand does not have the aerial grace of the bodiless and radiant crystal that builds the snow against the sky.

A strong and almost sandy crust has surfaced over the wintry countryside of snow. For three and even four steps, it bears one's weight like a white floor, and then, alas, it cracks, and one plunges through almost to the knee. As it is too glassy to be comfortable under snowshoes, and one cannot walk with much ease, we keep to our ploughed roads and shoveled paths and make the best of it. Held in its bright tension by the cold, and little troubled by the wind, the vast and shining floor is not without its own interest. For one thing, it is on such a surface that one can observe the shadows of winter, which are unlike all other shadows of the year.

Summer is the season of motion, winter is the season of form. In summer everything moves save the fixed and inert. Down the hill flows the west wind, making wavelets in the shorter grass and great billows in the standing hay; the tree in full leaf sways its heavy boughs below and tosses its leaves above; the weed by the gate bends and turns when the wind blows down the road. It is the shadow of moving things that we usually see, and the shadows are themselves in motion. The shadow of a branch, speckled through with light, wavers across the lawn, the sprawling shadow of the weed moves and sways across the dust.

*   *   *

The shadows of winter are astronomical. What moves them is the diurnal motion of the sun. The leafless tree may shudder through its boughs, and its higher twigs and small branches sway a little to and fro, but of that gaunt and rigid motion only a ghost of movement trembles on the snow beneath. Tree-trunk and tree shape, the bird-house and its pole, the chimney with its ceaseless smoke, the dead and nodding goldenrod—the life of their shadows comes with sunrise and with sunset dies. All day long beneath these winter suns, each austere and simplified image slides glancingly from west to east with the slow and ordained progress of the dial shadow on the wall.

Today having been spent outdoors from early morning to the close of afternoon, it is these shadows I have been watching on the hardened snow. They seem to me one of the most characteristic features of the winter, and I wonder that so little is said about them by dwellers in the country.

Today's tree shadows began with the image long, aslant, and blurred. The clearer and more definite shadow-image is always near the trunk, close, that is, to the object by which the shadow is cast. At noon, I thought, there came the maximum of definition. The sun is still rather low, and the shadow reached out from the tree much more than it would in June. As the afternoon lengthened, the shadows of the higher branches, always a little blurred, grew more indistinct, leaning to the east. The whole image died away on the snow in the winter twilight smoldering in the cloud-haze to the west.

I have not the painter's eye, but I could see that the shadows were blue even as the painters show them and that the blue varied in intensity. That night, I went out awhile to watch the moon shadows, which again are astronomical, and thought certain aspects of the tree images perhaps more definite than those I had seen by day.

The moon is now very high. Utterly silent, the huge landscape, glazed with the moon, rolled on under the heavens, the shadows foreshortened and falling due north. It might have been the phantom of a summer day.

*   *   *

The seed catalogues are arriving again, and as I take them down from their brown envelopes and study them at the kitchen table, I muse again on the dogmatic assertion I often make that the country-man's relation to Nature must never be anything else but an alliance. Alas, I know well enough that Nature has her hostile moods, and I am equally aware that we must often face and fight as we can her way-wardness, her divine profusion, and her divine irrationality. Even then, I will have it, the alliance holds. When we begin to consider Na-ture as something to be robbed greedily like an unguarded treasure or used as an enemy, we put ourselves in thought outside of Nature, of which we are inescapably a part. Be it storm and flood, hail and fire, or the yielding furrow and the fruitful plain, an alliance it is, and that alliance is a cornerstone of our true humanity.

[To Mrs. F. Morton Smith, his sister-in-law]

> . . . Last night we had an ice storm to coat the trees, our prize ex-hibit being Johnny the weathervane man, who was seen this morn-ing riding the sky on a crystal steed, with four aerial icicles hang-ing one from each hoof, and one midway from the tail, and the rider himself, a little man of bright diamond, facing the comfort-able glare of the Sunday morning sun. The youngish pines look just like court ladies of the eighteenth century in big, billowy, green and crystal gowns, with the plume atop for their fantastic headdresses. One lonely glade here, all aglitter in the blue sky and the sun, looked like a ballet.

It has always been our custom to take a little stroll before we put the house to bed, merely going to the gate and back when the nights are hostile with a bitterness of cold. Now that nights more mercifully human have come with the slow and dilatory spring, we go beyond the gate for perhaps a quarter or even half a mile, walking with miry feet down the farm road and through a sound of many waters.

Tonight under a faintly hazy sky and through a light wind one can feel, but not hear, the winter is flowing downhill towards the still frozen and imprisoned pond. Out of the forests and the uplands a skein of rills is pouring, the small streams now seeking their ancient courses, now following an hour's new runnel along the darkness of a wall.

If the opening music of the northern year begins with a first trumpet call of the return of light, and the return of warmth is the second great flourish from the air, the unsealing of the waters of earth is certainly the third. As we walked tonight in a darkness from which a young moon had only just withdrawn, the earth everywhere, like something talking to itself, murmured and even sang with its living waters and its living streams.

Between us and the gate, a torrent as from an overflowing spring, half blocked by a culvert heaved by frost, chided about our feet, and making another and smaller sound found its way downhill again in the night. Farther on, where woods close in to one side and the ground is stony and uneven, there tinkled out of the tree shapes and the gloom a sound of tiny cascades falling with incessant flow into a pool together with the loud and musical plashing of some newborn and unfamiliar brook.

Cold and wet, the smell in the spring air was not yet the smell of earth and spring. No fragrance of the soil, no mystery of vernal warmth hung above the farmland, but only a chill of sodden earth, water, and old snow. I knew that if I cared to look, I could find to the north of weathered ledges in the woods such sunken, gray-dirty, and gritty banks of ice as only the spring rains find and harry from the earth.

Yet spring somehow was a part of the night, the miry coldness, and the sound of water, a part of this reluctance of winter to break camp, a part of these skies with Sirius and Orion ready to vanish in the west. The long siege was broken, the great snows were over and gone, the ice was coming down from above tidewater in the current of the great rivers, and the colored twigs of the trees were at last awake.

* * *

Walking homewards toward the farm, now listening to the sound of water, now forgetting it as we talked, we both could see that much of the pond was surfaced with open water above its floor of ice. At the foot of our own hayfields a cove facing south and east showed in liquid and motionless dark, whilst beyond, and again above the ice, lay puddles and seas whose reflected quiet of starshine was a promise of the open water soon to come.

Across the pools, at the great farm on the hill, a light suddenly went out. Our own windows shone nearby, but we did not enter, so haunted were we both by the sense of the change in the year and the continuous sound of waters moving in the earth.

When we at length entered the house, using the side door and its tramped-over and muddy step, we found ourselves welcomed by something we are very seldom aware of summer or winter—the country smell of the old house.

All old farms, I imagine, have some such rustic flavor in their walls; country dwellers will recognize what I mean. A hundred and fifty years of barreled apples, of vegetables stored in a fieldstone cellar, of potatoes in the last of the spring, of earth somewhere and never very far, of old and enduring wood and wood-smoke, too, and perhaps the faintest touch of mold from things stored long, long ago in a bin—all these and heaven knows what other farmhouse ghosts were unmistakably present in the neat room with its lamp and books. The cold and humid night had stirred the house as well as ourselves: it had its own rustic memories.

Elizabeth presently brought in two slices of apple pie and two glasses of cold milk, and for a first time I did not bother to build up the fire.

[To his brother-in-law]

> Under this warm air, under this pleasant sky, the obstinate earth
> remains as wan and pale as if it had emerged but yesterday from

under February's snow. Who shall convince these gray ledges, these rusty junipers, these sodden pastures lifted and hubble-bubbled by the frost, that their six months of winter are over and done and that "the voice of the turtle is heard in the land"?

Only the lake seems to have heard. A week ago, the ice sheet had receded from the shore, leaving a winding path of open water between its edges and the land. Within this girdle of darker water lay the continent of ice itself, treacherous-looking, and rain-colored, a world of gray. Then open water began to appear to the leeward of islands and capes; soon the open places were larger than the ice, and at the end of a lovely warm day the surface was clear. There was no wind this time to break up the ice. It melted away like ice from a window pane; one looked in the morning, it was there; one looked in the evening, and there was the lake twinkling away as if nothing had happened all the winter long. And that night the geese came back, a great flock of them flying down the north and south channel of the lake, crossing the sky at sundown with multitudinous cries and a great rushing sound of wings. Far away dogs began to bark, and then all sounds died away, and I heard the sound of our own spring running its delicate treble in the advancing night.

On a dark and none-too-warm evening, the alder swamp rings with the triumphant chorus of a whole nation of spring peepers. The living, exultant noise sounds like a frenzy of tiny sleighbells, and through it one hears the musical trilling of the common toad, and the occasional *jug-o'-rum* of a bullfrog. Heard near by, the din from the swamp is almost deafening. It is a Dionysian ecstasy of night and spring, a shouting and a rejoicing out of puddles and streams, a festival of belief in sheer animal existence.

What has come over man that he has so lost this animal faith? If he wishes to stay alive as a creature of earth, it is to this faith that he must cling at all possible cost, for let him once relax his hold, out of his own being will emerge that brood of pessimisms and despairs that will bend back his fingers till they have broken his hold on life, and with it his vital and primitive strength. The body is not all of us, though a metaphorical animal carries us all upon its back, and even as the body keeps its own mysterious wills—even such as that of the heart to beat—so must it have its own appropriate and earthly faith. It was a fine music from the marsh, and in these our times I wish that all the world had been there to hear.

Not Winter

Ann Beattie

S ummer in Maine, like any other season in Maine, is filled with contradictions. The flowers are plentiful, but it seems that many people choose to plant annuals instead of perennials, then spend the summer fretting (or are they perversely happy?) that they'll have to plant their beautiful flowers all over again next year. If you live in Maine, you come to terms with long stretches of cold, dark days that gradually prickle with sunlit spots and soothe with some not-so-frigid breezes. Everyone looks forward to the joyous arrival of spring, which quickly leads into summer—always-too-short summer. Summer is the time to repaint, to replant, to enact a kind of charade of easy life, because soon enough the days will shorten, the light will change, the birds will migrate, and the cat won't be so eager to leave the house. Summer in Maine is postcard-beautiful: enjoyable, inspiring, demanding. Demanding because there is always the knowledge that summer days are few, and that what you do or don't accomplish will bring you a sense of pride or a feeling of frustration come fall.

When people think of Maine, they often conjure up the rocky coast, the lighthouses, the sailboats on fantastically blue water. Of course the beaches are crowded by day, with mothers gathering up beach toys and smearing suntan lotion on their children's pale skin. But nighttime at the shore can be even more fun. That's when dogs and their Frisbee-throwing friends are allowed. That's when the mothers have become less-frantic wives (the children having been

tucked in bed by baby-sitters), strolling hand-in-hand with their husbands at twilight. The idea of romance, I think, is not the first thing
people associate with Maine. With Venice, perhaps. Or Paris. But
Maine? Feisty, frugal Maine, with that frigid water and those rather
fearsome seagulls? I'm not much of a romantic, but part of the reason I'm seduced by the state is the fact that you have to search a little, you have to stay awhile, to discover the romance. It isn't apparent
on the surface. Sure, any place with moonlight on the water is romantic; but there's a certain mystery to the way Maine metamorphoses
from a daytime playground to a quieter, more enigmatic, more spacious place at night.

When I was a child, my parents would drive from Washington,
D.C., to Maine most summers to enjoy the three-mile-long beach in
Ogunquit, and to see summer theater and take walks along the sand.
Like many people, they also went for the crispy fried clams and the
cool night breezes. I remember that we always remembered the previous vacation wrong and therefore never had enough sweaters, and
that the greenhead flies on the beach at dusk sent us running. Maine
seemed exotic; it might as well have been another country, it was so
different from where I grew up. I don't think it ever occurred to me
that setting lobster traps and hauling them up was hard work—I just
thought of lobster as my dinner.

The July days I spent in Maine were easy, sunny, and breezy, and
the nights were refreshingly cool. Summer seemed to be there for the
taking, and most of the people who lived there year-round were de-
pendent enough on the tourist trade to be polite; if waiters and
innkeepers were not exactly effusive, well, that was the stereotype of
the New Englander. It never occurred to me that the services they provided were bracketed in their minds by difficult winters. I didn't
think about that, about what it must be like when the snows came,
followed by snowplows. The easy summer is for vacationers, not year-
rounders, who annually have to endure a bizarre sort of Christmas in
July, with tourists like hyperventilating elves busily having fun and
preparing presents for no one but themselves. At the end of the day,
so very many lobsters sent out on steaming trays to hungry diners

must make you think that Santa has gone a little strange and come up with the same gift idea over and over again.

It's not all that fanciful to associate Christmas with summer in Maine. There are more Christmas shops than you might expect, catering to the tourist trade. What is the assumption? That winter is coming faster than you think—so you need to be reminded? As well as a way to make money, aren't those shops a little elbow in the ribs? The decorations look so incongruous on a sunny, salty day: the icicles and glittering reindeer; the miniature Christ child in the crèche. What you see around you are intensely colored flowers and, outside the tourist centers (or at least I hope so), sleek foxes and plump rabbits; the Snuglee strapped to Mom's or Dad's chest and containing a slumbering baby is the modern-day manger.

I live in Maine now half the year. I'm there not so much because of fond childhood memories as because my husband likes to sail, and he has something of a history in the state (though it isn't counted in triple digits, so I realize it doesn't count). I'm a snowbird: I run away when it looks like things might get serious. Serious means: gray days; early (if spectacular) sunsets; cold. Those times I've lingered into winter, I've been stunned that summer seems farther behind than chronological time tells me it is. It's as if grayness erases your memory of all that summer color; it's as if the days fold in on themselves, instead of expanding the way a great summer day expands.

But again, it's Maine's contradictions that make it so interesting, at least for a writer. When you take in the view, your eye always moves between the general and the particular, the faraway and the up-close: the huge stretch of the Atlantic Ocean and the tiny snail on the rocks; the large expanse of marshland and the mosquito on the tip of your nose. There can be the seductive suggestion that things are endlessly plentiful: the wild blueberries; the sunny days; the perfect photo-ops; the seemingly constant supply of fresh fish. But it isn't so: there's poison ivy growing amid the blueberries; the rain and fog will come; the sun will disappear behind a cloud just when you've found your perfect photograph; there's been too much overfishing. Sadly, there are not so many mussels as there used to be. Or scallops. Or most anything else. The truth is, Maine is a serious place masquerading as a summer paradise. A place where the price of land has driven fishermen farther from the water. Where, in a booming economy, hotels and restaurants have to import workers—often from countries far from New England. And, increasingly, a place where people camp out only for the so-called good months. Workers in my town live in group houses; everything turns on the dollar. Time-share condominiums allow everybody a moment in the very, very upscale tent.

Of course, you can also camp in the woods. The woods are . . . woods. They're the paradoxical woods of Robert Frost's famous poem, woods that are at once "lovely, dark and deep." Nature in Maine is your friend or your enemy. It depends on how you view it. And also on your luck.

Summer is my favorite time of the year in Maine. Not just because it's Not Winter, but because the season is wonderful in its own right: that's what all those cars are doing on the highway. That's why the farmer's market is as crowded as Harrods' food court. Everybody loves the same season I love; they want to be hiking Mount Katahdin and sailing on Penobscot Bay and eating wild blueberries. The clichés are really quite pleasant: the gulls that are said to swoop (no mention of the racket they make, drowning out any attempt at conversation); the boats touchingly named for men's true loves, such as the *Lovely Lucinda* (as opposed to the boats bobbing in the water that commemorate men's other love, money—like the *Puts and Calls*).

Maine takes a lot of kidding: the reputedly taciturn people, ever the butt of jokes; the blackflies, exaggerated into single-engine planes by stand-up comedians; the water that curls your toes. What do all those daytrippers want to see? They often don't make it to the farther reaches of the state, where the wind on Isle au Haut can make your ears ache so much you wish you'd brought earmuffs, and where the cliffs seem to either magnetize you to the edge or propel you back instantly, depending on your testosterone level and/or your personality. Who are they, all those people—more and more every year—who come expecting sweet corn and sweet dreams? To them, Maine is the paintings of Fairfield Porter and the Wyeths; it is the poem they memorized, though they might not quite have understood it. What to say of a place that—according to *Fodor's 2000*—is so large that all the other states of New England could fit within its perimeters?

That it offers the possibility of space. Peace. Tranquility. That it is a sort of vanished America that nevertheless exists, partly in a time warp, partly as part of the modern age. The adventurous can have their adventures—rock climbing, kayaking, deer hunting. The timid can be catered to at imposing hotels, where there are flowery cushions on wicker rocking chairs. Some of these chairs will face the water, and over the water will appear lovely sunsets and a glowing moon. Those things might be present the rest of the year wherever the tourist lives, but in Maine the spectacle is something one stops for. Summer in Maine can easily be described through synesthesia: the dawn tastes delicious; the distant mountain hums. And much of the hard work that keeps it going—that keeps New York City going, for that matter—happens behind the scenes, under cover of darkness, from the deck of a lobster boat in the predawn, from behind the wheel of a long-distance truck transporting Maine's products. There is so much, you will never know it all. It is a world that is beautiful, colorful, drenched in an indescribable light: a world that could easily be unreal, except it is not. Maine is just far away—in both distance and spirit—from other places. It is a place we stop imagining to look, and look to imagine.

Ship, Dream, Pond, Talk

Wesley McNair

The Ship

There could be no better introduction to the camp in Temple, Maine, where my wife Diane and I spend each summer and early fall, than the private road that takes you there. The line of grass at the center tells you the road has nothing to do with the beaten path. Its single lane says this journey is for nobody but you. The corner it takes as it turns off the wider road into the woods stands for seclusion and anticipation.

In free verse poetry the drama comes from an interplay of the sentence and the line, the inquisitive and restless sentence pressing on, and the line, with its image or fragment of thought, tugging back as if to say, "Pay attention to this." The road in, a long, unfolding sentence of trees and green light, has this drama. Around one curve, a patch of high meadow rue and blackberries brush against the car; beyond another, in a dark space, the track widens to avoid a small dip that held water in the spring; up ahead, the road turns yet again, ascending a short hill to disappear. Then there is a clearing where a yellow wagon wheel rests against a birch tree, and the road takes you down to your first sight of the pond.

Rising up through the trees, the pond looks like the sky and, as every visitor sees parking in the driveway and getting out for a closer view, *is* the sky, its reflection printed from the near to the far shore.

And there, down among the trunks of birch, spruce, and pine, is the camp. The door of what appears to be the front of the building is actually at the back. The front has been the back of every New England house Diane and I have lived in. What we called the front door of our farmhouse in North Sutton, New Hampshire, was really a side door; the door at the front was seldom used. We enter our current home in Mercer, Maine, through a back door beside the garage; the tall Federal façade and front lawn are on the other side of the house. So it is with the camp. When you have followed the handrails made from straight saplings down the stone steps to arrive there, the front is still farther down, a zigzag of handrail and stone away.

Is the irony of entrance into the houses of northern New England related in some way to the inaccessibility of Yankees, echoed by the irony and understatement of their speech? I have always thought so. There are practical reasons for making the side or back the front as well, of course, the main one in this case being that the front is where the pond is. Yet entering by the back door, I can never avoid the feeling that the full expression of the camp is being kept even from me as I proceed toward the screen porch and its dramatic view. The mixture of privacy and expectation is delicious.

"It's like a ship," our old friend Malcolm Cochran tells us as we give him a tour on his first visit. Malcolm means how trim and compact the camp is, each area just large enough for its function. The back door opens beside a coat closet with overhead cabinets, then leads to the upstairs hallway, at the left of which are three bedrooms. One of them, a bunk-room with custom-made beds, you pass going down a short entryway to reach the second. Opening the door of the second, you find another snug sleeping compartment, with a full-size bed; a half-dresser and rocker at the bed's foot; a recessed mirror in the wall above the rocker where books and grooming accoutrements can be kept; and as deep as the mirror's recession, enclosed storage cabinets and a clothes closet. The gas lamp above the bed is perfectly situated for reading; nearby the lamp is a hook for your glasses when you're ready for sleep, and a small screw to hang your watch on. Lying here above the ship's hold, you have the distinct feeling of being held.

Behind my small typing desk in the hallway, the next door down, is the master bedroom containing its own strategically placed gas lamp; a chest and dresser; and to the left just inside the entrance, the *pièce de résistance*, a fieldstone fireplace, its stone first appearing below the woodwork in the outside hall. The upstairs fireplace, with its creamy mortar and variegated rock, prepares the eye for the larger fireplace, which stands directly beneath it in the living room. So there are two simple materials that dominate the interior of our camp: wood and stone. They become textures you touch or rub against moving from one intimate space upstairs to the next. Going downstairs, you reach to a banister made of peeled fir poles from the nearby forest. Putting kindling and logs in the downstairs fireplace and striking a match, you draw the screen and your hand across quartz and granite gathered just outside. The stones say the same thing the simple and intimate spaces of the camp say: What you require in your life is less complicated than you thought. They say, All you need is right here around you.

On early summer mornings when no fire is necessary except the flame I start for instant coffee on the gas range in the kitchen, I step out onto the porch above the pond for a full view of Drury Pond. Standing there in the prow of the ship, I look out on water always just right for the itinerary I have in mind. Tree-lined, with only seven other cottages, mostly unoccupied, the pond calls me away from the world just as the camp itself does. On rainy days a loon pops his head up near our dock, then goes right down under again, as if to demonstrate the pleasures of deep-diving. When the weather is fair, the sun chases clouds of vapor off the pond in perfect harmony with the burner in the kitchen as it brings water for my coffee to a boil. Rain or shine, I take my morning coffee, a notebook, and a pencil to my favorite rocker on the porch, from which I can see three ponds at once: the long curve of water stretching out to Lucy Point and beyond, the encirclement of sky that appears on the pond's surface, and the imagined underworld where the loon goes diving and flying. Opening to a new page, I begin the voyage into me.

*   *   *

Dick's Dream

Above the stairs of the camp is a picture of Tor House, the stone structure built by the poet Robinson Jeffers in Carmel, California. I bought the picture—the print of a watercolor—on a California trip Diane and I took to see our oldest son and grandchildren at the same time we were moving into the camp. As I go downstairs watching this lovely print hover for a moment above my head then pass from view, I often think of the history of Jeffers's Tor House, based on a dream that was fated to disappear.

Just eighty-five years ago when Jeffers arrived at the Carmel coast by stagecoach, it was entirely undeveloped. He later wrote that when he saw the hill of rock overlooking the sea where he would settle and raise his children, it seemed to him "the inevitable place." For the next few years, he built his house and then his tower, lugging many of the stones up from the sea by himself or with the help of his sons. As he constructed the place of rock on rock (*tor* is the Gaelic word for "stone"), he and his wife added ceramic and stone from spiritual and artistic locations in Europe; created gardens, bordering them with the shells of abalone, a mollusk central to the diet of coastal Indians; inscribed doorways and panels with verse, songs, and classical mottoes that consecrated the mythology of the poetic life. One inscription that was particularly moving to me appeared in the stone near a window in the dining room: the death date of Thomas Hardy.

When Jeffers etched it, in praise and sorrow, the development all around Tor House had long since begun, driving the natural world and its creatures away and making clear to this poet that his dream house was little more than a memorial to the vision that had earlier inspired him. Today, Jeffers's house can be found only after searching the streets surrounding the beach of Carmel. The large picture window on the second floor of a neighboring house looks down into Jeffers's gardens. Imposing structures built by the wealthy are everywhere. One of them, our tour guide told us, has been named "The Inevitable Place."

I can't help but wonder if what happened around Jeffers's house will one day happen around ours on Drury Pond, free as the pond now is of Jet Skis, motorboats, and on most days, activity on its few docks. For me, our camp is a house of poetry, just as Tor House was; for Diane, a jazz singer whose lyrical voice I hear upstairs when she practices in the afternoon, it is a house of song. Inevitable as retreating to this place seems to us, we are only the latest in a series of owners that have valued its unacculturated peace since it was built in the early fifties. The most recent was Dick Vaughan, who sold us the camp after showing me its long shoreline and sharing his stories about loons and a moose he and his wife, Peg, had seen there. Above the door to the porch he had printed his name for the camp on a square of wood: "Dick's Dream."

Because Dick, a man in his seventies, had a heart condition, he asked me to help carry a canoe to his truck on the day he packed up his belongings, and when I arrived on the appointed September afternoon, he told me, a little downcast, "I just took my last swim." I wrote him in a follow-up note, "Come back any time you please." Sadly enough, he held to his word, dying six months later. Dick Vaughan's death haunted me throughout the spring we moved in, for it suddenly turned the camp and the many things he had left behind there into his last effects. It was impossible not to see how much he and Peg had cared about the place in the stone walkways and handrails they had installed; their stone-bordered garden outside the kitchen window, where perennials now sprouted; and the cabinets of the kitchen itself, painted a bright yellow, with red handles to match the small red hand-pump beside the sink. I thought of the many breakfasts that must have begun with the sound of the coffee-grinder fastened at one end of the cabinets, and of guests served with the cups and dishes inside the doors. Behind other doors there was more of the Vaughan inheritance. In the closet under the stairs, which eventually became our combination oar-storage and pantry, we found a chain lock for a canoe, various hand tools, an organizer of nails and screws in all sizes, and touch-up paint for the kitchen and all the other rooms of the camp. The upstairs closet and overhead storage areas contained sheets, blankets, and sleeping bags; inside the small bathroom off the hall, with its chemical toilet, there was a bureau bearing a colorful array of washcloths and towels.

But the most intriguing treasure was the cache of games and puzzles in well-worn boxes, some dating back to the 1960s. Who could have predicted that entertainments with names like Parcheesi or backgammon would go so quickly out of fashion with great numbers of Americans? Yet the games we discovered seemed outdated, largely forsaken by a society whose leisure time, quickly vanishing, is spent by watching television, surfing the Internet, or playing video games. What these earlier pastimes lacked was electronics. You started and played them entirely by hand, opening a game board used by two to four people. They were no less interactive than the video game, but their interaction, unlike that of the electronic diversions, was communal. The competition they offered, executed by cards and dice and tokens, involved teasing, goading, defeating, being defeated by, and having fun with family and friends. Their legacy as part of Dick's Dream suggested the loneliness of our pursuits back on the grid, and the need to spend more of our leisure with those we love.

Dick also left behind a folder of plans for a septic system he showed me when Diane and I made our first tour of the camp, thinking they would be an incentive for us to buy the property. All we had to do was provide the camp with electricity, he said, then we could build the system and put in a flush toilet. The lady who owned the upper part of our road wouldn't allow him, he told us, to erect poles for electricity, but since he had managed to get two phones in the camp by running a cable down under the water from a camp across the pond, he didn't see why we couldn't drop an electric cable under the pond. Though we were initially intrigued by the idea, it seemed dangerous and impractical to us in the end, and anyway, Diane and I decided, the camp's pristine outhouse, with its tiled floor and the tufted lid-cover for the hole, was solution enough. After buying the place, we put our potential flush money into the purchase of an adjoining piece of property, increasing our acreage around the pond, and our shore frontage to 720 feet. We did not want more of the grid, which electricity would have brought us, but more of the world off the grid.

Rejecting Dick Vaughan's wish for electricity, I have often thought of his primary motive for installing it: taking the waste away. The small fortune it would have cost him, a retired school-teacher, to put in his septic system and flush toilet, and pump the daily deposits uphill to a level area off the driveway was apparently worth the satisfaction of being able to whisk the stuff away, out of sight. A friend of mine, Denis Culley, who is a vocal environmentalist with his own outhouse, claims that our problems with the environment begin with our inability to, as he puts it, "live with our own poop." Flushing the poop away so we don't have to deal with it leads, he says, to our irresponsibility toward all the environmental waste we create. We go on from installing our flush toilets to building smoke-stacks that pipe unwanted gases high into the air above our factories and toxic waste dumps that receive our discarded chemicals—if we can find locations for them far enough outside our own towns. I do not have the answer to our environmental problems, implicated as I myself am in them. Still, keeping the outhouse, where waste remains to decompose, makes me feel a little better about my relationship with the natural world.

In one of the loveliest poems he ever wrote, "The Purse-Seine," Robinson Jeffers speaks of the allure of city lights, likening them to the terrible beauty of sardines being netted at night off the California coast:

> . . . the crowded fish
> Know they are caught, and wildly beat from one wall to
>   the other of their closing destiny the phosphorescent
> Water to a pool of flame, each beautiful slender body
>   sheeted with flame, like a live rocket
> A comet's tail wake of clear yellow flame. . . .

At our camp we are a long way from urban America. Most summer nights, the only illumination besides the light from our gas lamps comes from a camp across the pond and the moon. Sitting on our porch in the dark, apart from storefronts, blinking towers, and computer screens, I am in an America that is not yet caught. Like Jeffers and like old Dick Vaughan, I concede the attraction of our technological civilization: without that civilization, I would not have the gas that powers the lamps or, for that matter, the computer back in Mercer on which I file my poems once they are completed. Yet like those two other dreamers, I am attracted nevertheless to a world that is more beautiful and more wild.

On Drury Pond and In It

A pond, my dictionary tells me, is nothing more than "a body of water usu. smaller than a lake." The problem with the definition is that it describes a pond as a static thing, seen on a map or from the air. Looking down on Drury Pond from my porch rocker during our first summer there, I find a body of water whose essence is movement and change. So the responses to it I have written in my notebook at odd hours of the day are very different from one another:

The pond is a place of risings, the sun rising, the trees rising out of their reflections on the water to meet the sun, a fish rising to make ripples in a reflected pine. Birdsong rising.

All afternoon the pond bears the print of the wind changing its mind, swiftly dimpling the water in one direction, then the opposite. Now a long island of crinkle drifts past the camp. On the far shore waves pick up sunlight like shifting constellations, like scores of fireflies.

Before bed I take the dogs out under the moonlight, daytime on an alien planet, everything around me turned to black and gray and loneliness. Beside the canoe, small waves wash over the moon as it rests in reflection. Far away on the pond the reflected moon appears again in an eerie strip of light. Inside the camp, I look back through the door's windowpanes and find the strip of light has disappeared; by the canoe, the moon, lengthened into an oval, is boiling with waterbugs.

Looking out to the pond this morning, I eventually notice that I am looking through five thin strands of spiderweb flung from the hummingbird feeder to the eaves. Lifting in and out of sunlight, they are less conspicuous than the distant waves, but also beautiful.

What is more peaceable than a canoe resting at the dock in the sunshine as the waves slip gently under it, swaying its cane seats and their elegant crochet of shadow?

A head of clouds moves simultaneously over the distant hill and its exact reflection on the pond. Then almost indistinguishable ripples turn the reflected sky and trees into an Impressionist painting. Across it, a great blue heron flies, startlingly right-side up.

In the gathering calm of twilight I see the image I have learned to look for: blue holes that gradually appear at the end of the point between the trunks of trees which had seemed full and solid before. Through that distance, the mystery of more distance. . . .

But there are times nothing will do but to be a part of the pond's fluctuating life yourself, as happens in this paragraph from my notebook about a canoe trip with my friend Peter Harris:

Paddling out from the dock onto the still pond to travel its length of about a half-mile, we pass the long necks of birches leaning over the water and see the forested hills shift around us, no sound except the water flowing from our paddles and canoe. Gradually, the camps to our right announce themselves, Bob and Rita Kimber's first, whose weathered front is barely distinguishable behind tree trunks; then on a steep bank the blond, rectangular front of the Vogel camp, up on stilts; and finally, as we circle the far end of the pond, the small, two-story cottage owned by the Judsons, and near it, an abandoned cabin. The redwing blackbirds are gone from the lily pads of the outlet, but there are Monet-like blossoms of yellow and white floating on the water.

We paddle past them and down to Lucy Point on the pond's other side, not the dramatic jut of land the word might imply, but a gentle protrusion, named after Bob and Rita's beloved dog, who often streaked out ahead of them as they all swam toward it from the opposite shore, so anxious was she to reach it. The red camp on the other side of the point and the three others that follow complete the unfolding narrative of pondside dwellings.

Then we are starting down the inlet between more lily pads; then we are poling our way toward the beaver dam like, I tell Peter, the Indian and trapper in a nineteenth-century canvas by George Caleb Bingham. It turns out he is thinking of the very same painting. Back so far in time, our senses tuned to blooming lilies and purple jots of pickerel weed, we re-emerge at the mouth of the inlet not far from the dock where we began, in the pond of the present. As we paddle toward home, the good green roundness of Derby Mountain ascends over the water and descends deep down into it, deep down into us. . . .

Agreeable as canoeing the pond is, nothing can match being in the pond. Our lives as landlubbers require that we travel upright, placing one foot in front of the other and using our arms to help balance ourselves. In the water we lie down, making swishing motions with our feet and using our arms as the fish its fins, or the bird its wings. Moving across the top of the fish's sky, we are as close as we will ever get to the old human dream of flying, as close as we can be to our first life in the womb and our ancient aquatic past in the cycle of evolution. Is it any wonder why swimming offers such deep pleasure, why when we come out of the water, we feel at once rested and transformed?

Our pleasure begins with discarding the clothes required by our life on land, getting down to the skin we were born with. What else can explain the smiles and laughter that always accompany "skinny-dipping" in the dark, or this childlike and joyful expression we have invented for swimming with nothing on? I have seen enough friends and members of my family whoop and holler and splash each other in ponds and lakes to understand that shedding clothes and jumping into the water makes people shed civilized behavior as well and take fresh delight in one another's company. The delight can have unusual forms. Each day we went swimming on his visit last summer, my ten-year-old grandson Kevin surged out to a certain warm spot beyond our dock so he could turn back to me and exclaim, in his comical imitation of an Irish accent, "'Tis loovely!"—to which I, arriving second, invariably answered, "'Tis grand!"—after which both of us shouted at the top of our lungs, "'Tis!"

Then there is the enjoyment of the long swim in the company of a friend or spouse, where one mixes socializing with a variety of strokes, lying on one's stomach to pursue one's course, then rolling over on one's back to enjoy the talk and the view of the retreating shore and the sky. The pond, just narrow enough to travel from one shore to another and back again in a single trip, is made for the long swim.

At four or five o'clock on summer afternoons, dried off from our own swimming, Diane and I often spot Bob and Rita on their way to the opposite shore. If it is four heads we see, they more than likely belong to Bill and Juliet and their dogs, Wally and Desi, all swimming across the pond from the Kimbers' dock, Wally in the lead.

Sometimes after turning back from the other shore, the four heads approach our camp, and the whole gang pull themselves up onto our dock. There the dogs throw themselves into a shake that moves from their hindquarters to their ears and sends our dogs, Charlie and Annie, to the porch door, whining and howling. Then all four dogs are romping joyfully off through the trees, and Jules and Bill are settling into chairs on the porch beside us.

On the afternoon I have in mind, it is near the end of our first camp summer, and Juliet is approaching the end of her pregnancy. Sitting in her two-piece bathing suit, she looks as if she is holding a giant egg in her lap.

"She's kicking," Jules says, already knowing that the egg contains a girl. "Can you see it?"

I'm not sure where to look until Bill leans over to point out where the feet are. "She's upside-down," he says, and suddenly I do see it, the tiny signal from inside the egg, understanding now that the reason Jules strokes her wide middle every so often during our conversation is to send her own message, her hello back.

"Isn't it hard to swim when you're carrying all that weight?" I ask her.

"The water buoys me up," she says. "Actually, the only time I'm free of the weight is when I'm swimming."

I imagine Juliet and the baby-to-be swimming at the same time, one outside and the other inside. Then I think about the birth that could happen any day now, though it is officially days away, excited, like everyone around me, by this event that will change our two friends from a couple into parents of a new child. Before they go, Diane wants pictures of them, and as they sit together in the two rockers, Juliet in her two-piece and Bill in his trunks, he presses his stomach out a little to help create what is destined to become the most famous snapshot on the roll: Mr. and Mrs. Pregnant.

When they leave, Wally is the first one into the water, and Desi, apprehensive as ever, the last. While Bill and Juliet swim farther away, calling him, Desi paces the dock and twitches and wags, becoming so upset that he jumps into the canoe, then out again. But at last he is in the water and swimming into the distance toward the others until they are all, once more, four heads. As they swim farther still, there are six heads: Wally, Bill, Juliet, Desi, and bobbing nearby them, unmistakable in our binoculars, two loons.

Talk

Most of Drury Pond's wildlife is difficult or impossible to see. That there are short-tailed weasels around us we know only because one awful day we found one, a small, exquisite creature our cat had killed and left as a gift outside the camp's back door. We know there are great horned owls because we hear them calling and responding to each other in the darkness with their eerie "whos." The whos that owls hunt—voles, shrews, and rabbits—must therefore be in plentiful supply. If you are outside at night at just the right time, you might see the wake of a beaver as it swims back home with a branch in its mouth under the moonlight. Walking along a pathway in the woods in the daytime, you might find a snake slithering into the leaves, or more rarely, a bright orange newt.

Occasionally Diane and I see moose foraging near Lucy Point, and once we were startled by the presence of a mother and calf, both staring curiously at us from the shore off our own dock. But the wild creatures most evident on the pond during the day are birds. Observe long enough and you're likely to catch, for instance, the gangly and graceful flight of a blue heron as it makes its way across the pond to one end or the other where the marshlands are. Loons are also a common sight. In early summer this year, when two of them were mating, they surprised me with a medley of strange tunes (loony tunes?) consisting of shrieks, sighs, and giggles I never knew loons were capable of. As Diane's petunias sprouted blossoms off the camp porch, hummingbirds appeared in tiny blurs. We have often seen pairs of ducks. And once there was a goose that landed in a tree.

"It's on one of the top branches, just off our shore," Diane told Bob on the phone. "I think it's gone to sleep up there." A member, with Rita, of the regional Audubon Society, Bob had never heard of a goose in a tree. The two of them drove over immediately from their house in Temple to see it for themselves. Sure enough, there on a high branch that seemed too small for it was a large bird with brown wings and an orange bill. Yet by the time the Kimbers arrived to circle the tree and search their bird books, even Diane had begun to question whether it was a goose: its color was too dark, for one thing, and besides, its neck was too straight and skinny. In the final verdict of the Kimbers, the goose was actually a double-crested cormorant. We all agreed as the Kimbers departed that even though Diane had gotten the bird's identity wrong, she deserved full credit for our shared wonder at this being none of us had ever seen on this pond before.

The discovery of wildlife is always more gratifying when you can share it with others, and some of my favorite talk at the camp consists of the agitated whispers inspired by, say, a gaggle of geese—real ones this time—skidding to a stop at the pond's center, or the sudden appearance of moose. Working on one of the puzzles inherited from the Vaughans with Bob or Bill, I engage in a different sort of talk. In her poem "The Moose," about a long bus journey in Nova Scotia that leads to a more northerly encounter with a moose, Elizabeth Bishop describes the "dreamy divagation" of "an old conversation / . . . recognizable, somewhere / back in the bus," the voices

> uninterruptedly
> talking, in Eternity:
> names being mentioned,
> things cleared up finally;
> what he said, what she said . . .

The passengers on Bishop's bus talk, she says, "the way they talked / in the old featherbed / peacefully, on and on." For me this leisurely and peaceful conversation is also like the kind that happens when people work together on a puzzle, their talk interspersed by comments on the puzzle's progress as someone locates a missing piece of landscape or sky and pats it into place. My guess is that a hundred years ago when the farm women of the region did their quilting or families shelled beans, they conversed this way, too. Their hands busy with mechanical activity, they were no doubt free to let their minds roam, just as we are doing our puzzle—as, for that matter, Elizabeth Bishop was when she worked on "The Moose," busying herself with the four- to seven-syllable count of each line while she talked and dreamed her poem's content.

Not all of the conversation at the camp is so peaceful as puzzle talk, but it is frequently wide-ranging and ruminative. I have often thought free verse poets could benefit from listening to the syntax of meditative conversation. When we ruminate aloud, finding with our eyes some area of the ceiling or wall that helps us match the right phrase with our thought, our sentences become longer and more elastic, expanded by words like "and," "but," "if," or "because," and punctuated by stresses of meditation and feeling that resemble the line breaks of free verse. On the porch of the camp in the afternoon, such talk is assisted by cold beer, the view of pond, woods, and sky, and a quiet so pervasive the occasional hummingbird at the feeder may seem too loud. At night in the living room, we exchange our long sentences with guests in the light of the gas lamps, which cast shadows on wood and stone. Robert Frost once remarked that poetry is "the art of having something to say," and that the poem's "better half" is "the wildness with which it is spoken." I sometimes hear in our camp talk this wildness—as if we are almost speaking poetry, as if this place wild enough to include a cormorant that sleeps in a tree had entered our speech.

It is no accident, given the natural surroundings of the camp, that our conversations with visitors sometime turn to the despoiling of nature and the senseless hunting of its creatures elsewhere. It was here Diane and Rita hatched the idea of involving PETA, the organization against animal cruelty, in an offensive to stop the practice of bear-baiting in Maine. On another afternoon Bob and I thought our way beyond the forested hills around the pond to the north of Maine, where every day more of the forest's diversity is cleared away and replaced—when it is replaced—by a narrow range of fast-growing trees that can be quickly harvested. But our talk is typically less somber and a lot less focused. When Diane's close friend Carol Hedden came for dinner, for instance, we covered family relationships; how she got involved with weaving; kinds of falling in love, including falling in love with the house where she and her husband now live; and last but not least, the migration of writers to the Temple area just before she arrived here in the late 1960s.

Since the writers who preceded me in the region included people like Hayden Carruth, George Dennison, Mitch Goodman, Theodore Enslin, and Denise Levertov, most of them poets, I was keen to know all she could tell me about their time here, and circled back to the subject as new questions occurred to me.

"Did they meet with each other regularly?" I asked her, and then,

"Was there a central figure in the group?"—wanting to know, and at the same time wanting to see Carol's earnestness as she tried to match my questions with answers, caught in the spell of memory.

"It wasn't like that," she said. "Oh, they knew each other, all right, and they would visit now and then. But there really wasn't any group," she added, shaking her head, "not as far as I remember."

Still, I am inclined to think these writers did more than social-ize—that they showed each other work in progress occasionally, just as Bill, Bob, and I do, and that having each other nearby made them feel less isolated by the solitude writing requires. This excerpt from "Questions," a recent poem by Hayden Carruth recalling his talks with the deceased George Dennison, gives proof that their relation-ship was more than incidental:

> Your voice comes to me, George, on the winter night
> In the faint mazy stars, a murmur of hesitant light
> In the air frozen solid, it seems, from here to Maine.
> . . . What are you saying, George?
> I strain to hear. Are you as smart and percipient
> As you were, can you tell me what I almost know
> In your words not mine as you used to, words
> So French and accurate I thought Descartes
> And Camus must live in you as well as Tolstoy
> And Kropotkin, words of fierce loyalties and loves
> for beautiful ideas and men and women? . . .

In any case, knowing from my own experience how this spot in West Central Maine favors solitude, with its wild places and distance from the world's traffic, I can easily see why the writers came here, and why many of them stayed—most of the rest leaving for other loca-tions off the beaten path. The rest include Carruth himself, who wrote those words to a dead friend at his farmhouse in Munnsville, New York, carrying on his conversation as all writers do, by convers-ing with himself.

Thinking of the authors who preceded me, and of my writer

friends Bill and Bob, I am never quite alone as I conduct my own interior conversation each morning on the camp porch. Besides, I have my dogs Charlie and Annie beside me; stretched out in the sun, they know that when I hold a tablet in my lap, there is nothing to do but sleep. Most importantly I have the pond, which encourages my writerly talk, just as it once encouraged George Dennison, who wrote in this passage from his book *Temple* of taking his canoe out on the pond and discovering other *isolati* like him:

> It was early evening. The pond was perfectly smooth and quiet. I paddled the full length of it, watching a beaver swim across . . . . A very handsome large loon, one we hear uphill at the house every day and every evening, swam placidly not far from me. Redwing blackbirds walked on the lily pads.

from The Sense of Wonder

Rachel Carson

One stormy autumn night when my nephew Roger was about twenty months old, I wrapped him in a blanket and carried him down to the beach in the rainy darkness. Out there, just at the edge of where-we-couldn't-see, big waves were thundering in, dimly seen white shapes that boomed and shouted and threw great handfuls of froth at us. Together we laughed for pure joy—he a baby meeting for the first time the wild tumult of Oceanus, I with the salt of half a lifetime of sea love in me. But I think we felt the same spine-tingling response to the vast, roaring ocean and the wild night around us.

A night or two later the storm had blown itself out and I took Roger again to the beach, this time to carry him along the water's edge, piercing the darkness with the yellow cone of our flashlight. Although there was no rain, the night was again noisy with breaking waves and the insistent wind. It was clearly a time and place where great and elemental things prevailed.

Our adventure on this particular night had to do with life, for we were searching for ghost crabs, those sand-colored, fleet-legged be-ings that Roger had sometimes glimpsed briefly on the beaches in daytime. But the crabs are chiefly nocturnal, and when not roaming the night beaches they dig little pits near the surf line where they hide, seemingly watching and waiting for what the sea may bring them. For me the sight of these small living creatures, solitary and fragile against the brute force of the sea, have moving philosophic overtones, and I do not pretend that Roger and I reacted with similar emotions. But it was good to see his infant acceptance of a world of elemental things, fearing neither the song of the wind nor the darkness nor the roaring surf, entering with baby excitement into the search for a "ghos."

It was hardly a conventional way to entertain one so young, I suppose, but now, with Roger a little past his fourth birthday, we are continuing that sharing of adventures in the world of nature that we began in his babyhood, and I think the results are good. The sharing includes nature in storm as well as calm, by night as well as day, and is based on having fun together rather than on teaching.

I spend the summer months on the coast of Maine, where I have my own shoreline and my own small tract of woodland. Bayberry and juniper and huckleberry begin at the very edge of the granite rim of shore, and where the land slopes upward from the bay in a wooded knoll the air becomes fragrant with spruce and balsam. Underfoot there is the multi-patterned northern ground cover of blueberry, checkerberry, reindeer moss, and bunchberry, and on a hillside of many spruces, with shaded ferny dells and rocky outcroppings—called the Wildwoods—there are lady's-slippers and wood lilies and the slender wands of clintonia with its deep blue berries.

When Roger has visited me in Maine and we have walked in these woods, I have made no conscious effort to name plants or animals, nor to explain to him, but have just expressed my own pleasure in what we see, calling his attention to this or that, but only as I would share discoveries with an older person. Later I have been amazed at the way names stick in his mind, for when I show color slides of my woods plants it is Roger who can identity them. "Oh, that's what Rachel likes—that's bunchberry!" Or, "That's Jumer (juniper), but you can't eat those green berries—they are for the squirrels." I am sure no amount of drill would have implanted the names so firmly as just going through the woods in the spirit of two friends on an expedition of exciting discovery.

In the same way Roger learned the shells on my little triangle of sand that passes for a beach in rocky Maine. When he was only a year and a half old, they became known to him as winkies (periwinkles), weks (whelks), and mukkies (mussels) without my knowing quite how this came about, for I had not tried to teach him.

We have let Roger share our enjoyment of things people ordinarily deny children because they are inconvenient, interfering with bedtime, or involving wet clothing that has to be changed or mud that has to be cleaned off the rug. We have let him join us in the dark living room before the big picture window to watch the full moon riding lower and lower toward the far shore of the bay, setting all the water ablaze with silver flames and finding a thousand diamonds in the rocks on the shore as the light strikes the flakes of mica embedded in them. I think we have felt that the memory of such a scene, photographed year after year by his child's mind, would mean more to him in manhood than the sleep he was losing. He told me it would, in his own way, when we had a full moon the night after his arrival last summer. He sat quietly on my lap for some time, watching the moon and the water and all the night sky, and then he whispered, "I'm glad we came."

A rainy day is the perfect time for a walk in the woods. I always thought so myself; the Maine woods never seem so fresh and alive as in wet weather. Then all the needles on the evergreens wear a sheath of silver; ferns seem to have grown to almost tropical lushness and every leaf has its edging of crystal drops. Strangely colored fungi—mustard-yellow and apricot and scarlet—are pushing out of the leaf mold and all the lichens and the mosses have come alive with green and silver freshness.

Now I know that for children, too, nature reserves some of her choice rewards for days when her mood may appear to be somber. Roger reminded me of it on a long walk through rain-drenched woods last summer—not in words, of course, but by his responses. There had been rain and fog for days, rain beating on the big picture window, fog almost shutting out sight of the bay. No lobstermen coming in to tend their traps, no gulls on the shore, scarcely even a squirrel to watch. The cottage was fast becoming too small for a restless three-year-old.

"Let's go for a walk in the woods," I said. "Maybe we'll see a fox or a deer." So into yellow oilskin coat and sou'wester and outside in joyous anticipation.

A child's world is fresh and new and beautiful, full of wonder and excitement. It is our misfortune that for most of us that clear-eyed vision, that true instinct for what is beautiful and awe-inspiring, is dimmed and even lost before we reach adulthood. If I had influence with the good fairy who is supposed to preside over the christening of all children, I should ask that her gift to each child in the world be a sense of wonder so indestructible that it would last throughout life, as an unfailing antidote against the boredom and disenchantments of later years, the sterile preoccupation with things that are artificial, the alienation from the sources of our strength. . . .

Many children, perhaps because they themselves are small and closer to the ground than we, notice and delight in the small and inconspicuous. With this beginning, it is easy to share with them the beauties we usually miss because we look too hastily, seeing the whole and not its parts. Some of nature's most exquisite handiwork is on a miniature scale, as anyone knows who has applied a magnifying glass to a snowflake.

An investment of a few dollars in a good hand lens or magnifying glass will bring a new world into being. With your child, look at objects you take for granted as commonplace or uninteresting. A sprinkling of sand grains may appear as gleaming jewels of rose or crystal hue, or as glittering jet beads, or as a mélange of Lilliputian rocks, spines of sea urchins, and bits of snail shells.

A lens-aided view into a patch of moss reveals a dense tropical jungle, in which insects large as tigers prowl amid strangely formed, luxuriant trees. A bit of pond weed or seaweed put in a glass container and studied under a lens is found to be populated by hordes of strange beings, whose activities can entertain you for hours. Flowers (especially the composites), the early buds of leaf or flower from any tree, or any small creature reveal unexpected beauty and complexity when, aided by a lens, we can escape the limitations of the human size scale.

Hearing can be a source of even more exquisite pleasure, but it requires conscious cultivation. I have had people tell me they had never heard the song of a wood thrush, although I knew the bell-like phrases of this bird had been ringing in their back yards every spring. By suggestion and example, I believe children can be helped to hear the many voices about them. Take time to listen and talk about the voices of the earth and what they mean—the majestic voice of thunder, the winds, the sound of surf or flowing streams.

And the voices of living things: No child should grow up unaware of the dawn chorus of the birds in spring. He will never forget the experience of a specially planned early rising and going out in the predawn darkness. The first voices are heard before daybreak. It is easy to pick out these first, solitary singers. Perhaps a few cardinals are uttering their clear, rising whistles, like someone calling a dog. Then the song of a whitethroat, pure and ethereal, with the dreamy quality of remembered joy. Off in some distant patch of woods a whip-poorwill continues his monotonous night chant, rhythmic and insistent, sound that is felt almost more than heard. Robins, thrushes, song sparrows, jays, vireos add their voices. The chorus picks up volume as more and more robins join in, contributing a fierce rhythm of their own that soon becomes dominant in the wild medley of voices. In that dawn chorus one hears the throb of life itself.

There is other living music. I have already promised Roger that we'll take our flashlights this fall and go out into the garden to hunt for the insects that play little fiddles in the grass and among the shrubbery and flower borders. The sound of the insect orchestra swells and throbs night after night, from midsummer until autumn ends and the frosty nights make the tiny players stiff and numb, and finally the last note is stilled in the long cold. An hour of hunting out the small musicians by flashlight is an adventure any child would love. It gives him a sense of the night's mystery and beauty, and of how alive it is with watchful eyes and little, waiting forms.

The game is to listen, not so much to the full orchestra as to the separate instruments, and to try to locate the players. Perhaps you are drawn, step by step, to a bush from which comes a sweet, high-pitched, endlessly repeated trill. Finally you trace it to a little creature of palest green, with wings as white and insubstantial as moonlight. Or from somewhere along the garden path comes a cheerful, rhythmic chirping, a sound as companionable and homely as a fire crackling on a hearth or a cat's purr. Shifting your light downward, you find a black mole cricket disappearing into his grassy den.

Most haunting of all is one I call the fairy bell ringer. I have never found him. I'm not sure I want to. His voice—and surely he himself—is so ethereal, so delicate, so otherworldly, that he should remain invisible, as he has through all the nights I have searched for him. It is exactly the sound that should come from a bell held in the hand of the tiniest elf, inexpressibly clear and silvery, so faint, so barely to be heard that you hold your breath as you bend closer to the green glades from which the fairy chiming comes.

The night is a time, too, to listen for other voices, the calls of bird migrants hurrying northward in spring and southward in autumn. Take your child out on a still October night when there is little wind and find a quiet place away from traffic noises. Then stand very still and listen, projecting your consciousness up into the dark arch of the sky above you. Presently your ears will detect tiny wisps of sound—sharp chirps, sibilant lisps, and call notes. They are the voices of bird migrants, apparently keeping in touch by their calls with others of their kind scattered through the sky. I never hear these calls without a wave of feeling that is compounded of many emotions—a sense of lonely distances, a compassionate awareness of small lives controlled and directed by forces beyond volition or denial, a surging wonder at the sure instinct for route and direction that so far has baffled human efforts to explain it.

If the moon is full and the night skies are alive with the calls of bird migrants, then the way is open for another adventure with your child, if he is old enough to use a telescope or a good pair of binoculars. The sport of watching migrating birds pass across the face of the moon has become popular and even scientifically important in recent years, and it is as good a way as I know to give an older child a sense of the mystery of migration.

Seat yourself comfortably and focus your glass on the moon. You must learn patience, for unless you are on a well-traveled highway of migration you may have to wait many minutes before you are rewarded. In the waiting periods you can study the topography of the moon, for even a glass of moderate power reveals enough detail to fascinate a space-conscious child. But sooner or later you should begin to see the birds, lonely travelers in space glimpsed as they pass from darkness into darkness.

What is the value of preserving and strengthening this sense of awe and wonder, this recognition of something beyond the boundaries of human existence? Is the exploration of the natural world just a pleasant way to pass the golden hours of childhood or is there something deeper?

I am sure there is something much deeper, something lasting and significant. Those who dwell, as scientists or laymen, among the beauties and mysteries of the earth are never alone or weary of life. Whatever the vexations or concerns of their personal lives, their thoughts can find paths that lead to inner contentment and to renewed excitement in living. Those who contemplate the beauty of the earth find reserves of strength that will endure as long as life lasts. There is symbolic as well as actual beauty in the migration of the birds, the ebb and flow of the tides, the folded bud ready for the spring. There is something infinitely healing in the repeated refrains of nature—the assurance that dawn comes after night, and spring after the winter.

I like to remember the distinguished Swedish oceanographer, Otto Pettersson, who died a few years ago at the age of ninety-three, in full possession of his keen mental powers. His son, also world-famous in oceanography, has related in a recent book how intensely his father enjoyed every new experience, every new discovery concerning the world about him.

"He was an incurable romantic," the son wrote, "intensely in love with life and with the mysteries of the cosmos." When he realized he had not much longer to enjoy the earthly scene, Otto Pettersson said to his son: "What will sustain me in my last moments is an infinite curiosity as to what is to follow."

In my mail recently was a letter that bore eloquent testimony to the lifelong durability of a sense of wonder. It came from a reader who asked advice on choosing a seacoast spot for a vacation, a place wild enough that she might spend her days roaming beaches unspoiled by civilization, exploring that world that is old but ever new.

Regretfully she excluded the rugged northern shores. She had loved the shore all her life, she said, but climbing over the rocks of Maine might be difficult, for an eighty-ninth birthday would soon arrive. As I put down her letter I was warmed by the fires of wonder and amazement that still burned brightly in her youthful mind and spirit, just as they must have done fourscore years ago.

The lasting pleasures of contact with the natural world are not reserved for scientists, but are available to anyone who will place himself under the influence of earth, sea, and sky, and their amazing life.

About the Contributors

Ann Beattie has written several novels and story collections. Her most recent book is *Follies: New Stories*. The recipient of REA and PEN/Bernard Malamud awards for her short stories, she divides her time between Charlottesville, Virginia, Key West, Florida, and York, Maine.

Henry Beston is the author of *The Outermost House*, the classic of nature writing that has been in print for more than half a century. During his years in Nobleboro, he wrote a book about Maine country life, *Northern Farm*, the source of his entry in this anthology.

Alice Bloom lives in Mount Vernon. She is an essayist and reviewer whose writing has appeared in several anthologies and a variety of national journals and magazines, including *The Yale Review, The Hudson Review, The New England Review,* and *Harper's Magazine.*

Gerry Boyle is a crime novelist, freelance writer, and editor of the Colby College magazine. He is the author of the Jack McMorrow mystery novels, set in Maine. A former columnist for the *Morning Sentinel* in Waterville, he makes his home in China Village.

Franklin Burroughs, from Bowdoinham, has had essays in the Pushcart Prize anthology and *The Best American Essays*. His books of nonfiction, reflecting experiences in Maine as well as his native South Carolina, are *Billy Watson's Croker Sack, The River Home,* and *Confluence.*

Rachel Carson, whose *Silent Spring* exposed the ecological impact of pesticides, was perhaps the most influential environmentalist of her time. Her many publications about the sea, including the essay reprinted here, are rooted in her experiences on the coast of Maine.

Deborah Joy Corey, from Castine, is completing a "nonfiction novel," from which her essay here has been excerpted. She has written two novels, *Losing Eddie*, winner of Canada's First Novel Award, and *The Skating Pond*, which won the Reader's Prize from *Elle* Magazine.

Carolyn Chute lives in North Parsonsfield. She has written four novels set in Maine, including *The Beans of Egypt, Maine* and *Merry Men*. She has recently completed a work of fiction titled *The School on Heart's Content Road* consisting of five related novels.

George Dennison, of Temple, wrote *The Lives of Children*, about the free school movement, two story collections, and two novels before his death in 1987. His nonfiction book, *Temple*, where "Dana Hamlin" first appeared, was assembled from a rural epic left unfinished.

Elaine Ford has written five novels and received two NEA grants and a Guggenheim Fellowship. Her recent story collection, *The American Wife*, won the Literary Fiction Award from the University of Michigan Press. A former resident of Milbridge, she lives in Harpswell.

Richard Ford was born in Jackson, Mississippi, and lives in East Boothbay. He is the author of nine books of fiction, including the trilogy that includes *The Sportswriter*, *Independence Day*, and *The Lay of the Land*. He has written many short stories and essays.

Bernd Heinrich's numerous volumes about the natural world include *A Year in the Maine Woods*, the source of his entry here. A recipient of the John Burroughs Prize, he has been elected to the American Academy of Arts and Sciences. He lives part of each year at his cabin in Weld.

Robert Kimber, from Temple, has written for *Audubon, Yankee, Down East*, and other magazines. He has published four books, most recently *Living Wild and Domestic*. His essay "Big Jim" won the *Missouri Review*'s 2007 Jeffrey E. Smith Editor's Award for nonfiction.

Cathie Pelletier has written eight novels and two screenplays. Her recent title, *Running the Bulls*, won the Patterson Prize. As K. C. McKinnon she has published two additional novels. A recipient of the New England Book Award, she lives in Eastman, Quebec, and Allagash, Maine.

Sanford Phippen, who lives in Hancock, has written four books, including *People Trying to Be Good*, from which his memoir here comes, and *Kitchen Boy*. The author of numerous essays and reviews, he is the editor of *The Best Maine Stories* and the letters of Ruth Moore.

Louise Dickinson Rich was the author of twenty-one volumes of nonfiction, fiction, history, and travel. She is best known for the book based on her experience in the Rangeley Lake area, *We Took to the Woods*, the first chapter of which appears in this anthology.

Bill Roorbach, from Farmington, is the author of eight books, among which are his recent novel, *The Smallest Color*, and a book of nonfiction, *Temple Stream*, winner of a Maine Book Award. He is the recipient of an O. Henry Award and the Flannery O'Connor Prize.

Richard Russo has published several novels, among them *Straight Man, Nobody's Fool, Empire Falls*, for which he received the Pulitzer Prize, and *Bridge of Sighs*. He has also written a book of short stories, *The Whore's Child*, and screenplays for the movies and television. He lives in Camden.

Susan Hand Shetterly, of Blue Hill, has published essays on issues of wildlife and wild land for *Audubon* and other magazines. The author of five children's books and two volumes of nonfiction, she has won fellowships from the NEA and the Maine Arts Commission.

E. B. White divided his time between New York City, where he wrote for *The New Yorker*, and Brooklin, Maine, which inspired many of the essays in his classic collection, *One Man's Meat*. The essay printed here, perhaps his best-known, comes from that volume.

Geoffrey Wolff has written the biographies *Black Sun, The Art of Burning Bridges*, and *The Duke of Deception*. His novels include *Providence* and *The Age of Consent*. A recipient of the Award in Literature from the American Academy of Arts and Sciences, he lives in Bath.

Monica Wood, from Portland, has written three novels, most recently *Any Bitter Thing*; a book of linked stories, *Ernie's Ark*; and two volumes on the craft of fiction. Her stories have been read aloud on NPR and have won a Pushcart Prize, among other literary awards.

Baron Wormser's entry in this volume comes from his recent memoir, *The Road Washes Out in Spring*, about his life off the grid in Mercer. He has published six books of poetry and won grants from the NEA and Guggenheim foundations. He was recently Maine's Poet Laureate.

Acknowledgments

Henry Beston. "Winter." From *Northern Farm*, copyright © 1970 by Elizabeth Coatsworth Beston. Reprinted by permission of Kate Barnes.

Ann Beattie. "Not Winter." From *Maine: The Seasons* by Terrell S. Lester, copyright © 2001 by Terrell S. Lester. Essays copyright © 2001 by Alfred A. Knopf. Reprinted by permission of Alfred A. Knopf, a division of Random House, Inc.

Alice Bloom. "Cold Spring Nights in Maine, Smelts, and the Language of Love." First published by *The Hudson Review*, copyright © 1988 by Alice Bloom. Reprinted by permission of the author.

Gerry Boyle. "The World from Bellevue Street." Previously unpublished, copyright © 2006 by Gerry Boyle. Printed by permission of the author.

Franklin Burroughs. "Of Moose and a Moose Hunter." From *Billy Watson's Croker Sack*, copyright © 1991 by Franklin Burroughs. Reprinted by permission of the author.

Rachel Carson. Excerpt from *The Sense of Wonder*, copyright © 1946 by Rachel L. Carson. Copyright renewed 1984 by Roger Christie. Reprinted by permission of Frances Collin, Trustee.

Carolyn Chute. "Maine Logging Truck." First published in *American Voices*, copyright © 1990 by Carolyn Chute. Reprinted by permission of the author.

Deborah Joy Corey. "Settling Twice." Previously unpublished, copyright © 2008 by Deborah Joy Corey. Printed by permission of the author.

George Dennison. "Dana Hamlin." From *Temple*, copyright © 1988 by George Dennison. Reprinted by permission of Susan Dennison.

Elaine Ford. "The Ogre and I." Previously unpublished, copyright © 2008 by Elaine Ford. Printed by permission of the author.

Richard Ford. "I'm New Here." Copyright © by Richard Ford. Reprinted by permission of the author.